AF608295

SETTLING DOWN AND SETTLING UP

The Second Generation in Black Canadian and Black British Women's Writing

Settling Down and Settling Up

The Second Generation in Black Canadian and Black British Women's Writing

ANDREA KATHERINE MEDOVARSKI

UNIVERSITY OF TORONTO PRESS
Toronto Buffalo London

Toronto Buffalo London
utorontopress.com

ISBN 978-1-4426-4037-5

Library and Archives Canada Cataloguing in Publication

Names: Medovarski, Andrea, 1973– author.
Title: Settling down and settling up : the second generation in black Canadian and black British women's writing / Andrea Katherine Medovarski
Description: Includes bibliographical references and index.
Identifiers: Canadiana 2018906577X | ISBN 9781442640375 (hardcover)
Subjects: LCSH: English literature – Black authors – History and criticism. |

LCSH: Canadian literature – Black authors – History and criticism. | LCSH: English literature – Women authors – History and criticism. | LCSH: Canadian literature – Women authors – History and criticism. | LCSH: Identity (Psychology) in literature. | LCSH: Postcolonialism in literature. | LCSH: Children of immigrants – Great Britain – Intellectual life. | LCSH: Children of immigrants – Canada – Intellectual life. | CSH: Canadian literature – Black Canadian authors – History and criticism
Classification: LCC PR120.B55 M43 2019 | DDC 820.9/35309051—dc23

This book has been published with the help of a grant from the Federation for the Humanities and Social Sciences, through the Awards to Scholarly Publications Program, using funds provided by the Social Sciences and Humanities Research Council of Canada.

University of Toronto Press acknowledges the financial assistance to its publishing program of the Canada Council for the Arts and the Ontario Arts Council, an agency of the Government of Ontario.

Canada Council for the Arts
Conseil des Arts du Canada

Funded by the Government of Canada
Financé par le gouvernement du Canada

Contents

Acknowledgments

A major endeavour such as this, although often lonely, is never a solitary pursuit. I am profoundly grateful to the colleagues, students, friends, and family (both biological and outer-biological) who have rooted for me and offered advice, criticism, reading suggestions, love, and support during the ten years it has taken me to complete this book.

A number of colleagues read and offered valuable feedback on some or all of the chapters. My greatest appreciation goes to Leslie Sanders, my first, last, and best critic and my ideal reader. I also thank Andrea Davis, Modupe Olaogun, Katherine McKittrick, Diana Brydon, David McNab, Vermonja Alston, and Terry Goldie for their keen eyes, reading and editing suggestions, and attention to detail. Each of you, in various ways, has made this work far better than it would have been otherwise.

I am also grateful for the friends and colleagues who have offered everything from professional advice and mentorship, to publishing and conferencing opportunities for some of the work in this book, to moral support, meals, and stress management while I was writing. Without you all I could not have brought this project to completion. I offer profound thanks to Brenda Spotton Visano, Selma Zecevic, Sailaja Krishnamurti, Cheryl Cowdy, Megan Hillman, Sharon Morgan Beckford, Guro Jun DeLeon, Guro Tetchie DeLeon, Evelyn Lamando, Anindo Hazra, Denise Handlarski, Janice Anderson, Lorin Schwartz, Eve Haque, David Chariandy, Hyacinth Simpson, Heather Campbell, Lily Cho, James Clark, Luciana Riciutelli, and Rinaldo Walcott. I extend huge appreciations to Bedour Alagraa for preparing the index. To Ari Belathar and Anne Yourt: thank you for becoming my sisters and for always caring about this project.

I have derived my greatest intellectual and creative sustenance from all of the writers on whom this study is based. But I am most grateful to Esi Edugyan, Tessa McWatt, and especially Dionne Brand for their willingness to talk to me about their writing and mine and for their ongoing enthusiasm about my research. I also offer profound thanks to some of the artists who have inspired me, including Jimmy Chiale, who has allowed me to use his magical painting on the cover, and Abdi Osman, who provided the photograph of this painting.

My team at UTP has been nothing short of amazing. My first editor, Siobhan McMenemy, although no longer with the press, remained committed to this project for many years. Mark Thompson brought the same enthusiasm and also new energy when he took over this role. The two of them sought out three phenomenally rigorous anonymous reviewers, whose in-depth feedback gave me the focus I needed to consolidate disparate ideas that evolved over many years. I am also grateful to my managing editor, Frances Mundy, and my copy editor, Matthew Kudelka, for all they have done to bring this book to fruition.

This book could never have been completed without the love and support of my immediate family. To my mother, Judith, and my late father, Andrew, who passed away during the writing of this manuscript: *Szeretlek, Anya meg Apa.*

I dedicate this book to my loving partner, Owen Lamando, and our beautiful son, Evan. Thank you both for showing me what conditions of possibility truly look like.

SETTLING DOWN AND SETTLING UP

The Second Generation in Black Canadian and Black British Women's Writing

"Settling Down and Settling Up": Conceptualizing the Second Generation

Settlement carries with it all the senses of coming to terms with conditions, terms, experiences, set-backs and promises; it is about settling what is contestable and what is acceptable, settling down and settling up.

Barnor Hesse, "Black to Front and Back Again: Racialization through Contested Times and Spaces"

In the early 1990s, Kobena Mercer, in an effort to rearticulate oversimplified political binaries and reinvigorate reductive conversations around social categorization, argued that "Just now everybody wants to talk about identity" (1994: 259). Since then, scholars examining a wide range of identity politics have consistently recognized the need to think about processes of racialization and constructions of gender in ways that are not fixed, bounded, or unified. One of the most significant ways cultural theory has moved beyond singular notions of identity is through explorations of diaspora and its invocations of movement and multiple identifications. The theoretical currency of diaspora as a concept has led to what at least one scholar has called a "diaspora explosion" (Brubaker 2005: 1), given the proliferation of the term both academically and, more recently, in popular contexts, over the last twenty years. Under such circumstances, it might now be more apt to claim that "just now everybody wants to talk about migration." In recent years, border crossings, diaspora, and other forms of literal and metaphorical movement have become privileged paradigms through which to understand the contemporary global and globalized conjuncture. However, while enabling in many ways, these are not always adequate frameworks within which to understand those who wish to remain "in place" or who have not directly experienced migration. The need for this shift is most clearly illustrated in an examination of literary production that engages with some of the concepts of diaspora. Notably, a number of women writers in Canada and the UK have begun to explore what happens to individuals and families *after* migration. Their fiction has focused increasingly on the second generation: Canadians and Britons descended from parents born elsewhere. These second-generation children of immigrants are often not moving, and have never experienced migration, yet they too trouble singular and fixed notions of cultural, ethnic, and national identities. My project considers possibilities for rethinking nation through the second generation by examining a cluster of these novels.

Through literary analysis I aim to explore the processes through which these texts conceptualize a second-generation presence in Canada and the UK, a critical pursuit that has yet to be taken up within the realm of theoretical production. A basic premise of this project, however, is that these novels also necessitate a rethinking of the arbitrary lines critics sometimes draw between the literary and the theoretical. Collectively, the novels in this study theorize a discourse of the second generation, and in so doing they facilitate significant epistemic reconceptualizations that might broaden conventional understandings of what it means to "theorize." My argument is informed by African American and African diasporic feminist critics such as Carole Boyce Davies, who suggests that black women writers can only go "a piece of the way" with Western theoretical concepts (38), and Barbara Christian, who points out that "people of color have always theorized – but in forms quite different from the Western form of abstract logic ... [O]ur theorizing (and I intentionally use the verb rather than the noun) is often in narrative forms, in the stories we create" (68).

Similarly, the novels I explore in this study can be readily inserted into existing theoretical debates, particularly in the ways they challenge migration, dislocation, and travel as paradigmatic frameworks of contemporary cultural analysis. Given their focus on grounding and rootedness, rather than migration and routedness, I want to place these texts into conversation with diaspora and postcolonial theories, cultural studies, and critical theories of race and nation, in order to question the premise that journeying is the most appropriate means through which to theorize a second generation. While this project makes use of diaspora as an enabling concept, it also aims to stretch its theoretical limits in its exploration of the complex, exclusionary, and sometimes participatory ways in which second-generation communities exist within various diaspora spaces. In thinking about the multigenerational processes of settlement for African-descended peoples, I articulate both Canada and the UK as diaspora spaces, just as Avtar Brah does when she suggests that "'diaspora space' (as distinct from the concept of diaspora) is 'inhabited' not only by diasporic subjects but equally by those who are constructed and represented as 'indigenous.' As such, the concept of *diaspora space* foregrounds the entanglement of genealogies of dispersion with those of staying put" (16). Brah focuses specifically on the UK, a space that for the last two decades has been readily understood as a site of diaspora. But it is equally useful to frame Canada in this manner, since it is not often understood to be a place of/for black peoples.

Many of the most historically influential theoretical conceptualizations of diaspora have framed their analyses through movement and dispersal. They articulate a counter-discourse to nationhood by invoking multiple spaces and border crossings, rejecting the notion of citizenship as either singular or localized. But any examination of the second generation disrupts some of these migratory discourses, challenging nation-based correlations between identity and place in ways that do not rely on literal movement. In his now-famous conceptualization of the Black Atlantic world, Paul Gilroy emphasizes that any understanding of diaspora must be premised on the tension between roots and routes. Nonetheless, his use of "ships in motion" (1993: 4) as the controlling metaphor for his extended argument in *The Black Atlantic* (1993) suggests a privileging of movement that has been called into question by other diaspora scholars such as Katherine McKittrick and Clyde Woods (2007) and Lily Cho (2007), feminist geographers such as Linda McDowell (1999), and cultural theorists such as Sarah Ahmed and colleagues (2003). Gilroy argues that invocations to "Keep on Movin'" (1993: 18) in various forms of black expressive culture "have created a new topography of loyalty and identity in which the structures and presuppositions of the nation state have been left behind because they are seen to be outmoded" (16). This is not always the case for second-generation children of immigrants, who often have a great deal invested in "staying put" in the places they were born. Gilroy also insists that the movement of black people, "not only as commodities but engaged in various struggles towards emancipation, autonomy, and citizenship ... provides a means to reexamine the problems of nationality, location, identity, and historical memory" (16). These problems can be examined as well through a discourse of groundedness, in which a desire to remain "in place," particularly within nations that are hostile towards non-white presences, can equally be seen as a strategy of resistance through which a second generation struggles towards autonomy and citizenship.

Carole Boyce Davies was one of the first literary or cultural critics to consider questions of diaspora from a feminist perspective; however, her significant theoretical interventions have also relied on the rhetoric of movement to conceptualize black women's cultural productions and their renegotiations of national identities. Her invocation of a "migratory subjectivity" (4) disrupts national, colonial, and patriarchal hegemonies when she insists that "[b]lack women's writing ... should be read as a series of boundary crossings and not as a fixed, geographical, ethnically or nationally bounded category of writing" (4). In this conceptualization of black female agency, movement itself is seen as a liberatory politics, a means to understand black women's writing as transnational and translocal, and to frame it outside of the limiting categories of minority literature. While this recontextualization provides a significant counter-discourse to the hegemonic and often troubling paradigms of national literatures, the novels in my study are not easily understood within this framework since none of them embrace a migratory subjectivity as a means through which to imagine a post-migrant second generation. They are certainly an extension and complication of Davies's feminist project insofar as they reveal the need to consider the gendered implications of diaspora. The etymological origins of that term, in evoking the scattering of seed, have clearly masculine resonances. But perhaps this language might be expanded by also emphasizing planting and cultivation, as a means through which to understand the ways the women writers in this study root their second-generation characters firmly within, rather than outside, the nations in which they were born.

I deploy diaspora as a strategic concept, rather than as a descriptive narration of an experience of migration, in order to historicize and politicize outer-national thought in particular ways that perhaps come closest to those of Richard Iton, who reminds us that "politics is, among other things, a contest about what matters and what ought to be the subject of consideration and debate" (9). His invocation of diaspora, like mine, "aims to transcend ... the predominance of the state as the sole frame for subject-formation and progressive and transformative discourse and mobilization" (17), but it does so in order to reinvigorate conversations that most typically happen within the taken-for-granted frameworks of nation-states and the privileged place of the nation as a site of collectivity and identity formation. For me, the greatest value in diaspora lies in the ways it can be used to conceptualize a different kind of political terrain through which to understand oppositional, transformative, and also constitutive collective action and resistance. Iton articulates "diasporic potential" in "the capacity to imagine and operate simultaneously within, against, and outside the nation-state" (202), and this best describes the complex and sometimes ambivalent ways in which a second generation engages with the nations of their birth. Understanding the children of immigrants through this potential perhaps best illustrates the ways in which diaspora is, above all, "a commitment to a form of resistance: an attempt to forge and maintain connections among those disconnected, disturbed, and unsettled in a particular fashion by the intersections of coloniality and race" (203).

In a project based in the diaspora spaces of Canada and the UK, this intersection also suggests a need to engage with concepts of the postcolonial. But a migratory framework must be renegotiated to account for the children of immigrants; most postcolonial discourse is unable to account for their experiences. As a theoretical framework that developed in response to anti-colonial resistance struggles, it is informed by a critique of colonialism and a rhetoric of oppositionality between European colonizers and the "Third World" colonized in which the second generation cannot be easily located. David Scott, in *Refashioning Futures: Criticism after Postcoloniality* (1999), observes that postcolonial theory emerged as a critical elaboration of the anti-colonial movements of the 1960s. This political moment demanded "a theory of *liberationist* politics" (12, emphasis Scott's), as colonized nations sought to overthrow European rule and newly independent nations strove towards material and cultural sovereignty. Scott claims that the shift from anti-colonial to postcolonial theory emerged in the late 1970s as a different "problem-space" (8), based on a different set of epistemological assumptions: "As a political-theoretical project, postcoloniality has been concerned principally with the decolonization of the West's theory of the non-West. Postcoloniality … provided a new set of conceptual tools with which not merely to revive colonialism as a going problematic, but to reframe it in terms of the relation between colonial power and colonial knowledge" (12). This language of decolonization, literal or discursive, does not often account for the struggles of a second generation, whom Gilroy has described in the British context as "the stubbornly *non-colonial* descendants" (1999: 60, emphasis mine) of postcolonial migrants who arrived during and after the collapse of the European empires. This generation faces a different set of challenges, in which resisting the oppression of fading colonial power is no longer the main preoccupation as new, globalized hegemonies arise.

Contemporary cultural criticism, according to Scott, operates within a different problem-space from that which preceded it, and the current conjuncture demands a new set of questions that move beyond the realm of colonizer–colonized binaries: "If the question that animated the nationalist/liberationist histories of the colonial turned on the question of the colonial attitude toward the colonized, or the extent of inclusion/exclusion practiced by colonial power, the question that now animates the new demand [of criticism] is a different one, namely, what are the conceptual and institutional dimensions of our modernity?" (15). Second-generation considerations might be better understood within this transitional problem-space, in which questions are based on formative instead of oppositional concerns. The second-generation children of immigrants might be better understood as engaging in constitutive acts that are reshaping the dimensions of modernity through a re-evaluation of some of its most significant post-Enlightenment institutions, such as the nation, the state, and the citizen.

Diana Brydon does not follow Scott's argument that postcolonialism has become normalized as a critical paradigm, nor does she feel that the current global capitalist conjuncture has entirely moved away from the problem-space he has articulated. She does, however, agree that the critical edge of postcolonial studies "need[s] to be revived and redirected" (693). Focusing on the issues and concerns of a second generation might take the field in alternative directions, providing different discursive terms through which to understand the colonial histories that have shaped Canada and the UK. For example, a project about the children of immigrants might entail looking beyond the ways in which a liberationist postcolonial politics has historically used the notion of resistance nationalism as a counter-narrative to colonial hegemonies. In Scott's transitional problem-space, it might now be equally important to engage with what Iton (similarly following Scott) calls a "substantive postcoloniality" (198), one that develops "if not a committed resistance to the existence of the state, at least an anarchist-inflected imagination, a pragmatic understanding of the constraints and limitations of this category of institutions, and a disinvestment in the conception of the state" (198). This rejection of national paradigms is not always articulated as a driving concern within postcoloniality,[1] particularly in its focus on discourse analysis. I argue that turning to the children of immigrants might reveal new ways of thinking about postcolonial projects within the productive intersections of discourse analysis and political analysis, given the ways their engagements with the nation are neither wholly oppositional nor hegemonic.

Some of the most influential theorizations of race and nation have strived to account for these complex histories of colonization, immigration, and racialization; nonetheless they too rarely address a second-generation presence. In the Canadian context, Sunera Thobani's *Exalted Subjects: Studies in the Making of Race and Nation in Canada* (2007) uses Foucauldian concepts of the subject and power to trace the ways the Canadian nation produces, and is simultaneously produced by, a narrative of "exalted subjects," Anglo- (and sometimes Franco-) white-descended citizens who are constructed as the personification of national values and the "legitimate heir[s] to the rights and entitlements proferred by the state" (3).[2] This discourse of exaltation is contrasted to that of the "outsider," whom Thobani describes as "'Indians,' immigrants and refugees ... cast in the trope of the 'stranger' who 'wants' what nationals have" (4) – political and economic rights, as well as the "ontological and existential capital" (5) that accompanies citizenship. Thobani challenges this binaristic thinking on which post-Enlightenment concepts of nationhood are built by examining the concealed histories of violence – both gendered and racialized – on which the discourse of exaltation is based, and by foregrounding ongoing processes of colonization as she explores the complex relationships between exalted national subjects, immigrants, and Indigenous peoples. Hers is a provocative and important examination of Canadian national identity formation, one of the few to account for the complex relationships of power between Aboriginal, "settler," and immigrant in the context of Canadian settler colonialism; yet it too seems unable to account for the second-generation children of immigrants. While Thobani does acknowledge that "the racialization that constructs immigrants as less worthy of citizenship means that all people of colour are likewise perceived as outsiders, regardless of whether they are born in Canada or whether they have citizenship status" (139), the relationships between subsequent generations in immigrant families and the nation are perhaps more complicated than this. Nowhere does Thobani even mention the children of immigrants, who remain unaccounted for in her categorizations of citizenship. I am arguing that we must account for these subjects, who often become something other than exalted citizens or abject outsiders as they negotiate their place in the nation. This project asks: What are they becoming? How can we understand the complexities of their ambivalent insider–outsider status? And how are their processes of racialization, marginalization, or belonging different from those of their immigrant/refugee parents or their exalted and legitimized "Canadian" or "British" counterparts?

This study developed out of a sense that the second-generation children of immigrants seem to be an absent presence in many areas of contemporary theorizing – lurking at the margins and providing fruitful possibilities for thinking differently about the problem-space of the nation within globalized capitalist modernity, but rarely named or explored in any detail. By bringing fictional texts into conversation with diaspora theory, postcolonial theory, and critical studies of race and nation, I hope to engage in a literary analysis that "makes room" for the children of immigrants. By decoupling the concept of diaspora from the concept of migration, by challenging late modernity's too often assumed correlation between nation and identity formation, and by asking that we think in more complex ways about the relationship between the fictional and the theoretical, I aim to explore how novels about the second-generation children of immigrants might be used to expand existing conceptual boundaries and, more broadly, challenge the boundaries of theory.

Settlement on Different Terms

The processes of settlement are a significant preoccupation in each of the primary texts in this study: Dionne Brand's *What We All Long For* (2005); Tessa McWatt's *Out of My Skin* (1998); Andrea Levy's *Fruit of the Lemon* (1999); Esi Edugyan's *The Second Life of Samuel Tyne* (2004); and Zadie Smith's *White Teeth* (2000). Rather than "giving up on land to light on" (45), to borrow Brand's often-cited phrase from *Land to Light On* (1997), these writers rewrite the nation-spaces of Canada and the UK to reflect the realities of a second generation who can sometimes invoke, but never return to, a "back home" the ways their immigrant parents sometimes can. While they occasionally draw on familial histories of migration, these novels are far more interested in the places in which their characters are currently situated than they are in the places the first generation left behind. Most of these texts focus largely on Canada and the UK and are extremely local in their geographical considerations and spatial (re)mappings. In these localities, the second generation is consistently shown to inhabit space in very different ways than their immigrant parents. Most notably, they often (although not always) lay claim to the spaces of Canada and the UK with much more certainty and confidence, even when they face marginalizing comments such as "Where are you from?" that cast them as outsiders to the nation. But although their definitive answers to this question assert their insider status, the second generation also has a much more complicated understanding of the concept of "home" than their parents. The immigrant figures in these novels assert a linear trajectory that moves from their former lives "back home" to their current experiences, whereas for their Canadian- and British-born children, "home" and "foreign" are often shifting, ambivalent, and contradictory terms, which they sometimes embrace and at other times reject as they struggle to situate themselves, locally and globally. Rather than engage in direct comparisons between "here" and the places in which the first generation was born, these novels insistently contextualize the local spaces of the second generation within broader transnational frameworks. Brand's Toronto is conceptualized as a global city, one that is perpetually being remapped by waves of immigrant arrival and second-generation settlement. McWatt situates Montreal in the broader context of the Americas through her evocations of the history of transatlantic slavery and the ongoing colonization of Indigenous peoples. Levy's novel frames England as inextricably linked to its former colonies even as the nation tries to deny that their histories and geographies are deeply intertwined. Edugyan represents the Canadian prairie frontier as a complex space in which Canadian, African American, and continental African migrations converge. Smith's portrayal of multicultural London sheds light on a city that has been shaped by centuries of colonialism and the arrival of people from all over the globe. The dynamism and complexity with which all of these spaces are written suggests a need to think beyond the notion that migration and settlement exist in opposition to each other. Rather, these texts demonstrate that, to borrow from Ahmed and colleagues, "being grounded is not necessarily about being fixed; being mobile is not necessarily about being detached" (1).

Conceptualizing the unique experiences of a second generation also necessitates looking beyond some of the earlier paradigms through which "immigrant literatures" have been understood. The texts in this study operate differently than earlier waves of "immigrant" writing in Canada and the UK, in which migrants' struggles to belong are engaged in on quite different terms. Brand, Edugyan, and McWatt have produced narratives that extend the concerns of, for example, Austin Clarke's Toronto trilogy (*The Meeting Point* [1967], *Storm of Fortune* [1971], and *The Bigger Light* [1975]), Frederick Philip Grove's *Over Prairie Trails* (1922), John Marlyn's *Under the Ribs of Death* (1957), and Rohinton Mistry's *Tales From Firozsha Baag* (1987). Similarly, Levy and Smith may draw upon earlier waves of British immigrant writing such as Sam Selvon's Moses trilogy (*The Lonely Londoners* [1956], *Moses Ascending* [1975], and *Moses Migrating* [1983]), and George Lamming's *The Emigrants* (1956), but their preoccupations differ significantly. In these earlier Canadian and British texts, as immigrants struggle to settle in Canada or the UK, they face two limited and limiting options: assimilation to their new countries and cultures, or the maintenance of a long-distance ethnonationalist attachment to their countries of origin. Too often, assimilation is presented as the most favourable and socially acceptable route towards social citizenship. This rigid binary, with its attendant reliance on ethnic absolutisms, is unable to account for the much more complicated and fluid processes of settlement engaged in by the second generation, for whom neither of these options is truly viable.

The texts under consideration here consistently seek to move beyond the limited and often binaristic either/or choices available to immigrants. Instead, these novels all ask, through the perspective of their Canadian- and British-born protagonists, how settlement might occur *on different terms* for a second generation. Critical work on migration in the last decade has made a point of differentiating among various migratory experiences, most notably on the basis of class and gender, so that it is now readily understood that the cross-border movement of a privileged cosmopolitan cannot be compared to that of an illegalized migrant worker, for example. Far less attention has been paid, however, to the varying terms of their settlement. Migration cannot be homogenized; settlement also needs to be conceptualized as a heterogeneous and uneven phenomenon, one that can vary substantially on the basis of class, race, gender, sexuality, and – of particular importance to this study – generation. These novels ask how settlement might take place *without* assimilation.

To extend a term Barnor Hesse uses to articulate British multiculturalism, the second generation might best be described as *un/settled*.[3] Lily Cho suggests that for some diasporic subjects, such an experience is visceral and corporeal: "To live in diaspora is to be haunted by histories that sit uncomfortably out of joint, ambivalently ahead of their time and yet behind it too. It is to feel a small tingle on the skin at the back of your neck and know that something is not quite right about where you are now, but to know also that you cannot leave" (19). Discomfiture and uncertainty are apt descriptors of a second generation, who must negotiate a sense of place within their current locations while also dealing with the memories of migration that haunt their lives and those of their families. They are repeatedly "immigranted" (43) – to use Lillian Allen's term from *Psychic Unrest* (1999) – by a dominant population that assumes them to be from elsewhere, and they resist this externalization by demonstrating a specifically post-immigrant sensibility, one that neither embraces their parents' cultures wholeheartedly or unquestioningly (long-distance ethnonationalism) nor rejects them entirely (assimilation). Though influenced by various geographies and histories from West Africa, the Caribbean, Europe, and the Americas, the second generation in these texts is far more interested in taking up questions of nationhood and citizenship, and articulating collectivity, in the places where they are currently situated.

Their active rearticulations of the nation necessitate a rethinking of the very concept of "settlement" itself in a manner that might account for its non-hegemonic possibilities. For the second generation, this process does not have to involve a displacement of earlier presences or an uncritical desire to indigenize oneself to a place at the expense of other communities.[4] Thobani, for example, suggests that the immigrant is a complex figure in settler societies such as Canada, arguing that global economic conditions and desires for advancement have meant that "migrants have been party to the ongoing colonization of Aboriginal peoples" (16). Having become – sometimes knowingly, other times not – complicit in colonial processes of dispossession, "the more immigrants have sought their own inclusion and access to citizenship, the more invested they have become, with very few exceptions, in supporting the nation's erasure of its originary violence and its fantasies of progress and prosperity" (16). This is a provocative argument, but again, Thobani does not consider a second-generation presence. As evidenced by the texts in this study, the children of immigrants very often attempt *not* to rehearse these colonial gestures as they strive to settle in more ethical ways than their parents. They often illustrate that settlement on different terms can also be counter-discursive, can be based in radical re-envisionings of the nation-state, and is a complex and discontinuous process in the course of which subjects both engage with and work against the nation.

The strategies pursued by a second generation might be best described, to borrow from Barnor Hesse, as those which illustrate the "heterographies of settlement" (167). Hesse's suggestive term, heterography, draws attention to a migrant-descended second generation that is neither interested in nor able to access hegemonic processes of settlement – those that occur in the "generally accepted manner" – and must instead generate alternative relationships to the spaces of their birth. The term also calls to mind the idea of *heterogeneity*, which emphasizes that settlement involves multiple processes rather than a teleological and singular route from foreigner to citizen. In considering the generational heterogeneities of settlement, I also follow Hesse, who rejects "a narrow, temporalized notion of settlement, as if it were a discrete moment or an ephemeral legacy of immigration, disappearing generationally like a 'foreign' accent" (168). Finally, Hesse's term is suggestive of *heterogenesis*, a biological term describing generational variance. Heterogenesis, or "the birth of a living being otherwise than from parents of the same kind,"[5] emphasizes the differences between migrant parents and their second-generation children, who are not "of the same kind" as their parents in that they do not self-identify as Jamaican, Vietnamese, Ghanaian, Guyanese, Bangladeshi, and so on. Their processes of settlement must instead mediate provisional access to Canadian-ness and British-ness that intersects with these other identities to reconceptualize what belonging to the nation might mean.

In this regard, the transformative possibilities of second-generation settlement are closely related to questions of social citizenship. For their migrant parents, settlement is more often related to questions of legal citizenship: the right to vote, to own property, to hold a passport, and other such rights conferred by the state. Their children, whose access to these rights is indisputable by virtue of their birth in Canada or the UK, desire not just legal citizenship but social citizenship as well: a sense of belonging to the nation and a perception that they can participate actively and meaningfully in the body politic. Their political engagement often results from the dramatic dissonances they experience between legal and social citizenship and from their desire to rearticulate social citizenship to accommodate their un/settled, post-immigrant experiences. A second generation does not seek entry into the imagined communities of Canada or the UK on the terms established by the nation; but neither can they reject those terms entirely since they have no other nations to which they might turn.

Rinaldo Walcott, in "Land to Light On? Making Reparation in a Time of Transnationality" (2006), argues that in this age of global capitalism, nations continue to be "spaces of tremendous human troubles" (87), fundamentally unethical political formations based on exclusion and injustice. This is, in large part, why a second generation does not desire citizenship per se. Rather, they demonstrate a desire to "settle up" with the nation,[6] to *remake* citizenship on other, more ethical or more inclusive terms. The primary texts in this study attempt to imagine other grounds for political and social organization that might challenge nations to reimagine community in ways that can accommodate multiple and shifting identifications. The second generation situates these struggles firmly within, rather than outside of, national formations, in an acknowledgment that laying claim to a nation that casts them as outsiders can be a powerful act of political insubordination.

As they struggle to remake social citizenship in these texts, a second generation also calls into question other collectivities that have played significant roles in political struggle in the past but that may no longer be effective in enabling alternative conceptualizations of community. Most notably, their cross-cultural dialogues and rejection of ethnic absolutisms demonstrate a consistent scepticism about "race" as a meaningful political discourse through which to speak a counter-poetics of nationhood. A second generation rejects what Gilroy calls "invocations of incommensurable otherness" (2005: 8) and searches instead for means through which to bend, stretch, and renegotiate the conceptual boundaries of nationhood. This is why they are often unwilling to form "race"-based political affiliations with later waves of migrants, who may prefer to organize on the basis of ethnic particularity. As Gilroy points out, the second-generation descendants of migrants are often "trapped in the vulnerable role of perpetual outsider, but their local sense of entitlement leaves them reluctant to make common cause against racism and xenophobia with more recently arrived refugees and asylum seekers. To do so would be to accede to the secondariness and marginality with which racism associates them" (123). In these texts, second-generation characters of various ethnicities most often find the greatest commonality with one another as a result of their shared experiences. Rather than drawing the boundaries of collectivity along ethnic lines, these texts postulate the value of trans-ethnic connections; "race"-based solidarities are often looked upon with suspicion as reproducing an essentialist discourse that is unable to account for other, more complex social or cultural affiliations. A rearticulated notion of diaspora provides those of the second generation with one alternative possibility for articulating collectivity. Cho observes that "diaspora brings together communities which are not quite nation, not quite race, not quite religion, not quite homesickness, yet they still have something to do with nation, race, religion, longings for homes which may not exist" (13). This uncertainty encapsulates the multiple identifications of a second generation, who embrace the potential enabled by their "not quite" status.

Scale Politics: Space, Race, Gender, and Nation

Dominant discourses of the nation, by contrast, often define "race" in far more rigid and exclusive terms, and quite often "the discourses of race and nation are never very far apart" (Balibar and Wallerstein 37). This is in part why some theorists who are nonetheless interested in critical explorations of nation formation have shifted their analyses to focus on geographic space. Imre Szeman, in *Zones of Instability* (2003), points out that space has become a widely accepted locus of analysis "in a contemporary academy trying either to undo the tyranny of time (modernity) or to come to grips with the meaning and significance of globalization" (6). He argues that a focus on space better enables an exploration of literature's significant counter-discursive and counter-national possibilities:

> One of the reasons to think about space before nation is in order to open up a different way of conceptualizing the nation: not as a performed political structure that everybody already knows the shape of (say, the modern European nation-state), but as a problematic that draws together the hope of forming new collectivities, the role of culture and literature in these collectivities, the political problems of organizing space, and, finally, the relationship of the writer or intellectual to the people. (5-6)

Like Szeman, I want to explore the ongoing processes through which national formations are variously upheld, undermined, and constantly (re)negotiated through cultural production. This approach questions the premise that nations are predetermined, fixed entities. Given the ways that black diasporic cultural production so often exceeds the boundaries of nation, a turn to the spatial offers another means for examining the ways in which the second generation inhabits the spaces and places (in) which they have un/settled, and the strategies they engage in to reconceptualize those spaces to reflect their own needs and experiences.

A turn to the spatial, however, "cannot be simply metaphorical, cognitive, or imaginary" (McKittrick 2006: 17). While scholars working in the humanities now readily understand identities as complex, multifaceted, and perpetually under construction, in part by having drawn on the notion of "conceptual spaces" as a kind of discursive framework for these examinations, we do not always think about space itself in the same complicated ways. The spatial metaphors that have come to abound within literary analysis in the last decade too often assume that space is a "given" – an uncomplicated and taken-for-granted concept that does not need to be interrogated or analysed. Neil Smith, however, points out that "the central danger in an unreflective use of spatial metaphors is that it implicitly repeats the asymmetries of power inherent in traditional social discourse" (63). This is why my examination of space in this project draws in particular from the ideas of social geographers such as Smith, as well as feminist geographers such as Doreen Massey, Linda McDowell, Sallie Marston, and Katherine McKittrick, whose work has significantly altered the field of human geography over the last two decades. Literary scholarship that examines space might be similarly reinvigorated by these geographers' willingness to think about the spatial implications of social processes, identity formation, and power relations. In particular, their complex understanding of geographic scale informs my own thinking about space in this project. I borrow from McKittrick's articulation of black women's geographies, which relies in part on this critical examination of scale politics:

> Geographic divisions, or scales, range from the psyche to the globe. Coherently hierarchical in their implications (psyche, body, home, community, region, nation, globe), scales identify a planetary organization. While hierarchically organized, scales are interconnected and socially produced: the body does or does not occupy the home; bodies, consciously or unconsciously, assert and define the meaning of community; regional boundaries are produced by bodily politics and home-and-work economies; the nation and nationalism produce material and ideological boundaries, which impact upon the psyche, homes, communities, bodies, regions. (2006: 74)

Thinking in this manner about the ways in which scales are intertwined helps us see spaces as historicized, shifting, fluid, and malleable, just as we understand identities and social identifications to be. Or, to put it another way, there are gendered and racial implications in examining space, and I am particularly interested in exploring these via a second generation, whose spatial practices and processes of settlement are often multiscalar and illustrate the spatiality of both the social and the political. According to Massey, thinking across spatial scales is also a means of challenging nationalist, exclusivist conceptualizations of place that have been "attempts to fix the meaning of particular spaces, to enclose them, to endow them with fixed identities and claim them for one's own" (4).

This project often foregrounds geographic scales, such as the body and the home, that have historically been associated with women. Understanding space as multiscalar, however, helps us examine the ways in which these spaces have always been related to nation-building projects and how these projects can be disrupted by a second generation. As Sallie Marston points out, the home "is a socially produced scale – a scale that is throroughly implicated in wider social, political, and economic processes" (232). Linda McDowell elaborates: "A focus on the social relations within a domestic space crosses the boundary between the private and the public, between the particular and the general, and is not, as is often incorrectly asserted, a focus on the 'merely' domestic or the private sphere" (73). The social relations of a household are mediated by capitalism, gender relations, and patriarchy, all of which are intertwined in the writing of national narratives. But if we take seriously the notion that scales reproduce one another, then unsettlement at one scale will enable unsettlement on others as well. Thus the ways in which a second generation challenges, renegotiates, and reinterprets conventional notions of the domestic have broader implications in rearticulating the hegemonies of nation-space. As Neil Smith observes: "the state … polices the borders of lower spatial scales, especially the body, home and community, and challenges to state power emanate from these and other sources of oppression … even if they are rarely or so neatly defined" (75). To put it simply, what happens at the scale of the household matters in the broader context of the nation. A further implication of this corollary is that "challenging certain of the ways in which space and place are currently conceptualized implies also, indeed necessitates, challenging the currently dominant form of gender definitions and gender relations" (Massey 2). The texts in this study, in their narration of second-generation women characters in particular, question assumed hegemonies regarding which spaces women may or may not occupy. They often reject the binaristic and culturally reductive assumption that domestic spaces are feminized while masculine spaces are public spaces by instead portraying second-generation women characters confidently laying claim to the spaces of their cities and nations, and also rejecting some of the conventional gender roles that have historically been intertwined with the domestic.

In the context of this project, it is important to think critically about scale politics through both a gendered and a racialized lens, given the ways "space works to condition the operation of power and the constitution of relational identities" (Delaney 6). Geographers who examine critically the relationship between race and place have observed that, like gender, racial boundaries very often correspond to spatial ones. David Delaney, for example, argues that ideologies of race "are integral to the formation and revision of *all* … spatialities at all scales of reference, from the international … to the corporeal" (7). Like other social geographers who have emphasized the ways in which the social and the spatial are mutually constitutive, he contends that "elements of the social (race, gender, and so on) are not simply *reflected* in spatial arrangements; rather, spatialities are regarded as *constituting* and/or *reinforcing* aspects of the social" (7, emphasis Delaney's). Thinking through scale, however, offers one means by which to interrogate the spatial workings of race and racism: "racial identities, for example, may be differentially constructed at various scales, and this process may have political significance. A given subject may be 'raced' differently in the context of the national … or local … scales of reference" (8). These complex processes of racialization play out in particular ways for a second generation, who must negotiate various iterations of social identity as they inhabit the ambivalences of being both insiders and outsiders to the nation, and often have these ambivalences reiterated within their familial and domestic contexts as well.

Historicizing the Familial: A Poetics of Relation

Questions of kinship and the family are of particular importance in any study of the second generation, as the term immediately invokes a multigenerational familial context. My use of the term in this study, however, extends beyond sociological classifications that identify the second generation only as the children of immigrants. I invoke a far more complicated, messy, and historically inflected understanding of multigenerationality that, again thinking through multiscalar geographies, considers the political and national implications intertwined within the familial. As I have already observed, a number of cultural theorists have drawn attention to the correlations between gender, family, and nation.[7] Patricia Hill Collins, for example, argues that there is a connection "between family as a gendered system of social organization, race as ideology and practice, and ... constructions of national identity" (157). She and others recognize that the family is often the micropolitical level at which subjects are disciplined in particular ways to produce and reproduce – both literally and figuratively – certain types of citizens. This study asks: What kinds of nations are being (re)produced in families wherein migrant parents and second generation children self-identify according to different cultural, national, or ethnic collectivities? And conversely, how might these families provide an alternative model for heterogeneous nationhood? Collins suggests there is political value in "transforming the very conception of family itself" (172), and this project aims to enact such a transformation so as not to reproduce the hierarchical, patriarchal formations on which both family and nation are often constructed.

Edouard Glissant's Poetics of Relation – a resonant metaphor in the context of this project – offers a productive means of thinking differently about the familial. Glissant contrasts relational identity to root identity, which is often based in aggrandized myths of a distant past and is sanctified by the "hidden violence of filiation" (1997: 60), thus invoking the linearity, hierarchy, legitimacy, and genealogical sequence on which Western epistemologies are often based. Glissant claims that a Poetics of Relation, by contrast, rejects these hierarchical structures[8] and is based instead in contingency and fluidity: "all cultures are equal within Relation" (1997: 163). Significantly, he traces the emergence of Relation to the history of transatlantic slavery in the Americas, stating that "the Plantation is one of the focal points for the development of present-day modes of Relation. Within this universe of domination and oppression, of silent or professed dehumanization, forms of humanity stubbornly persisted" (1997: 65). On the plantation, "the multilingual and frequently multiracial tangle created inextricable knots within the web of filiations, thereby breaking the clear, linear order to which Western thought had imparted such brilliance" (1997: 71).

I argue that even though mine is a contemporary project, there is an imperative to think about multigenerationality in the wake of this history of slavery, particularly in a project that focuses in part on the geographies of the Americas. The "tormented chronology" (Glissant 1989: 64) that is the consequence of four centuries of colonial conquest continues to haunt many black diasporic peoples, as well as others who have been caught in the tangled, multiracial genealogies of conquest. Many second-generation children of immigrants might well reject the origins they associate with their parental cultures. Nonetheless, for black diasporic subjects in particular, this refusal must be contextualized within a legacy of tangled, untraceable genealogies, their attendant fragmentations of subjectivity, and a diasporic longing to transcend this history of traumatic rupture, a rupture that began with the Middle Passage and that plantation economies only intensified. Understanding a second generation through a Poetics of Relation offers a means through which to acknowledge the role played by these complex histories in contemporary subject formation, for both black and non-black peoples; it also provides a framework within which to understand a second generation's ambivalent relationships to current national formations, given the erasures of such histories from dominant national narratives.

Glissant's Poetics of Relation, based in the rhizomatic thought of Deleuze and Guattari, offers a productive way of complicating the ostensibly genealogical explorations that are foregrounded in some of the novels in this study. Smith, Levy, and McWatt in particular include extended discussions and/or illustrations of family trees in their narratives, but they also disrupt assumptions of linear, patriarchal descent and reject the idea that long lineages are necessary for a legitimate claim to a nation. I read these textual moments instead as "family rhizomes." Deleuze and Guattari propose that the trope of the rhizome, an underground stem bearing both roots and shoots, be conceptualized as an "anti-genealogy," arguing that "[t]o be rhizomorphous is to produce stems and filaments that seem to be roots, or better yet connect with them by penetrating the trunk, but put them to strange new uses. We're tired of trees. We should stop believing in trees, roots and radicles. They've made us suffer too much" (15). This shift to non-hierarchy, to scattered assemblages, to an insistence that any line can be connected to any other, is a better description of the anti-genealogical projects in which these texts engage, as well as a more suitable way to characterize families whose members are scattered across many nations. Instead of offering linearity, homogeneity, and assumptions of second-generation cultural "inheritance," their depictions of multiethnic families challenge the singularizing and unified discourses through which national narratives are conceptualized. These texts do not use family trees to establish pedigree or to draw correlations between familial identities and particular spaces or places; instead, the family rhizomes in these texts explore dramatic disjunctures between family, identity, geography, and biology.

These disjunctures are another significant means through which the familial can be conceptualized on different terms for a second generation. The texts in this study also postulate other, outer-biological possibilities for establishing kinship bonds. Brand, Edugyan, and McWatt in particular often look beyond traditional understandings of the familial, rejecting the importance of blood as a sacred fluid, be it for the family or for the nation. But all of the texts in this study also consider the social and political value of various collectivities based on friendship, shared experiences, and communal ties that traverse biological boundaries. Donna Haraway, in *Modest_Witness@Second_Millennium* (1997), points out that scientific, genetic, "racial," national, and familial discourses all utilize the language of kinship to "produc[e] the material and semiotic effect of natural relationship, of shared kind" (53). She argues that we need to denaturalize these discourses, drawing attention to the counter-discursive possibilities engendered by thinking beyond the biological. Haraway writes:

> I am sick to death of bonding through kinship and "the family," and I long for models of solidarity and human unity and difference rooted in friendship, work, partially shared purposes, intractable collective pain, inescapable mortality, and persistent hope. It is time to theorize an "unfamiliar" unconscious, a different primal scene, where everything does not stem from the dramas of identity and reproduction. Ties through blood – including blood recast in the coin of genes and information – have been bloody enough already. I believe that there will be no racial or sexual peace, no livable nature, until we learn to produce humanity through something more and less than kinship. (265)

The texts in this study, through their willingness to imagine alternative ways to frame ethical relationships, loving bonds, and collective solidarities, speak to Haraway's demands. Faced with a dearth of contemporary familial vocabulary to describe such outer-biological relations, these writers strive to articulate other paradigms through which kinship might be expressed. In trying to write these alternative forms of relationality, they are again involved in constitutive rather than oppositional acts, imagining other possibilities through which to understand the familial, the spatial, and the national.

Haraway's propositions, however, while immediately resonant in the context of the texts being considered here, are not without precedent. This reimagining of kinship must again be historicized within the modes of Relation that emerged in plantation contexts, in which outer-biological family bonds were not only sites of resistance to an economic system built on a violent disregard for the familial structures of the enslaved, but also a necessary means of survival. I am not suggesting that a contemporary second generation's reconstituted notions of kinship can be easily or neatly mapped onto this historical legacy. Nonetheless, such a history continues to resonate within the second generation's current modes of relation, providing a different lens through which to understand contemporary manifestations of anti-black violence, and can help us appreciate the ongoing need for alternative forms of relationality in the wake of current manifestations of social and political marginalization.

Comparative Approaches

This study is based in a comparative analysis of Canada and the UK, two diaspora-spaces that converge through a shared colonial history but also diverge in the ways they have conceptualized nationhood and race, and in the ways twentieth- and twenty-first-century state policies and attitudes have governed and disciplined their racialized subjects. They vary in the processes through which they have consolidated their dominant national narratives, a difference that has emerged in part as a result of Canada's need to account for – and manage – its original inhabitants. Thus, these two nations have very different understandings of what "indigeneity" means. Britain, the imperial centre, has historically espoused "the nineteenth century romantic-nationalist idea that equated each nation with a single culture" (Coleman 4). It has constructed itself as unitary, singular, and white, so that, as Gilroy observes, "to speak of the nation is to speak automatically in racially exclusive terms" (1993b: 27). That said, while Englishness has often been articulated as the indigenous, undefined and undefinable "norm" against which all other ethnicities are understood in the UK, Stuart Hall points out that "the so-called homogeneity of 'Britishness' as a national culture has been considerably exaggerated. It was always contested by the Scots, Welsh and Irish, challenged by rival local and regional allegiances, and cross-cut by class, gender, and generation. There have always been many different ways of being 'British'" (2000: 217).[9] Hall also observes that, particularly since the eighteenth century, defining itself against its colonial "others" has been "a constitutive element of British identity" (218). Thus, despite sustained effort on the part of Britons, both a local and an overseas colonial history have disrupted the dominant discourse of a unified, homogenous, and singular national identity.

Canada's history as a settler colony has resulted in a different national trajectory. The long-standing narrative of Canada's "two founding nations," the French and the English, and the originary presence of Indigenous peoples, have meant that this national space has always been constructed through a discourse of plurality and multiplicity. As a consequence, consolidating a unified and normative concept of a specifically English Canadianness has, according to Daniel Coleman, been a sustained cultural project since the nineteenth century. In *White Civility: The Literary Project of English Canada* (2006), he observes the processes through which Anglo-whiteness has become Canada's "fictive ethnicity" (7),[10] one that is based on an attempt to reinvent the English concept of "civility." But from its beginnings, this imitative model has rendered Anglo-Canadian whiteness ambivalent, inconsistent, and unstable: because it is "a cultural field [that] is never univocal but is a space of contest and competition" (20), English Canadian identity must constantly work to rehearse and reinforce its constructed singularity and cultural dominance. While the singularity and homogeneity of England's national identity has also been challenged, particularly in recent years,[11] Canada's position as a settler colony has meant that the narrative of Anglo-Canadian singularity has been vexed since its inception, always already threatened by both those who were here before the English settlers and by those who have come after: "By representing himself as already indigenous, the settler claims priority over newer immigrants and, by representing himself as already civilized, he claims superiority to Aboriginals and other non-whites" (16).

Any comparative study of the second generation in Canada and the UK must also consider their divergent immigration histories. While acknowledging the centuries-old black presence in both nations, I also explore the differing patterns of twentieth-century global migration to Canada and the UK from various diasporic locations, including continental Africa and the Caribbean. The dominant discourse in the UK suggests that the arrival of the *Empire Windrush* in 1948 represented an inaugural moment in both Caribbean migration to, and (post-)colonial "race" relations within, the nation. Without rehearsing such misleading arguments, it is nonetheless necessary to observe that migration from England's former colonies did increase substantially in the two decades after the Second World War. By contrast, the (white) face of Canadian immigration did not start to change until the introduction of the points system in 1967, as a result of which non-white migrants were able to enter Canada in substantial numbers for the first time. As a result of this difference, the second-generation presence in the UK is far more established and far more mature. "By 1975, 40 percent of the black population in Britain were British-born" (Osborne 11), and it is now possible to speak of a third generation whose struggles to un/settle in many ways echo those of the second. Arguably, this is not yet the case in Canada, where, demographically, two-thirds of Canadian-born racialized minorities are under twenty-five years old (Gregg 47).

Canada and the UK have framed official state policy surrounding their racialized and ethnicized citizens in substantially different terms. Canada has enacted an ostensibly benevolent liberalist policy of accommodation through the Canadian Multiculturalism Act (1971; 1988); by contrast, the very naming of the British Race Relations Act (1965, amended 1968, 1976) suggests a far less generous discourse based in exclusion and conflict management. Nonetheless, while the language in these acts may differ, both nations use their policies largely to discipline and contain their "others" and to reinforce the centrality of certain ethnicities. Academic criticisms of Canadian multiculturalism have ranged from Himani Bannerji's argument that it is "a governing discourse" (9), used "to manage a colonial history, an imperialist present, and a convoluted liberal democracy" (10); to Rinaldo Walcott's observation that "[o]fficial multicultural policy in Canada ... textually inscribes those who are not French or English as Canadians, and yet at the same time it works to textually render a continued understanding of those people as from elsewhere and thus as tangential to the nation-state" (1997: 77); to Sunera Thobani's sustained analyses of the ways in which multiculturalism's discursive regulations have attenuated anti-racist activism by focusing on culture instead of addressing genuine issues of social, political, and economic inequality.[12] Moreover, Canada's Multiculturalism Act does little to address the concerns of second-generation children of immigrants, whose demands for social citizenship extend far beyond its extended rhetoric of cultural preservation. Through a second generation, I interrogate state-sanctioned multicultural policy by considering what it might mean to attempt to legislate belonging. More to the point, if legislating belonging is not possible, how and towards what ends does such legislation exist?

In Britain, the various incarnations of the Race Relations Act were intended to promote not multiculturalism but rather what is vaguely called "good relations" between racial communities and the dominant society. The act was designed to protect the rights of visible minorities by preventing racial discrimination and reinforcing social citizenship through legally sanctioned practices. Hesse argues that this ostensibly benevolent narrative "incorporates yet disavows its indebtedness to a racist discourse ... [It] identifies the problem of 'race' not as racism but as the condition of being the racialized other" (2000: 11–12). This has been of particular concern to a British-born second generation that is not interested in being narrated either as "other" or as a "problem." Furthermore, the supposed benefits of the Race Relations Act were undercut by the implementation of an increasingly restrictive Immigration Act in 1968 (amended 1971), and by the British Nationality Act (1981), both of which led to progressively more selective definitions of legal citizenship that often excluded the descendants of those from Commonwealth nations. As with the Canadian Multiculturalism Act, British policies either have not accounted for a second-generation presence or have done so in detrimental ways.[13] Moreover, as Paul Gilroy argues, there has been little effort in the last three decades "to take political discussions of citizenship, belonging, and nationality beyond the dual prescription of assimilation and immigration control: the left-over categories of the 1960s debate" (2005: 123). He also observes that "[i]nterestingly, neither Britain's politicians nor its media are prepared to acknowledge that almost two additional generations have passed since anybody sat down and tried to make sense of the politics of race as a matter of policy" (123). Perhaps, however, there are other forums besides legal ones through which to take up these questions. I would argue that fictional texts play an important role in establishing different terms for talking about citizenship, nationality, and belonging, terms that make it possible to imagine other possibilities through which these concepts might be redefined. In Canada and the UK, cultural production has enabled new conversations to emerge that foreground questions and concerns that are often foreclosed in policy and political discourses.

Partly in response to the nature of various political struggles, understandings of blackness in both Canada and Britain have undergone notable shifts in recent decades. The term "black" has had a different history in each of these nations, albeit those histories overlap; in both spaces, however, the concept is now most usefully understood as a fluid, shifting, flexible signifier rather than a rigid categorization. In Britain, "black" emerged in the 1970s as an oppositional category of cultural and political identity, one that encompassed people of African, Caribbean, and also South Asian descent. As Alison Donnell has pointed out, "as an identificatory category black never really has fitted neatly into national boundaries" (11), and this has been part of its usefulness in the British context; by the mid-1980s, however, "there was ... a more sustained questioning of the usefulness of black as an organizing category" (14). This has been because, as Hall argues, "the new cultural politics is operating on new and quite distinct ground – specifically, contestation over what it means to be 'British'" (1996a: 447). Such political ground has necessitated that blackness be decoupled from notions of ethnic absolutism that developed in the political climate of the 1960s. Gilroy argues that these earlier ideas about racial kinship might have served particular purposes in the past, providing a basis from which to mobilize an oppositional politics, but that they "appear now as naïve, outdated and sentimental" (1993b: 12).

Many scholars of black Canada also utilize a malleable and fluid understanding of blackness that is, to borrow from Rinaldo Walcott, "wholly outside the biological and the national" (1997: 120). Walcott argues that "[w]hen I use the term blackness, I mean to signal blackness as a sign, one that carries with it particular histories of resistance and domination. But blackness is also a sign which is never closed and always under contestation ... I deploy blackness as a discourse, but that discourse is embedded in a history or a set of histories which are messy and contested" (xiv–xv). Because this discursive category is in a perpetual state of becoming, its conceptual boundaries are always alterable, while nonetheless remaining historicized in very specific ways. This study similarly invokes Walcott's unruly discursive understanding of blackness, in order to explore its resistant, outer-biological, and non-hegemonic possibilities – ones that can disrupt conventional understandings of both the familial and the national. Regarding the primary texts in this study, "black" is a (sometimes) phenotypical label that is thrust upon some characters, who either embrace it, reject it, or pay little regard to it, while other characters may or may not be characterized in this way at all. My interest in Walcott's notion of messy, contested discourses is in thinking about blackness as an unstable – and destabilizing – signifier. The primary texts in this study do not suggest a preoccupation with "black" as a subject-position, so much as a preoccupation with what thinking *through* black*ness*, in a discursive sense, might enable for reconceptualizing the nation-spaces of Canada and the UK.

McKittrick similarly invokes blackness in Walcott's discursive and historicizing sense in order to explore "critical geographic possibilities" (2006: 96) regarding black Canada and to write against dominant histories of erasure and spatial containment. She argues that "[m]any black Canadian geographies offer a way in to the nation without positing finished and transparent geographic projects; the struggle of asserting black in/and Canada necessitates an understanding of geography that is ongoing, connected to yet displaced from, white geographic domination" (96). Thinking about black Canadian geographies in this way helps illustrate that "Canada is in fact racially produced – sometimes on different terms than expected" (95). This observation brings much to bear on the British context as well, and while I am not suggesting that their geographies are neatly or simply commensurable, I am trying in this project to think similarly about the implications of articulating blackness and/in Canada and the UK in order to consider what altering and alterable geographic and discursive terrains might look like for a second generation.

The demographic differences in immigration and the varying articulations of racialization in Canada and the UK have had differing political and policy implications; they have also resulted in somewhat different cultural and literary landscapes. In Britain, Andrea Levy and Zadie Smith can be situated within a substantial constellation of African, Caribbean, or South Asian descended second-generation writers and post-immigrant writers who grapple with issues of generational difference and un/settlement. They include, among others, Diran Adebayo, Patience Agbabi, Monica Ali, Bernardine Evaristo, Jackie Kay, Hanif Kureishi, Courttia Newland, Meera Syal, and Alex Wheatle. In Canada, by contrast, literary conversations by or about the second generation are less common – Brand, McWatt, and Edugyan are among only a handful of cultural producers to take up these questions. I anticipate that in the coming years and decades, as a second generation in Canada matures, discussions regarding the nation's native-born, nonwhite citizens will accelerate.

In a comparative literary study it is important to consider the aesthetic convergences between the primary texts. Given that most existing studies about the second-generation children of immigrants are largely demographic and sociological, the focus here on expressive culture suggests that it is important to think about the formal aspects of the novels in this study, and the ways in which literary form may echo content in the creation of alternative sites of possibility for a second generation. This is one area in which notable similarities arise between the Canadian and the British texts in this study, given that they all demonstrate an engagement with realism – albeit in deeply negotiated terms. Writing about the UK context, Magalena Maczynska observes that most Caribbean- and African-descended writers in Britain have been, in the second half of the twentieth century, "committed to realist representation, drawing on genres developed in the classical realist tradition and adhering to a mimetic ontological agenda" (135). In recent decades, however, many women writers in particular have challenged this realist aesthetic as they consider "the possibility of new directions for that writing" (135). Arguably, Maczynska's observations bring much to bear on the Canadian novels in this study as well. "Realism's privileging of reason and scientifically inspired epistemological and ontological models," she continues, "has been denounced as a … restrictive, totalizing paradigm. Realist writing came under attack for failing to question, or mendaciously concealing, its own artistic strategies and ideological agendas" (137). This is why the label "realist" cannot be simply or uncritically applied to the works in this study – or to previous generations of immigrant writing, for that matter. The novels in this study, both Canadian and British, demonstrate much more complex motivations; they might better be described as reflecting a critical realism rather than an unquestioningly mimetic one. This critical realism seeks to document injustice and to challenge established structures of power and is often carefully grounded in the specificities of place, in order to illustrate the complexities of migration and its familial legacies, as well as the persistence of racism and marginalization faced by the second generation.

Moreover, the writers in this study also demonstrate that these critical modes of writing are not incompatible with other forms of narrative expression or other literary techniques. According to Pallavi Rastogi, many Black British women writers in the late twentieth century and beyond have used prose fiction "to achieve literary self-determination" (77). They have done so in part by invoking postmodern literary techniques "including: the use of metanarrative techniques to reflect on identity, rewriting history from the margins, forgoing chronological and sequential storytelling techniques to create disjointed, interrupted narratives; and speaking from multiple perspectives to compose a fictional mosaic" (77). Many of these techniques are used in the Canadian and British texts in this study. To be clear, however, I am not suggesting either "realist" or "postmodernist" as labels to describe or categorize any of them. Rather, I am suggesting that in drawing from multiple narrative traditions, which are sometimes seen as incompatible, these writers push against conventional boundaries of genre even while they push against the boundaries of nation.

Settling Down and Settling Up

This project, via Barnor Hesse's notions of "settling down and settling up," aims to look beyond the assimilationist–ethnonationalist binaries that foreground many of the debates on immigration, to consider instead what "settling down" on different terms might look like for a second generation and the ways in which settlement might occur without assimilation. At the same time, these processes of second-generation settlement work to *un*settle hegemonic discourses of nationhood, particularly their predominant correlation to whiteness in both Canada and the UK. Importantly, however, this project also recognizes that settlement is often difficult work, especially for racialized minorities. Hesse points out that part of the process of negotiating "what is contestable and what is acceptable" – to return to the opening epigraph of this book – means paying attention to "the equivocations and ambivalences in the conditions of settling" (167). A second generation's ongoing experiences of racism, inequalities, and exclusions all point to the ways in which conditions of settling are profoundly uneven. Hence the processes of settling down are often paralleled with the processes of "settling up" with the nation – challenging and holding it accountable for these ongoing marginalizations of its legal citizens. Part of this process involves calling into question some of the dominant ways in which "race" and difference are understood, conceptualized, or managed, and challenging some of the hegemonic narratives of inclusion, benevolence, and racial tolerance that circulate in both Canada and the UK.

The experiences of a second generation demonstrate that belonging is far from being automatic by virtue of being born in a nation or possessing legal citizenship. Despite these obstacles, a second generation nonetheless engages in a constitutive and not simply an oppositional project, as they seek to remake, rework, and rethink citizenship on different terms than those they are offered through official state-based discourse. This is not a naive or prematurely optimistic process; it is part of the process of "settling up." As they lay bare the racial antagonisms that make social citizenship difficult – and sometimes even unattainable – they also demonstrate that for racialized citizens, struggles to belong are an ongoing negotiation. Out of their difficult and uneven "conditions of settling," a second generation looks towards creating new and different ways of being-in and being-of the nation. In so doing, they begin to articulate what Michel de Certeau, in *Culture and the Plural*, calls "conditions of possibility." De Certeau states that "[f]or every constructive desire (and every group assumes one), signs of recognition and tacit agreements about the conditions of possibility – if a practicable space is going to be opened – need to be made" (11). He argues that conditions of possibility must be created to enable different forms of political action than those allowed by dominant, hegemonic discourses, so that "new fields [of] collective existence" (12) can emerge, not only for minority groups but also for nations as a whole. And he further claims that "it is not possible for a minority movement merely to confine itself to a political demand. It also has to change the culture" (78).

The novels in this study engage with this often non-linear and ultimately transformative process. Each of them narrates one or more second-generation children of immigrants who are settling down, settling up, and bearing witness to the ways in which conditions of settling are uneven for, and sometimes hostile to, non-white presences. In my analyses, I consider the ways in which each novel challenges or interrogates one of the hegemonic narratives of Canadian or British nationhood or one of the ways in which immigrants and their families are typically conceptualized. While these discourses are grounded in the specificities of one nation-space, they are sometimes invoked in similar ways in the other. In each chapter I also consider how these novels, in various ways, contemplate different conditions of possibility for, and through, second-generation citizens.

Chapter 1, which focuses on Dionne Brand's *What We All Long For*, challenges the dominant and celebratory official narrative of Canadian multiculturalism while also interrogating global discourses of cosmopolitanism, one of the paradigms into which Brand's novel is most often interpolated. I argue that the novel proposes a different articulation of "on the ground" or everyday multiculturalism that might reinvigorate the as yet unfinished project of thinking through racial difference for the children of immigrants, and that the city of Toronto, as represented in the novel, is an important site where such renegotiations happen. In chapter 1, I suggest that *What We All Long For* explores conditions of possibility in which a second generation is able to rethink what constitutes "the political," opening a space to begin imagining different sites of engagement for social citizenship than those offered by the nation. The four second-generation protagonists also contemplate the political value of friendship and of cultural production as means through which to realize political, cultural, and familial possibilities.

Chapter 2 considers Tessa McWatt's *Out of My Skin*. This novel challenges the dominant Canadian narrative of peaceful settlement, revealing the violences that are often concealed within discourses of settler colonialism. McWatt's novel, through its protagonist, Daphne, and its examination of the Oka Crisis, contemplates difficult but hopeful conditions of possibility for the children of immigrants to belong ethically in a hemisphere built on colonial violence and the ongoing colonization of Aboriginal peoples. This novel also interrogates one of the attendant premises advocated by state multiculturalism: the notion of ethnic hyphenation. McWatt's novel rejects this oversimplified premise, calling into question the assumption that a second generation should or will have "roots" attaching them to the place of their parents' birth. Daphne's rejection of Guyana, a space of trauma and refusal, necessitates her renegotiation of a more ethical relationship to the city of Montreal and its Indigenous inhabitants, to the Canadian landscape, and to her Anglo-white adoptive parents.

Chapter 3, focusing on Andrea Levy's *Fruit of the Lemon*, considers similar issues in an English context. Levy's novel is the only one in my study to narrate an act of journeying when its protagonist, Faith, travels from England, her birthplace, to Jamaica, the place her parents continue to call "home." In this novel Levy challenges one of the dominant British discourses around racialized immigrant families and their descendants: the assumption that "home" is inevitably somewhere else. Levy's novel tests the myth of return to a familial "back home" and finds it an inadequate paradigm through which to understand the second generation in the UK or to theorize their place in the nation. Instead, the novel proposes conditions of possibility not through a return to mythic Jamaican origins but rather through a diasporic engagement with Faith's various familial and colonial legacies, to arrive at a more complex understanding of England and her place in it. Levy's first three novels are, in this regard, important efforts to redefine Englishness in order to create a space for the nation's black subjects. While there has been extensive discussion in recent years of black Britishness, Levy is one of the few writers paying attention to the specificities of black Englishness by insistently disrupting dominant correlations between Englishness, ethnicity, and the pastoral tradition. The earlier novels in Levy's body of work are perhaps not as rich or as sophisticated as her subsequent, award-winning novels, *Small Island* (2004) and *The Long Song* (2010). Their significance lies in having initiated certain conversations regarding the role played by a second generation in rethinking national identities.

Chapter 4 focuses on Esi Edugyan's *The Second Life of Samuel Tyne*. Here I argue that Edugyan offers a trenchant examination of anti-black racism on the Canadian prairies, challenging the dominant premise that Canada is a nation built upon benevolence, inclusion, and racial tolerance. While unpacking the multiple, contradictory, and contested narratives of prairie settlement, this novel also challenges "racial," spatial, national, and familial boundaries. In its extended exploration of domestic spaces, it offers a detailed examination of the struggles faced by immigrant women in mothering their Canadian-born children. The second-generation twin daughters, Chloe and Yvette, also face a different kind of struggle to belong in the midst of an increasingly unmanageable mental illness. Their turbulent lives point both literally and symbolically to the pain and difficulty that are often involved in remaking social citizenship, and the costs of attempting to belong to a nation that enacts profound erasures of blackness. Despite its seeming cynicism, I argue that this novel also explores conditions of possibility through a representation of outer-biological, trans-racial, and trans-ethnic kinship bonds.

Chapter 5 looks at the ways Zadie Smith's *White Teeth* portrays a Britain destabilized by its own melancholic, postcolonial confusion regarding the place of its "others" and by its own declining global importance. This chapter challenges the assumption that immigration and settlement are neat, tidy, or easily concluded processes for the children of immigrants. This chapter, like the previous one on Edugyan's novel, also insists that we understand settlement in the UK as a process differentiated by gender. *White Teeth* has received substantial critical attention, but the novel is rarely taken up in gendered or feminist terms. Yet, I argue, it is largely the women characters of both the first and second generations who work to reconceptualize the nation, by confidently occupying the public spaces of London, by looking towards their future in Britain rather than their families' past "elsewheres," and by refusing to police cultural or familial boundaries as their male counterparts do. Among the second-generation protagonists, Magid and Millat Iqbal remain caught between the binaries of assimilation and long-distance ethnonationalism; it is Irie Jones who looks beyond these debates to articulate a different version of British multiculturalism, one based in outer-national, outer-biological, and non-patriarchal terms. The novel ultimately proposes conditions of possibility by looking beyond the very notion of "roots," and by extension generationality, altogether, in ways that usefully extend the premise of my project.

This desire to think beyond nation, identity, ethnicity, genealogy, and geography is shared by all of the writers in this study. Their disparate experiences of migration and/or un/settlement inform their writing. Brand arrived in Canada from Trinidad at age seventeen, but for much of her literary career she has been concerned with questions of nation, identity, and belonging in a Canadian context. McWatt came to Canada from Guyana when she was three years old and lived much of her life in Toronto and Montreal. While she currently resides in London, England, she has publicly stated that "[t]he more I live in Britain the more Canadian I feel."[14] Edugyan, the youngest author in this study, is the second-generation child of Ghanaian immigrants to Canada. Levy and Smith are both second-generation Britons with ties to Jamaica through one or both parents, but their experiences have differed as a result of the fact that Levy is Smith's senior by nearly an entire generation. Levy came of age at the height of Powellism in the late 1960s and 1970s; Smith's early years saw the rise of Thatcherist conservatism in the 1980s. Nonetheless, despite their disparate experiences, these five writers all share a post-immigrant sensibility that looks beyond the places they or their families came from in order to take up questions of social citizenship in the places they now live. As they have "un/settled down" in Canada and the UK, through their writing they are also "settling up" by establishing new grounds for conceptualizing the nation.

Chapter 1

"A Kind of New Vocabulary": Dionne Brand's (Re)Mappings in *What We All Long For*

Being on the threshold of these cities, of these new cities that would be something other than "*new* cities," a certain idea of cosmopolitanism, an *other*, has not yet arrived, *perhaps*.

– If it has (indeed) arrived …

– … then, one has perhaps not yet recognized it.

Jacques Derrida, *On Cosmopolitanism*

Dionne Brand's *What We All Long For* (2005) occupies an important place in this project, as it speaks in profound ways to the experiences of the second-generation children of immigrants. The novel has provoked a flurry of scholarly and popular criticism that considers the ways Brand complicates dominant national narratives of citizenship and belonging, and has extended the popular discourse of multicultural Toronto as a city of immigrants. Much of this scholarship is decidedly conclusive, offering specific arguments about the ways the novel expresses Brand's anti-national political commitments. I want to take a different approach in my reading of this text. I suggest instead that *What We All Long For* is a novel of possibility, one that ponders, to borrow Derrida's deceptively simple phrase, a "democracy to come" (2004: 325), contemplating different models of urban relationality that are perhaps not yet recognizable, as Derrida states in the epigraph above. Brand's novel is not a definitive articulation of either a local, urban citizenship or a global, cosmopolitan citizenship; it focuses on processes rather than political labels, and on the potential that lies in becoming, thereby opening a textual and fictional space for what has not yet been articulated in the formal political realm. Rather than ascribing to a particular *kind* of outer-national politics (global, local, or both), it asks us to think differently about how we understand politics and the potential that lies in a rearticulation of what constitutes the political.

My reading of the novel, following Richard Iton, aims to "bring into view and into the field of play practices and ritual spaces that are often cast as beyond the reasonable and the relevant – to the point, indeed, of being unrecognizable as politics" (16–17). I explore Brand's engagements with the geographic scales of the city and the home, and the ways the second-generation protagonists – Tuyen, Jackie, Carla, and Oku – renegotiate these spaces in order to explore their political potential. I argue that the possibilities expressed in the novel are explored most extensively through the second generation's intertwined spatial, social, and artistic practices. In particular, I want to focus on four aspects of the novel: the manner in which the second generation inhabits the public spaces of the city, their rearticulations of ethnicity, their renegotiations of the familial, and the possibilities that might be enabled by their artistic pursuits.

"[B]orn in the city from people born elsewhere" (20), the second-generation protagonists illustrate the complexities of an ethnic and racial diversity that is not "imported" and can no longer be cast as external to the Canadian nation. In Brand's novel, "second generation" is a fluid and flexible category rather than a straightforward designation of lineage or biological descent from immigrant parents. While Tuyen and Oku were born in Toronto of Vietnamese and Jamaican immigrants to Canada respectively, Carla and Jackie are less explicitly delineated. Instead, they function in the narrative to expand this label, troubling any easy correlations between identity, place, and familial origin. Carla is the child of Derek, an immigrant from Jamaica, and Angie, a second-generation Canadian-born woman of Italian descent. Jackie is also not second-generation in a literal sense, having arrived in Toronto with her parents at age five from Nova Scotia. Nonetheless, Jackie's frustration with her parents' invocations of elsewhere is not unlike that of her three immigrant-descended friends. All four protagonists reflect a similar attitude towards their families and cultural origins that insistently looks beyond the places from which their parents have come, to emphasize instead the transformative potential of the city in which they have grown up.

Some of the criticism on *What We All Long For* runs the risk of appearing prematurely celebratory, particularly in the ways some scholars interpolate the novel into cosmopolitan discourses. Allison Mackey, for example, suggests that the second-generation protagonists ultimately experience a sense of "belonging as informed by planetary consciousness" (228). Emily Johansen similarly argues that the second generation demonstrates a kind of "territorialized cosmopolitanism" that enables them to espouse the liberatory fluidity of "cosmopolitan citizenship" (48). Kit Dobson, suspicious of these celebratory labels, instead foregrounds the "struggle work" involved in the protagonists' ongoing negotiation of belonging within the Canadian nation. Complicating Marlene Goldman's argument that Brand's earlier writing expresses a "politics of drifting" as a liberatory resistant practice (13), Dobson's reading of *What We All Long For* suggests that the second generation explores alternative forms of anti-national consciousness by espousing "open conceptualizations of urban citizenship" within Toronto (91), which Dobson reads, via Saskia Sassen, as a "global city" (89). While Dobson's examination of the globalizing forces within the novel is considerably more nuanced than those of some critics, I am wary of the extent to which he and others have attempted to consolidate the complexities of Brand's novel under the rubric of expressing a "politics *of*" something or particular kinds of local/global citizenship. My concern is that these too easy labels or assertions of what is being articulated regarding belonging and citizenship actually foreclose the novel's open-endedness and the possibilities it creates for developing what Brand refers to in the novel as "a kind of new vocabulary" (154), to think differently about these issues, these politics, and these discourses.[1]

There are other, broader, and perhaps even more urgent reasons to think critically about the recent proliferation of cosmopolitanism as a seemingly progressive discursive framework through which to (ostensibly) think differently about, and offer alternatives to, the limits of the nation and/or the destructive globalizing contours of late modernity. I echo Rinaldo Walcott's concerns when he states that "[c]ontemporary conversations of cosmopolitanism do very little to unsettle the present coloniality of our being. In fact, I argue that beneath many of the conversations of cosmopolitanism are pedagogies that are built upon – and not even in opposition to – raciological subgenres of humanness" (2015: 192). Walcott advocates instead for what he calls "a cosmo-political ethics" – "one that is only possible if we take seriously our multicultural present" (193). This is an important conceptual shift to consider given that scholars often create "a false separation between the idea of multiculturalism and the idea of cosmopolitanism" (195), resuscitating the cosmopolitan as a solution that seemingly moves beyond the failings of state-sanctioned forms of multiculturalism. He argues instead that "each idea inflects the other, and thus it is not possible to have one without the other" (195).

Walcott urges scholars in the humanities (and other fields) to grapple seriously with the idea of multiculturalism rather than simply bypassing it in favour of cosmopolitanism – which he argues many scholars do without considering the ways this discourse is deeply implicated in the racialized orderings of modernity. His call is particularly resonant in a Canadian context given the ways state policy on multiculturalism has often set the terms through which official conversations around race and ethnicity happen in this country. Regarding Brand's novel specifically, Heather Smyth has turned critical attention to the issue of multiculturalism, suggesting that "[b]y situating her narrative explicitly in cosmopolitan urban rather than national space, and by exploring a variety of dynamics foregrounding community and identification, Brand ... may help us imagine our way out of the limits of multicultural discourse" (274). Like Smyth, I want to look seriously at the various manifestations of everyday multiculturalism practised by the second generation in Brand's novel, which might offer alternatives to state-sanctioned narrations of racialized and ethnic difference.

My engagement with the second-generation protagonists in the novel is spurred by Walcott's important question: "What kinds of new questions might we ask of multiculturalism?" (2015: 189). Walcott suggests that some everyday forms of multiculturalism in the Americas are "unfolding into creolization" and into "new ways of coming into the world" (186). His thinking is informed by Caribbean cultural critics such as Edouard Glissant and Sylvia Wynter, who similarly grapple with the legacies of physical and epistemological brutality on which the Americas have been built, but also with the new ways of being that are emerging within and between the cultural collisions that have created this space. Walcott states that "[t]he importance of creolization, conceptually, is that it locates our lives, histories and experience between brutality and something different – something more possible, if I can use such a phrase" (188). Viewed through the lens of creolization, vernacular multiculturalisms offer very different possibilities than those which are circumvented by the static narrative of muliticulturalism promoted by official state policy. I read the practices of everyday multiculturalism espoused by the second-generation protagonists within this framework, in order to offer a different kind of globalized historical context through which to think about their actions. This necessitates situating them, and the contemporary Toronto they inhabit, in the broader context of the Americas, and within the historical legacy of "four centuries of expansion, exploration, conquest, colonization and imperial hegemonisation which constituted the 'outer face,' the constitutive outside, of European and then Western capitalist modernity after 1492" (Hall 1996b: 249).

The Second Generation's (Re)Mapping of Toronto

Understanding the city in the context of the Americas offers another dimension through which to think about Brand's powerful indictments of nation-centred parameters of belonging and the state apparatuses that attenuate them. Those who are part of the second generation, in turning to Toronto rather than the Canadian nation as a site of affiliation (as many critics have observed), echo the speaker in Brand's *Land to Light On* (1997), who famously states that "I don't want no fucking country, here / or there and all the way back, I don't like it, none of it / easy as that" (48). Brand's rejection of the nation as an imagined community is also evident in *A Map to the Door of No Return* (2001), in which she claims: "Belonging does not interest me. I had once thought it did. Until I examined its underpinnings" (85). Nonetheless, if we are to take seriously the forms of possibility the novel opens up, we need to consider what might be enabled by Brand's urban turn and how and to what end she might offer the city as a counter-discourse to nationhood.

Derrida suggests that the emergence of new types of cities – what he refers to in the European context as cities of refuge – also enables particular kinds of political reimagining: "We would ask that these new cities of refuge ... *reorient the politics of the state*" (2001: 4; emphasis mine). Brand's turn to Toronto might be similarly understood as an attempt to reorient existing state-based political discourses. To be clear, I am not suggesting the need for a reinvestment in states and their "ever more evident bankruptcy" (Bauman 1992: 692). According to Walcott, for Brand, "giving up on land to light on is to give up on the promise that nation building can ever be an ethical project in the context of the contortions of late global capitalism" (2006: 89). He argues that she instead turns to "a political geography" (88) as a means of foregrounding questions of the ethical in her work. Through this alternative spatialization and conceptualization of politicality, we can think about the important role that Toronto, as a city in and of the Americas, plays in the possibilities for a democracy to come. The city is foregrounded from the first line of the novel, revealing the complexity with which Brand will represent its political geographies: "This city hovers above the forty-third parallel; that's illusory of course" (1). By referring to a line of latitude as "illusory," Brand un-maps the city, marking it as simultaneously a physical and an imaginary space,[2] in a cartographic reconceptualization that foregrounds the potential in the imaginary rather than asserting geographic specificity.[3] It is, arguably, in the imagined that Brand highlights possibilities for Toronto (and for other cities) to re-envision new affiliations and alternative parameters for belonging that might reorient state politics, as Derrida urges.

Brand's first description of Toronto as a multicultural city places it firmly in the context of the Americas, drawing attention to the legacies of colonial violence that have underpinned subsequent waves of global migration:

> There are Italian neighbourhoods and Vietnamese neighbourhoods in this city; there are Chinese ones and Ukrainian ones and Pakistani ones and Korean ones and African ones. Name a region on the planet and there's someone from there, here. All of them sit on Ojibway land, but hardly any of them know it or care because that genealogy is wilfully untraceable except in the name of the city itself. They'd only have to look, though, but it could be that what they know hurts them already, and what if they found out something even more damaging? These are people who are used to the earth beneath them shifting, and they all want it to stop – and if that means they must pretend to know nothing, well, that's the sacrifice they make. (4)

These recent migrants, who desire nothing more than to stand still, express a need for regrounding that echoes Hardt and Negri's observation that in the contemporary global capitalist conjuncture, "huge populations see mobility as an aspect of their suffering because they are displaced at an increasing speed in dire circumstances" (154). Particularly for those who have been forced to migrate as a result of political or economic instability, "a stable and defined place in which to live, a certain immobility, can on the contrary appear as the most urgent need" (155). Yet Brand's description, which pointedly distinguishes between the originary Indigenous presence and the later waves of multicultural arrivals in Canada, provokes some difficult moral questions about what belonging and citizenship might mean in the context of the Americas – questions that are too often elided in cosmopolitan discourses. If migrants wilfully ignore the Indigenous occupants of this land, what might this suggest about the processes they undergo to root themselves in this place? Or, to put it more simply, who, or what, is being sacrificed in the construction of this fiction of settlement? Also, is the trauma of their cross-border upheaval meant to be commensurable to the traumatic displacement of Aboriginal peoples who do not have the same history of migrancy? (Can it ever be? How can it *not* be?) And, finally, to what extent might the exigencies of migration in a globalized world provoke, or even necessitate, unethical forms of belonging?

The migrants Brand describes in the passage above have, arguably, become complicit in a colonial project based on Aboriginal displacement and historical erasure, as Thobani illustrates in *Exalted Subjects* (2007). The second-generation protagonists, however, through their alternative spatial practices and engagements with the spaces of the city, work towards a different and more ethical form of settlement that operates very differently from that of their immigrant parents, a point on which I will elaborate below. Nonetheless, Brand's novel does not make simple condemnations about the plight of migrants such as those described in the passage above. Through Quy, and through the first-generation immigrant parents represented in the novel, she examines the complexities of contemporary globalized migration and is attendant to the traumas that are sometimes its cause and sometimes its consequence, offering a multifaceted portrayal in which there can be no easy binary between oppressors and oppressed.

It is Quy's migration that the narrative explores in the most detail. After being separated from his family during their escape from Vietnam, he spends his childhood at the Pulau Bidong refugee camp, where for seven years he wonders what will become of him. Eventually joining a small gang of petty criminals posing as monks, he spends his adolescence as an undocumented migrant, becoming a "noncitizen," one of many "who fall between the cracks of a state-based membership system" (Brysk and Shafir 3), or what Bauman, in *Globalization: The Human Consequences,* calls "vagabonds": "the waste of the world" (92), who are forced into migration due to circumstance and usually are not welcome to stay anywhere. Recalling the Thai pirates who attacked his boat en route to Pulau Bidong, Quy wishes they would have taken him, despite their brutality, for then "I would have had a destination" (9). Eventually joining any gang from which he feels he might benefit, Quy descends deeper into the criminal underworld. Every border crossing he makes comes of necessity and self-preservation. He also becomes involved in human smuggling/trafficking, which complicates any simple understanding of his precarious position. Illegalized himself as an undocumented migrant yet also facilitating the cross-border migration of others through various illegal acts, Quy casts himself through his endeavours as both exploiter and exploited, a victim who nonetheless exercises some agency – albeit criminal – in a globalized world in which border crossings are heavily policed. His experiences speak to the need to understand the complexities of contemporary migrancy in a way that neither homogenizes migrants' experiences nor reduces them to moral absolutes. Brand's representation of Quy, in highlighting both the traumas of his childhood and the cruel, violent, and ethically questionable behaviours of his adulthood, rejects any easy categorization of him as either victim or agent.[4]

Thousands of kilometres away in Toronto, Quy's parents, Cam and Tuan Vu, continue to mourn the loss of their son, having spent the last two decades unsuccessfully trying to locate him. Their experience of global migration is in many ways the obverse of Quy's. While he is forced to stay on the move from country to country, Cam and Tuan experience what Bauman refers to as a "forced territoriality" (1998: 23). The emotional trauma resulting from the loss of their son ties them to the city, which they have not left since their arrival from the Chi Ma Wan refugee camp in Taiwan. As Tuyen's older brother, Binh, reminds her, by way of explanation of his planned trip to Thailand to try to find Quy, "It's not for me. It's for Ma, you know, and Bo. They can't leave here. They're … Ma's terrified …" (13). Immobile but nonetheless deeply unsettled, Cam and Tuan are painfully grounded by their terror, and their fear of returning to Asia inhibits their search for their son and compounds their original guilt for having lost him. They eventually attain Canadian citizenship and purchase a large suburban house, but the terms under which they settle render impossible any attempt to put down new roots. Both Cam and Tuan experience severe bouts of insomnia, which is common in trauma survivors, and Cam demonstrates an obsessive preoccupation with "birth certificates, identity cards, immigration papers, and citizenship papers and cards. She checked incessantly and duplicated them tenfold, keeping them in cookie jars, vanity drawers, and breadboxes" (63). The Vus' history of migration continues to haunt their lives as legal citizens, and their ongoing anxiety pervades their lives despite the class status they have achieved. They too are among those "who are used to the earth beneath them shifting, and they all want it to stop" (4). Brand demonstrates that their lives are shaped by the traumas of their refugee experience and their grief over their lost son.

Cam and Tuan's traumatic existence is echoed, with varying degrees of intensity, within the other families in the novel. The immigrant parents spend much of their time in their houses or apartments, disengaged from the city's daily ebb and flow, yet these dwellings are not spaces of comfort either for themselves or for their children. Jackie's parents live in a small, dingy unit in the public housing project of Alexandra Park, in a continuous cycle of poverty and domestic violence. Oku recognizes that his parents' house, largely because of his father, Fitz, is pervaded by a bitterness he can only describe as "toxic" (187). When Carla looks back to the St. James Town apartment she once shared with her mother, Angie, and her brother, Jamal, her childhood idealization of this space dissipates with the recognition that "this was not a home where memories were cultivated, it was an anonymous stack of concrete and glass" (110). The years she spends living with her father, Derek, and her stepmother, Nadine, are no better. She feels "not like a daughter but like a clerk" (250), despite Nadine's manic domesticity, which does little to turn the house into a home for anyone who lives there.

Nonetheless, the most pronounced discomfort is reflected in the enormous suburban house that Tuyen's parents have purchased in an attempt to reconfigure their own relationship to space. Richmond Hill "is one of those suburbs where immigrants go to get away from other immigrants, but of course they end up living with all the other immigrants running away from themselves – or at least running away from the self they think is helpless, weak, unsuitable, and always in some kind of trouble" (54–5). Suburban living offers them no respite from the anxieties they carried with them to Canada. Nearly everything in the house is covered in plastic, and each room is overflowing with duplicates of household items and paperwork because Cam "didn't throw away anything" (62). Fitz, too, displays this tendency towards hoarding; his yard is filled with old car parts because he similarly "threw nothing away" (84). Tuyen's and Oku's parents believe that owning a house is a sign of "arrival" in more ways than one, marking both newfound economic stability and spatial permanence. Yet they fill the space in these houses with the things they can't "let go of," either literally or figuratively.

The two generations have very different attitudes towards the space of their homes, and also towards the space of the city. The first-generation immigrant parents express a profound distaste for the city in which they have lived for decades. Oku's father extols the masculine virtues of manual labour, yet spending years doing it for others in the city has, in his son's estimation, left him "an unhappy man" (84). Jackie's parents arrived from Nova Scotia with high hopes for a better life, but they now refer to the city as a "wretched hellhole" (93). Tuyen's parents' misery is encapsulated in the statement Cam utters during every fight with Tuan: "We shouldn't have come" (64). Carla's mother Angie finds her life in Toronto so unbearable that she finally kills herself. Obversely, while the traumas that haunt their parents' lives in the city are palpable, and despite their own material and emotional hardships, the second generation repeatedly expresses a deep affection for Toronto. Carla often broods over her mother's lost dreams and suicide, her father's emotional withdrawal, and her brother's troubled youth, "[b]ut she loved the city" (32). Oku is too often stopped by the police if he is out late at night, yet despite this he also reflects on "how he loved the city" (164). Tuyen is unable to cope with her parents' emotional baggage and her ongoing fights with her siblings, so she moves downtown, where she contemplates "the beauty of this city, it's polyphonic, murmuring. This is what always filled Tuyen with hope" (149). But the friends are not naively idealizing, nor do they falsely construct the city as a utopia. They recognize its systemic problems: racial profiling, cultural discrimination in the high school system, housing inequality, unequal treatment at the hands of the repressive state apparatus. Despite these harsh realities, they still display an attachment to Toronto their parents have never experienced.

From the opening scene, in which Tuyen, Carla, and Oku burst onto a subway and into the novel, the second generation is confident and self-assured about their ability to occupy the city's public spaces:

> It's 8 A.M. on a Wednesday of this early spring, and the subway train rumbles across the bridge over the Humber River. People are packed in tightly, and they all look dazed, as if recovering from a blow ... Mostly people are quiet, unless they're young, like the three who just got on – no annoying boss to be endured all day. They grab hold of the upper handbars and as the train moves off they crash into one another, giggling. Their laughter rattles around in the car, then they grow mockingly self-conscious and quiet, noticing the uptightness on the train, but they can't stay serious and explode again into laughter. (2)

The sense of physical and verbal containment exhibited by the commuters is not evident among the three friends, whose unruly voices and bodies defiantly fill the subway car, attracting both the passengers' and the reader's gaze. Tuyen is described as "Asian, she's wearing an old oilskin coat, and you want to look at her, she's beautiful in a strange way" (2). Oku is said to have "an enviable loose physical allure to him" (3). Refusing the invisibility and marginalization of their parents' generation, they negotiate a different relationship to public spaces, rejecting the premise that racialized bodies should be rendered invisible. That they first appear on a moving transit vehicle also underscores their complex realities as the children of immigrants, suggesting that their relationship to the city encompasses both rootedness and unsettlement as they strive to understand their immediate family histories of migration.

Throughout the novel, unlike their parents, the second-generation children spend little time in their homes. Instead they travel the streets of the city, inhabiting its public spaces at all hours. In so doing, they engage in what Michel de Certeau, in *The Practice of Everyday Life*, refers to as "pedestrian speech acts" (1984: 97). Arguing that "the act of walking is to the urban system what the speech act is to language" (97), he contends that walking the streets of the city is one effective means of engaging in everyday practices that enable inhabitants to write an alternative urban narrative: "The walking of passers-by offers a series of turns [*tours*] and detours that can be compared to 'turns of phrase' or 'stylistic figures.' There is a rhetoric of walking. The art of 'turning' phrases finds an equivalent in an art of composing a path [*tourner un parcours*]" (100). Tuyen's and Carla's neighbours, also second generation, call themselves the Graffiti Crew and spray-paint the city with their "emblems of duality" (134). The friends engage in similar enunciatory acts with their urban wanderings. Carla's feverish bike rides and Tuyen's and Oku's walks, often used for artistic inspiration, are corporeal utterances that mark the streets with their presence. Their pedestrian speech acts, in which they both "speak" and "speak up" about their lifelong presence in Toronto, become a means of reshaping public space and constituting a different type of city, one that reflects their unique experiences.

The second generation's spatial practices are also a means for them to negotiate and respond to Toronto's colonial legacies. Jane Jacobs argues that cities in settler colonies such as Australia and Canada "provide distinctive and useful variants on the First World City. These cities display many of the hallmarks of what is understood as postmodernity ... Yet these same cities are also products of a colonial past, and they exist in nations that are struggling toward a postcolonial future" (253). Henri Lefebvre would concur, arguing for the need to consider "real differences ... between the types of cities resulting from history" (1996: 109). In the case of Toronto, its colonial past has informed its spatial layout. Jacobs observes that colonial cities were often designed in such a way as to "creat[e] familiar copies of home," and to that end, planners "order[ed] these unknown spaces into knowable gridded plans" (265). Toronto's streetscape is based on this model, and its residents often navigate by referencing the major intersections on this grid. Brand's second-generation characters often defy this geography, instead meandering between and alongside the main arteries, taking shortcuts through parks and the city's railway lands. Their movements are an example of the ultimate failure of colonial urban planning to create homogeneity by ordering space.

Rearticulations of Ethnicity

For the second generation, inhabiting the streets of the city is also a way to escape from their parents' immigrant narratives and their rigid understandings of identity and ethnicity:

> They all, Tuyen, Carla, Oku and Jackie, felt as if they inhabited two countries – their parents' and their own – when they sat dutifully at kitchen tables being regaled with how life used to be "back home," and when they listened to inspired descriptions of other houses, other landscapes, other skies, other trees, they were bored ... Each left home in the morning as if making a long journey, untangling themselves from the seaweed of other shores wrapped around their parents. Breaking their doorways, they left the sleepwalk of their mothers and fathers and ran across the unobserved borders of the city. (20)

Their parents' source of inspiration is consistently the second generation's source of listlessness as they reject the nostalgic anecdotes of interchangeable elsewheres that seem always to be better than here. Privileging the present over their parents' pasts, the friends are far more invested in the place they currently inhabit, and they describe their daily emergence into the city in terms of escape. They are frustrated by their parents' inability to realize that, in Kwame Appiah's terms, "the identifications that give rise to our ethical concerns aren't simply inherited" (242), and they resist their parents' belief that they too belong to a time and place outside of the nation in which they were born. This insistence that their children are cultural outsiders, just as they are, is best expressed in Tuan's inaccurate reference to Tuyen's natality: "You bring these children here and this is what happens to them. They disobey" (56). As Tuyen reminds him, "You didn't bring me here, Bo, I was born here. Wellesley Hospital. Remember?" (56).

The oversimplified cultural binaries of the second generation's parents are unsatisfying and do not reflect the children's far more complex realities. The friends spend their adolescent years longing to leave their parents' homes, longing for "[n]o more stories of what might have been, no more diatribes about what would never happen back home, down east, down the islands, over the South China sea, not another sentence that began in the past that had never been their past" (47). They reject their parents' ethnic identifications with other countries; they are unable to participate in their elders' imagined communities or share in their requisite histories. Yet assimilation is neither possible nor desirable for them. Immediately following their rejection of long-distance nationalism, they express a similar refusal of its domestic manifestations:

> They'd never been able to join in what their parents called "regular Canadian life." The crucial piece, of course, was that they weren't the required race. Not that that guaranteed safe passage, and not that one couldn't twist oneself up into the requisite shape; act the brown-noser, act the fool; go on as if you didn't feel or sense the rejections, as if you couldn't feel the animus. They simply failed to see this as a possible way of being in the world. (47)

The second generation is unable and unwilling to accept membership in the nation under the terms it has been offered to them and recognizes the emotional and psychological costs of participating in this imagined community, based as it is on exclusion and long-standing assumptions of British or French descent. The city offers a space of possibility for articulating community and belonging, and also for moving beyond the assimilation–ethnonationalism binary on which conventional understandings of Canadian multiculturalism are based. Unwilling and unable to assimilate to the dominant culture, the second generation is also uninterested in the static discourse of "preserving" cultural origins, a recurrent trope in the Canadian Multiculturalism Act.[5] Instead, they work towards developing new forms of identification.

The second generation engages in a powerful rearticulation of nation- and race-based notions of ethnicity that are most evident in the ways they enter – under their own terms – the 2002 World Cup celebrations and participate in the various street parties that spontaneously erupt in the "ethnic" neighbourhoods when a nation's team wins a match. For many in these enclaves, "[r]esurgent identities are lifted and dashed. Small neighbourhoods that seemed at least slightly reconciled break into sovereign bodies" (203). But for Tuyen, Oku, and Carla, the celebrations linked to soccer are laden with other meanings and significances. C.L.R James writes eloquently about the political implications of sport, and his extended examination of West Indian cricket in *Beyond a Boundary* considers the ways in which athletic competition is "charged with social significance" (66). He argues that "social and political passions, denied normal outlets, expressed themselves so fiercely in cricket (and other games) precisely because they were games" (66). His observations hold true for World Cup soccer in Toronto in 2002.

For some, including the many Koreans (both immigrant and second-generation) who take to the streets to celebrate an unexpected victory against the Italians, attending a street party becomes an allowable outlet for expressing their ethnicity in a nation that too often demands assimilation or invisibility. As one radio commentator states: "I didn't even know we had a Koreatown in the city" (204). For Tuyen and Oku specifically, however, the party in Koreatown has other corollaries: "Tuyen felt elated, infected by the mood on the street. It reminded her of a year ago, when she and Oku went to Quebec to demonstrate against globalization" (204). Their invocation of the anti-globalization protests denies a straightforward reading of the street party as apolitical or as a simple expression of Korean ethnonationalism. In de Certeau's terms, they enact different "procedures of 'consumption'" (1984: xiii) for the street party. De Certeau argues that in practices of everyday resistance, "users make [*bricolent*] innumerable and infinitesimal transformations of and within the dominant cultural economy in order to adapt it to their own interests and their own rules" (xiii–xiv). Tuyen and Oku adapt the cultural coding of the World Cup in this manner, rejecting the notion that these parties must be read solely as depoliticized ethnic gatherings.

Jane Jacobs has observed that too many postmodern theorizations of the city have failed to consider questions of ethnicity and marginalization, claiming that "there is little sense of the ways in which the concerns of racial and ethnic minorities, say, might *not* be placated by the introduction of ethnic festivals, nor is there any hint of how such groups might transform these new arenas of *play* into more familiar arenas of *politics*" (257–8). Taking to the streets during a victory party is, for a few hours at least, sanctioned by the police in a way that more overtly political demonstrations never would be. During the 2002 and subsequent World Cups, Toronto police regularly closed neighbourhoods such as Koreatown, Little Italy, and Little Portugal to traffic for a few hours (and in a few instances, even for two days) in response to such celebrations, in part because they were assumed to be apolitical. They have been far less generous towards explicitly politicized anti-globalization, anti-war, or anti-poverty demonstrations that have caused similar traffic disruptions. Thus, although not propelled by politics, the playful celebration in Koreatown might also be understood, in Jacobs's sense, as a political intervention into mainstream discourses that persist in Anglicizing the city or partitioning it into supposedly impermeable ethnic enclaves.

For Tuyen and her friends, the street party also offers an opportunity to articulate their own understandings of ethnicity; for them, during World Cup, the boundaries of "Korean-ness" are decidedly flexible. Tuyen's response to the television announcer's ignorance about Koreatown is not just a rant; it is an articulation of her own position regarding the permeability of ethnic boundaries: "Asshole, she thought ... You fuckers live as if we don't live here. She wasn't Korean, of course, but World Cup made her feel that way. No Vietnamese team had made it so today she was Korean" (204). She arrives on Bloor Street and eventually runs into Oku and "the usually subdued Carla waving a Korean flag and singing *'Oh, Pil-seung Korea'*" (209), untroubled that the Italian team has been defeated. At this moment, all three of them can become Korean in a manner that is joyfully subversive rather than appropriative. Because they have a malleable understanding of ethnicity and community that is very different from the "sovereign bodies" soccer sometimes encourages, they transform nationalist symbols and anthems into tools for celebrating the diversity and conviviality of the city. Under different circumstances, Tuyen has resented assumptions that she has much in common with racialized "Others" of any ethnicity. In her parents' restaurant, "when the customers were Vietnamese or Korean or African or South Asian, she hated ... the sense of sameness or ease she was supposed to feel with them" (129–30). At the street party she and her friends embrace that sense of sameness, now chosen by them rather than thrust upon them by the dominant culture. This ethnic rearticulation marks perhaps the most cogent political possibility for the street party; Tuyen, Carla, and Oku's cultural fluidity looks beyond "sovereign bodies" to express the potential for other grounds of affiliation.

After the celebration the friends articulate an important realization about their unique way of being in the city: "Carla had said it all, not just about her mother but about all of them. Trying to step across the borders of who they were. But they were not merely trying. They were, in fact, borderless" (213). Again turning to territorial metaphor to express their cultural fluidity, the friends acknowledge the possibilities enabled by their living in this city as post-immigrants with multiple spatial and cultural affiliations. They live in a city populated by "ex-West-Indians, ex-Eritreans, ex-Somalis, ex-Vietnamese, and ex-South Asians" (316), just like themselves. Collectively, they can identify what they are *not*: they are not of the places their parents were from; they are not immigrants and can lay no claim to a migratory subjectivity to understand their experiences; yet they are not "Canadian" either, refusing the limits this imagined community will place on them. But how can the second generation express who, and what, they "are" when bounded, nation-centred paradigms of identity are so inadequate? Their "borderless-ness" speaks to the need for what Brand refers to in the novel as "a kind of new vocabulary" (154) to articulate their experiences. This new vocabulary cannot just be a rejection of any correlation between identity and place, since aspects of their identities and identifications are actively enabled by their strong connection to Toronto. Nonetheless, the second generation's lives and experiences necessitate a very different understanding of collective and political affiliation through which they can negotiate their own paradigms for belonging.

Reimagining the Familial and the Political

In *What We All Long For*, Brand's representation of the second generation is quite different than it was a decade earlier in "Brownman, Tiger ..." In her 1994 essay she writes of a generation that is "restless" (101): "They're not immigrants so they're not grateful for the marginal existence they're afforded. They were born here, or they can't remember any place else" (101). She also suggests that these young people are not politically engaged: "They're not on the street like my generation before them; their view is inward, nursing wrath" (102). Her criticisms of the second generation are sometimes harsh, and while she strives to understand their plight she is sceptical of their motivations. *What We All Long For* reflects a very different view of the second generation's political engagements. Tuyen, Carla, Oku, and Jackie do not turn inwards; they *are* on the streets, but on different terms than Brand's own generation, and their activism takes different forms. While Brand's generation was involved in explicitly anti-racist, socialist politics, her protagonists are politically engaged in other ways, through their creative pursuits and in their day-to-day relations with one another. Oku's and especially Tuyen's artistic reimaginings are important discursive interventions (a point on which I will elaborate below), while Jackie's consignment store, in which she sells recycled "post-bourgeois clothing" (99), is a small-scale local means of rethinking global capitalist modes of production and consumption. Even their ongoing game of "Word" demonstrates an insistent re-evaluation of the world in which they live and a consistent rejection of racism, sexism, and homophobia. In de Certeau's terms, the friends engage in everyday practices of resistance, collectively adapting the dominant culture's discursive constructions of the city and of themselves. In so doing, they reshape the city while also expanding conventional understandings of what "political engagement" might mean.

This rearticulation of the political plays out at multiple, intersecting geographic scales, including the city and the home, and the novel illustrates these as mutually informing each other through the ways they complicate discourses of the familial. In part because of the difficulties within their biological families, the second generation turns to, or is thrust into, a city that is sometimes represented as a surrogate family. Even their parents, despite their fears and anxieties about Toronto, occasionally perceive the city as a necessity in their children's lives. Brand makes use of a powerful metaphor to explain how Cam and Tuan view Binh and Tuyen differently than their eldest daughters, who were born in Vietnam. They look at Tuyen and Binh "[a]s if assuming a new blood had entered their veins; as if their umbilical cords were also attached to this mothering city" (67). This is not the first time the city is personified, but it is the only moment in the novel that the city is feminized. For the second generation, the city is their lifeblood, a sustaining force that makes dealing with their familial struggles a little bit easier. The city as surrogate mother is also important given the ways the first-generation parents "abandoned them to the rough public terrain that they themselves couldn't handle" (19). This abandonment seems less harsh, less dangerous, when viewed in the context of the mothering city, which can nurture their children in ways they themselves, as cultural outsiders, know they cannot. Toronto can sustain the second-generation children, but the birthing image also suggests that in some ways, the city can create certain types of subjects and constitute – "raise," so to speak – the second generation in particular ways. As David Harvey emphasizes, "We individually and collectively make the city through our daily actions and our political, intellectual and economic engagements. But, in return, the city makes us" (237). Brand's maternal metaphor draws attention to the inevitable intertwining of the emotional, the familial, and the political in this process of creation.

If extended, Brand's metaphor of the city as a nurturing mother also speaks to the complex intersections, in both geographical and nationalist discourses, of space, place, kinship, gender, and nationhood. Sidonie Smith and Gisela Brinkler-Gabler, in "Gender, Nation, and Immigration in the New Europe," question the naturalized correlation of these factors by challenging Benedict Anderson's masculinism in *Imagined Communities* and by problematizing his conceptualization of nationhood as fraternity. They argue that

> [a]ccording to Anderson, there is a sense of fatality about national identity as there is a sense of fatality about the ties of kinship. Neither is chosen; both are inherited. Since fatality lies outside the realm of choice and agency, national identity seems "natural." And this kind of fatality lies close to the fatality of a "femininity" and "motherhood" aligned almost exclusively with the natural world. (13)

Brand's reconceptualization of the city as a nurturing mother disrupts a number of these supposed fatalities. The friends' relationships to one another and to their "mothering city" reject the inevitability of either nation or family as determining factors of imagined community, since they actively choose one another and the city as alternative sites of affiliation. In Brand's novel the city provides a foundation for these new collective paradigms, "mothering" its second-generation children through its multiple cultures, ethnicities, and histories. Brand's gendering of the city also troubles the fatality of a Eurocentric cultural tradition that has historically constructed the natural landscape as feminine, and by extension the city, and its mastery over space, as masculine. For example, Derek Gregory has observed that by the nineteenth century, "Western 'nature' is made ever more elaborately feminine – particularly through constructions of landscape – whereas Western 'space' is made over in the image of a masculine, phallocentric power … Thus, space is itself represented as the physical embodiment of (masculine) rationality whose structures are to be imposed over 'nonspace'" (131).[6] In feminizing urban space, Brand challenges long-standing Western philosophical assumptions of masculine spatial dominance and disrupts the binaries that have historically constituted some spaces as "natural" and others as "constructed."

In renarrating the social constructions of urban space, Brand renders the city as an important site for articulating outer-national solidarities that might question established correlations between citizenship and the state. In her extensive work on citizenship, Saskia Sassen has observed a nascent political dynamic, one that is "producing operational and rhetorical openings for the emergence of new types of political subjects and new spatialities for politics" (191). She argues that the city is playing a key role in this transformative process, insofar as it can be "reconfigured as a partly denationalized space that enables a partial reinvention of citizenship" (193). The second-generation friends are certainly among these new types of political subjects, and their daily activities in the city, what Sassen would call "as yet informal citizenship practices" (192), play an important role in reconceptualizing social processes to create alternative understandings of what being-in, and being-of, the city and the nation might mean. Nonetheless, Brand is careful when articulating possibility in urban affiliations. In the current global capitalist conjuncture, and as Quy's very different experiences suggest, cities are also dangerous and unethical places; this is perhaps why Brand focuses consistently on the possibilities for citizenship enabled by their most ordinary inhabitants.

In this regard, the second-generation friends can be seen as new political subjects in other ways as well, shaped not only by the ways they inhabit the city but also by their interactions with one another. Ash Amin and Nigel Thrift theorize what they call the "emancipatory city," arguing that urban sociality provides a space for considering "new forms of molecular politics" (234) that may not fall under the rubric of conventionally defined political engagement, as well as for "taking more seriously the minor forms of association that abound … allowing these kinds of politics to subsist" (234). One of the most important and undertheorized forms of relation, they claim, is friendship:

> Friendship, and friendship-based associations have become increasingly important elements of the urban social glue, many of whose pleasures lie in simply relating to others ... [S]uch bonds also take us back to the very roots of cities as sites of association, and through this, political organization. Thus, what may seem routine, even trivial, may have all manner of political resonances that we are only just beginning to understand – and mobilize. (234)

The novel's representation of the four friends explores this very potential, as they turn to one another for alternative forms of affiliation – rather than filiation – to those ascribed by their families and by the nation. Through them, Brand considers the ways friendship might enable a new type of ethical political vocabulary, one in which solidarities are chosen rather than linked to blood, birth, or soil. Their routine and trivial activities together, including walking, cooking, eating, and listening to music, can all be layered with other political implications as they utilize these activities to work through their issues with their families and their questions of belonging to the nation. The micropolitics of how they relate to one another, with trust and respect, intervening in one another's lives only upon request, might well provide an effective model for wider forms of macropolitical organization. Through friendship, the second generation can begin to express what Rinaldo Walcott calls an "ethical relationality" (2006: 97) – a sense of collective identification that challenges existing national or ethnic vocabularies of community.

The Possibilities of Art

These new and intertwined political, familial, and spatial practices are also reflected in the second generation's artistic pursuits, through which the novel metafictionally explores the political potentialities of the creative. In particular, Tuyen's practices as a performance artist offer a provocative renarration of both domestic and urban space. To facilitate her multimedia installations, she reorganizes her apartment according to her own spatial principles rather than any sort of convention. Witold Rybczynski, who traces the evolution of houses and their changing uses and functions from the Middle Ages to the late twentieth century, points out that "privacy and domesticity [were] the two great discoveries of the bourgeois age" in the eighteenth century (77) and still largely inform domestic architecture today. Tuyen rejects these characteristics as she reworks her studio apartment to serve her personal and creative needs. The boundaries between the ostensible privacy of the apartment and the semi-public space of the hallway are blurred by her photographs, which are displayed on the walls of the stairwell, and by the piles of shoes she and Carla leave outside their doors. Tuyen also reconfigures her interior space in a manner that challenges its domestic functions: "She had surreptitiously broken down the wall between her bedroom and the kitchen, making one large room for her installations. One thing with Mrs. Chou's slum apartments – the ceilings were high. Tuyen's dark room was a thick black velvet curtain. The dishes were in the bathtub as the countless paintbrushes were in the sink" (25). Reorganizing rooms in a manner that privileges her art over any other aspect of her life, she has rejected what Elizabeth Grosz, in "Bodies-Cities," has observed as "the division of the home into the conjugal bedroom, separated off from the other living and sleeping spaces, and the specialization of rooms" (301). Tuyen lives downtown in part so that she can inhabit her lesbian identity without her family's knowledge, and her refusal of the conjugal bedroom and its traditionally attendant use for marital procreation is one way she uses space to construct this identity. She most often refers to her living space as her "studio" rather than her apartment, regularly mounting artistic installations in it. Both her arrangement and her use of her home question any assumed division of living and working space, consistently blurring the boundaries between public and private, artistic and domestic.

Her art, the most significant pursuit in her life, is also a means for Tuyen to understand her relationship to the space of the city, to her family, and to her fluid and shifting notions of ethnicity. She spends much of the novel working on a variation of a *lubaio*, a traditional Chinese column used for posting messages. It is carved from a railway tie, a symbol that resonates with the exploited Chinese labour on which the Canadian railway infrastructure was built, and which the nation actively writes out of its dominant narratives. Historical erasure is not the specific subject of her art; nonetheless, it speaks to one of the reasons why the nation is such a troubling site of affiliation for Tuyen and her friends. Tuyen has taken this railway tie, a vehicle for movement, and has fixed it in one place by upending it and fastening it to her ceiling.

In its contradictory gestures to both mobility and settlement, the *lubaio* is an interesting and perhaps unintentional metaphor for her own life.

When she first envisions her installation, Tuyen plans to "have the audience post messages on the *lubaio*. Messages to the city" (17). Over the course of the novel, the nature of her installation changes and develops, and it is not until the final pages that she finally has a clearer vision of her project:

> She would need a larger space for the installation, three rooms really, very high ceilings. In the middle of each room a diaphanous cylindrical curtain, hung from the ceiling, that the audience could enter. At the centre of one cylinder would be the *lubaio* with all the old longings of another generation. She would perhaps do something with the floor here too, perhaps rubble, perhaps sand, water. In another cylinder there would be twelve video projections, constantly changing, of images and texts of contemporary longing. This one would be celebratory, even with the horrible. Again here the floor, the path, what material? The last cylinder would be empty, the room silent. What for? She still wasn't quite certain what she was making; she would find out only once the installation was done. (309)

Tuyen's work demonstrates a significant preoccupation with both space and time as she strives to work through generational differences. The first cylinder, devoted to her parents' generation, negotiates the traditional, and her potential floor covering gestures to those "other landscapes" and "other shores" (20) to which this generation remains attached. The second cylinder considers her own generation's longings, which are constantly shifting and changing. Finally, the last empty cylinder speaks to both hope and possibility, offering a space for the audience and subsequent generations to participate in creating meaning out of this work of art and out of the city. Tuyen's insistence that her representation is "celebratory, even with the horrible," encapsulates the second generation's attitude towards their lives and towards the city they love. It is also potentially a self-reflexive comment about Brand's own representation of the city, and of the second generation, in the novel itself.

Henri Lefebvre insists that "[w]ork on the urban cannot limit itself merely to recording what has been produced. We must also look ahead and propose things" (1996: 211). Brand's novel, itself "celebratory even with the horrible," does precisely this. Focusing consistently on possibility, she proposes a number of alternative political paradigms through which to understand the engagements and commitments of the second generation, as well as a range of solutions to current urban problems. The very difficult ending of the novel needs to be considered in this light. The final pages, which reveal that Quy has made his way to Toronto, continued his criminal involvement, and plans to take his newfound brother Binh "for everything he's got" (311), debunk the myth that family reunions and "homecomings" (whatever those might mean in this context) are automatically celebratory. The novel ends with a dramatic rupture of these assumptions: Quy is attacked by Jamal and one of his friends, who steal Binh's BMW and leave Quy beaten and bleeding on a Richmond Hill sidewalk minutes before he is to be reunited with his parents. Yet despite this turn of events, Brand continues to look ahead, devoting one final paragraph to Carla's newfound sense of peace. In the last two sentences of the novel, she articulates the most important longings all of the friends share: "Tomorrow she would miss work and have everybody over. She longed to hear Tuyen chipping and chiselling away next door" (319). Friendship, community, and the promise of art – are these the things "we" should all long for after reading the novel?

The final pages resonate with the fulfilment of these possibilities. Tuyen, in the midst of escalating familial crisis and anxiety upon Quy's return, reminds herself, "She had her art, she had her life" (305). Similarly, after years of Carla's asking the Graffiti Crew to paint "[s]omething more" (32) than their usual tags and initials, something that encapsulates her and Angie's hopes and dreams, they finally comply by spray-painting her entire apartment building: "On one side there was a flowering jungle, lianas wrapped around the CN Tower, elephants drinking by the lake, pelicans perched on fire escapes. On the other side there was a seaside, a woman in a bathing suit and hat shading her eyes, looking out to sea" (302). Graffiti, a predominant expression of hip hop culture, has historically been used to express oppositional and resistant identities and to respond artistically – and politically – to the spatial management and containment of some communities. Here, the Graffiti Crew, in that resistant tradition, expresses the kinds of possibility, and desires for "more," that encapsulate all of the second-generation characters in the novel. In episodes such as these, hopeful even in the midst of crisis and chaos, Brand looks ahead to propose the transformative possibility of the artistic and the imaginative. Rather than a retreat from the political, such creative reimaginings speak to the intersections between the aesthetic and the political and to the ways art both produces and is produced by the new political subjects Brand articulates in this novel.

Brand's corpus has repeatedly confronted the difficult moral and ethical questions of what belonging, migration, and settlement might mean in Canada and in the wider context of the Americas. She consistently foregrounds the violence on which this hemisphere has been built, yet she also narrates moments of optimism. These glimmers in *What We All Long For*, itself "celebratory even with the horrible," can be glimpsed in her essay "Bathurst," published more than a decade earlier. Even then, "this city" held promise for her and for the other immigrant populations of which she speaks, despite their marginalization and hardship. In 1994, she writes: "In a weird way this is a very hopeful city. When you think of all the people living in it – the Chinese, the Italian, the Portuguese, the South Asians and us – you've got to wonder how all of that is happening. And you've got to be hopeful despite people ... People make room and people figure out how to do the day-to-day so that life's not so hard" (77). Although she is now far less interested in defining the differences between "us" and "them," in *What We All Long For* she continues to explore the political and creative potential enabled by Toronto's cultural convergences. She has also looked beyond the exigencies of migration to explore the second generation's negotiation of these trans-ethnic collisions and how they too can enable conviviality through everyday practices. While a major problem of state-sanctioned multiculturalism lies in its always already impossible attempts to legislate belonging, Brand's novel points towards other grounds on which to articulate collectivity and other sites of belonging that might offer different possibilities for community, engagement, and collective action. These continuities in Brand's corpus speak to Henri Lefebvre's belief that in the city, "the past, the present, the possible cannot be separated" (2004: 30).

Chapter 2

"Belonging Is What You Give Yourself": Tessa McWatt's *Out of My Skin*

[B]elonging is ... for Black Diaspora people (and other diasporas as well) a project of ethical political positionality. What does it mean to belong to the Americas? How does staking such a claim reproduce and replicate the violence which gave birth to the Americas as we have come to live and know this place? How does a Black claim to the Americas – anywhere in the Americas – differ from and partake in the on-going processes of colonial practices? Is there a place for uttering different and competing discourses for Black belonging in the Americas?

Rinaldo Walcott, "Rhetorics of Blackness, Rhetorics of Belonging: The Politics of Representation in Black Canadian Expressive Culture"

This chapter, which examines Tessa McWatt's first novel, *Out of My Skin* (1998), builds upon my analyses of Dionne Brand's *What We All Long For* in two ways. First, McWatt's novel facilitates a more detailed discussion of the implications of contextualizing Canada in the context of the Americas, and, second, it allows me to extend my conversation about what possibility does – and does not – look like for the children of immigrants, who must learn to situate themselves within these "new world" geographies. Set mainly in Montreal during the 1990 Oka Crisis, McWatt's narrative centres on the protagonist, Daphne, a racially indeterminate woman who has been adopted by Anglo-white parents, and her attempts to learn about her birth family's Guyanese background and the circumstances of her biological mother's immigration to Canada. In its narrative parallels between Daphne's search for her identity and the events at Oka, the novel grapples directly with what it means for second-generation diasporic subjects to inhabit unceded

Aboriginal land. Through its invocation of several colonial histories, including the conflicting "settler" discourses of French and English Canada, the turbulent history of Aboriginal land claims, and the legacies of slavery and colonization in the Caribbean and South America, *Out of My Skin* confronts the traumatic upheavals on which the Americas has been built.

In this chapter I make two interrelated arguments regarding the novel: one is textual, the other metatextual. First, I argue that through Daphne's emotional journey the novel explores possibilities for staking a different and more ethical claim to the geographies of the Americas – a "different discourse of belonging," as Walcott suggests in the epigraph above, than those espoused by white Canadian settler discourses. Second, in taking seriously my goal to stretch the boundaries of theory, I suggest that *Out of My Skin* also makes a notable intervention into theoretical discourses of diaspora, which do not always account for indigeneity in meaningful or substantial ways. I aim to illustrate the ways the novel narrates a complex trajectory in the course of which Daphne must learn to renegotiate the intertwined geographic scales of her body, the city of Montreal, the mutually informing discourses of the family and the nation, and the geographies and myths of the "Northern" Canadian landscape. In so doing, Daphne must confront directly her stereotypical perceptions about the Indigenous presence in Canada, as well as revise significantly her preconceived notions about Aboriginal peoples and their claims to the land, to consider how they complicate her own struggles to belong on more ethical terms as the descendant of immigrants.

Interpolating an adoption narrative into a project about the second-generation children of immigrants might appear to be an unusual move, given that for much of the novel Daphne is not aware of her biological family's Caribbean background. Nonetheless, her search for information about her birth family reveals that her biological mother immigrated to Canada while pregnant with Daphne, and this realization that she could be conceptualized – albeit in messy and complicated terms – as the child of an immigrant, must become one of the ways she understands herself within the Canadian nation. Moreover, her adoptive parents' attitudes towards her demonstrate their participation in an intertwined familial and national narrative of assimilation coupled with a troubling disavowal of Daphne's markers of racial difference. These are evidenced, for example, in her adoptive father's exasperated and uncritical response to Daphne's sustained confusion about her racial identity – "You're a Canadian, and don't you let anyone tell you otherwise" (16) – and her adoptive mother's inability to confront her own frustration in dealing with Daphne's hair (161). Daphne's search for her biological family is provoked in part by her sense of feeling like an outsider within her adoptive family, a marginalization that is echoed in the ways she is unable to negotiate a place for herself within hegemonic narratives of national belonging. Intertwining an adoption narrative with a discussion of the second generation also has notable symbolic resonances. In a popular Canadian discourse in which immigrants, and – problematically – their children, are often encouraged to integrate themselves into their "adopted country,"[1] McWatt's disruption and complication of the adoption narrative challenges the ways in which this language is used to render racialized minorities, even those born in Canada, as outsiders to the nation, as not actually part of the "real" national family.

McWatt has taken up the intersecting scales of the body, the family, and the nation in many of her subsequent works, and the literary conversations she inaugurates in *Out of My Skin* are sustained throughout her corpus. Several of her novels represent various forms of adoptive and outer-biological families that work to trouble notions of biological kinship, and disrupt the ongoing remnants of scientific racism which assume that "race" is biologically determined. Her work also narrates diasporic migrations and connections, considering both real and imagined border crossings between Kenya, Canada, Guyana, Barbados, the United States, France, Italy, and the UK. Some of her works explore black Atlantic connections between Canada, the Caribbean, and the UK (e.g., *Dragons Cry* [1998] and *This Body* [2004]), while her more recent work (e.g., *Higher Ed* [2015]), focuses on diasporic, transnational London, where she has lived for nearly two decades. But it is her first novel, set largely in Ontario and Quebec, that offers the most extensive examination of the violent colonial processes through which Canadian nation formation takes place. *Out of My Skin* also offers the most sustained engagement with Aboriginal issues I have encountered by a black/Canadian/diasporic writer. The broader conversations McWatt stages in and through this novel make a notable intervention into dominant paradigms of both Canadian and black diasporic literatures and theories.

McWatt's novel, like Brand's, challenges the dominant Canadian multicultural rhetoric of "preserving, enhancing, and sharing" one's cultural heritage, a national project that is shown to be deeply problematic both for the children of immigrants and for mixed-race subjects such as Daphne, whose "heritage" is neither simple, singular, nor desirable, laden as it is with the traumas of her biological family. Through its representation of the Oka Crisis and the character of Surefoot, the Aboriginal woman Daphne meets at the adoption agency, the novel also reminds readers that "the First Peoples of Canada are not multicultural minorities; they are descendants of the original inhabitants of the land. Their demands for self-determination and land rights and the resolution of treaty disputes go beyond the demands for the removal of barriers to equitable participation in society" (Saloojee 411). In this regard, a broader question informs my reading of the novel: What does it mean in a Canadian context that the Canadian Multiculturalism Act, which encourages immigrants to maintain their linguistic and cultural heritage (albeit on the problematic terms established by the nation), exists simultaneously alongside the Indian Act, which has historically legislated the cultural genocide and forced assimilation of Aboriginal peoples? Although not the explicit focus of the novel, we can see the ongoing impacts of the Indian Act play out in Surefoot, who lives the consequences of cultural genocide. Her experiences as an urban Aboriginal unable to trace her roots to any specific Indigenous nation, and the physical and sexual abuse she faces from the nuns at an orphanage and a foster family, invoke the legacies of the Residential School system and the Sixties Scoop. Thus, while there are similarities between the experiences of Daphne and Surefoot, their differences reveal that Canada's management of its racialized "minorities" and of its Aboriginal "others" has historically played out in very different ways.

As Daphne learns about her Guyanese ancestry, she must come to terms simultaneously with a history of slavery and forced migration to the Americas as well as the violent legacy of Canadian settler colonialism that has displaced Indigenous peoples from their land. In intertwining these issues so closely, the novel also stages a broader conversation about the relationship between diaspora and indigeneity in the Americas, one that is rarely taken up within the realms of theory. James Clifford, in one of the first attempts to address this question, suggests that diasporic and indigenous concerns are largely incommensurable. He argues that "[d]iasporas are caught up with and defined against (1) the norms of nation-states, and (2) indigenous, and especially autochtonous, claims by 'tribal' peoples" (1994: 307). While he suggests that "tribal-diasporic opposition is not absolute" (310), he also claims that "the specific cosmopolitanisms articulated by diaspora discourses are ... in tension with indigenous, and especially autochtonous, claims" (308). Given my project's scepticism regarding cosmopolitan discourses, as I explored in the previous chapter, I suspect that I articulate a very different understanding of diasporic claims and longings than does Clifford, one that perhaps offers a greater opportunity to think about the ways in which the concerns of diasporic and indigenous peoples might intersect or overlap, albeit in sometimes uneasy or troubling ways. To extend Clifford's terminology, what possibilities might arise from confronting directly some of these diasporic–indigenous tensions, as McWatt does?

Out of My Skin, in taking up these complex debates, is part of a small but growing body of writing that attempts to explore the potential confluences between indigenous and diasporic discourses within Canada. It builds upon the explorations of ethical black diasporic belonging articulated by Walcott, as cited in this chapter's epigraph, as well as on subsequent work, such as Kim, McCall, and Baum Singer's edited collection, *Cultural Grammars of Race and Nation: Diaspora and Indigeneity in Canada* (2012). Recognizing that theirs is a contentious project, the editors proceed carefully in their attempts to explore "the ways in which diaspora and indigeneity put pressure on discourses of nation and the potential transformations they make possible" (6). Most of the articles in their collection are a bipartite challenge to the hegemonies of Canadian literary and cultural nationalisms, focusing on either diasporic or indigenous discourses and epistemologies. The book lays important theoretical groundwork, but future theoretical/literary studies might push further the ways in which diaspora and indigeneity also pressure *each other*. This, I argue, is what makes McWatt's literary contribution to these debates so unique: her novel examines these competing pressures, nearly two decades before such issues were taken up within the realms of theory or literary criticism. The novel might also be read in conversation with another recent literary text that similarly considers diaspora–indigenous relations: Sto:Loh writer Lee Maracle's volume of poetry, *Talking to the Diaspora* (2015). Maracle simultaneously facilitates black diasporic–Aboriginal conversations (e.g., in poems like "On the 25th Anniversary of Martin Luther King Jr.'s Death") and attenuates them by referring to all non-Indigenous Canadians as "part of some diaspora" (n.p.), in a manner that erases the fundamental power differences between white and non-white peoples in this hemisphere.

McWatt's novel is at times similarly fraught and likewise offers no easy answers to such contentious questions. Nonetheless, it provides an important textual staging ground through which to consider the costs and consequences of belonging for both diasporic and indigenous peoples in these "new world" conjunctures. In the remainder of this chapter, I trace Daphne's narrative trajectory by focusing on four key moments of dialogue, uttered by various characters, which illuminate her trajectory from ignorance and appropriation towards more ethical forms of belonging and a greater awareness of the colonial histories and power dynamics that have shaped the spaces she inhabits.

"What Are You Anyway?" The Micropolitics of the Body

Daphne is portrayed as a character who, like many black female subjects, experiences "social lives which are often displaced, rendered ungeographic," to borrow from Katherine McKittrick (2006: x). In describing Daphne's sense of social isolation and un-belonging, the narrative similarly utilizes (un)geographic references: "her connection to others seemed like a tightrope on which she teetered, surrounded by empty space, no ground in sight. Gaps everywhere: stepping and missing" (McWatt 1998: 64). This trope of "stepping and missing" is sustained through the first third of the novel, in which Daphne reflects on her formative experiences as the racially indeterminate child of white adoptive parents. Daphne's adult dysfunctions (an inability to connect to people, masturbating in times of emotional crisis, infantilizing herself by plucking her pubic hair, and the signs of an eating disorder) are intertwined with her lifelong inability to answer the question, "What are you anyway?" (16), first asked by her grade two teacher and by countless others since then. Her self-infantilization and disordered eating practices in particular reflect her desire to return to an emotional place before "the appearance of the crack, the question *what are you* nudging it wider each time she asked it of herself" (17).

Imitation is another extended trope surrounding Daphne, revealed in her hobby as an audubon imitating bird calls and in her employment at a Montreal photocopy shop. These adult activities have their origins in Daphne's childhood attempts at cultural construction. Never able to answer the question of her cultural origins, she spends her preadolescent years superficially and arbitrarily assuming a variety of cultural identities including East Indian, Egyptian, Chinese, and Aboriginal: "Soon invention was separated from her quest for belonging and thrived on its own impetus" (20). Having gleaned her information from Eurocentric research sources like encyclopedias and Henry Wadsworth Longfellow poems, she bases her bedsheet saris, foot-binding, and other acts of cultural appropriation in deeply troubling cultural essentialisms, which are encouraged by her adoptive father, who refers to her affectionately as "my own little Hiawatha" (69). They are also a precursor to a new foray into cultural invention. At the outset of the novel, some of Daphne's thoughts have begun to take on a Caribbean accent, and she hears "an invented voice with the playful rhythm and scorn of the islands" (5), but again she lacks the specificity of which island or region of the Caribbean she now imitates.

Daphne's cultural and racial uncertainty is manifested in her profound corporeal discomfort, which provides one interpretation of the novel's title. Feeling "out of her skin," she is uncomfortable with the ways she inhabits her body and is constantly rubbing her belly, buttocks, and thighs as if to ensure that they exist despite her racial indeterminacy. Her struggles can be read through what Ahmed and colleagues refer to as "the micropolitics of the body" (10), the wider historical contexts and discourses that play out on her corporeal surface. Her inability to offer specifics about her racial identity points to the problem of defining "race" according to either blood or phenotype. As Paul Gilroy observes in *Against Race* (2000), "[t]he history of scientific writing about 'races' has involved a long and meandering sequence of discourses on physical morphology. Bones, skulls, hair, lips, noses, eyes, feet, genitals, and other somatic markers of 'race' have a special place in the discursive regimes that produced the truth of 'race' and repeatedly discovered it lodged in and on the body" (35). Daphne meditates over nearly all of these somatic markers throughout the narrative, but none are able to provide the answers she and others seek to the question of her identity. Daphne's lifelong inability to answer the question "What are you?" is equally unnerving to those who ask it, and this points to a profound cultural anxiety about the racial script that, according to remnants of nineteenth-century pseudo-scientific biological and semiotic narratives of racialization, "should" be evident on her body but obviously is not. In other words, phenotypical indicators "should" provide adequate clues to her racial make-up even in the absence of information about her birth parents. But, as Gilroy further argues, "[t]he desire to fix identity in the body is inevitably frustrated by the body's refusal to disclose the required signs of absolute incompatibility people imagine to be located there" (104). Daphne's body has similarly refused to yield the concrete evidence that will allow others to categorize her within preconceived racial paradigms or insert her seamlessly into established racial hierarchies; this points to the dangers inherent in assuming that the body is a repository of racial truth. Rather than offering the safety or security of knowability, Daphne's body is described in precarious and potentially explosive terms as having a "minefield mapped on to her features" (McWatt 1998: 73).

Daphne's corporeal instability is also reflected in the ways she inhabits the space of Montreal. She spends hours walking alone along streets that have become familiar after eight months but nevertheless preclude any sense of arrival. Unlike Brand's protagonists, who find empowerment through the ways they inhabit and renarrate the streets of Toronto, Daphne's experiences in Montreal reflect her sense of displacement. She is what de Certeau might call a "*Wandersmänn*," one of those urban wanderers "whose bodies follow the thicks and thins of an urban 'text' they write without being able to read it" (1984: 93). While Brand's second-generation protagonists demonstrate the possibility of rewriting the urban script, Daphne is, at the outset of the novel, unable to see or realize this possibility. For her, to again borrow from de Certeau, "the city itself is an immense social experience of lacking a place – an experience that is, to be sure, broken up into countless tiny deportations/displacements and walks compensated for by the relationships and intersections of these exoduses that intertwine and create an urban fabric" (1984: 103). De Certeau's migrant rhetoric and his reference to "deportation" speak to the ways Daphne experiences life as a not-quite-citizen, marginalized from any ethnonational community and from the wider body politic. While the deportation metaphor resonates, Daphne also has no human connections through which to form relationships or intersections with others that might compensate for her sense of alienation. Daphne's wandering might further be read for its symbolic resonances. As Riva Kastoryano observes, "the practice of citizenship goes beyond its legal definition, for it finds expression in quite different terms and in a distinct domain. More specifically, the politics of citizenship pertains to agents' political engagement, to their participation in public space" (121). This tangible and spatialized experience of citizenship eludes Daphne, who, feeling suspended in "empty space" (McWatt 1998: 64), never actively participates in or engages with public spaces but merely meanders through them. She is oblivious to processes through which other citizens' political actions reconfigure these spaces, for example in the public rallies in support of the Mohawk protesters.

Daphne's marginalization is also reflected in her repeated acts of voyeurism. The novel opens with her gazing intently into an apartment window. Her realization that "she was on the outside" (2), can be read both literally and symbolically and, like her wandering, gestures towards issues of citizenship and belonging. The first line of the novel, "Up close it was all disappointing" (1), is ostensibly a reaction to the apartment she sees through the windows; a literal reading reveals her profound disenchantment with the private lives of the "real" (in other words, Anglo- or Franco-white) citizens. A symbolic reading of the vague referent "it" might also point to the ways nations, based on regulatory regimes of exclusion, are inherently dissatisfying for those outside their conceptual boundaries. Her voyeurism, however, which marks her as standing outside the national body politic, might also be read for its resistant possibilities and for the ways in which it challenges post-Enlightenment paradigms. Nancy Duncan argues that "the idea of privacy is deeply embedded in Western political theories of freedom, personal autonomy, patriarchal familial sovereignty and private property" (128). Not coincidentally, these elements have historically been deemed some of the necessary prerequisites for access to citizenship. Daphne, in peeping into other people's private spaces, demonstrates a blatant disregard for these principles, an irreverence that might be read as an act of defiance against her own not-quite-citizen status.

"Propa' Hyphenation": Ethnicity, Geography, Family, Nation

In many ways, Daphne also feels like an outsider peering in at her adoptive family. Peeping into other families' lives provides her with a counterpoint to her inability to trace her own biological lines of descent. She is fascinated by the pictures on the wall of the home she later learns is Michel's. Drawn to his photographs, Daphne is intrigued by "a portrait of a big family. It was the kind of family which was full, bursting over, generation into generation of the same faces. Sisters ... so many. Their faces varied, but each had something that connected it to the others: a line of the chin or a fold over the eye" (75). In this picture, Daphne witnesses the multigenerational continuities that she can never experience in her own adoptive family, but that she nonetheless longs for.

This longing, coupled with her ongoing desire to answer the question "What are you anyway[?]," leads Daphne, through an adoption agency, to find her birth aunt, Sheila Eyre, whom she learns is an immigrant from Guyana. Her biological family's surname, most obviously evocative of the Charlotte Brontë novel *Jane Eyre,* is a homonym for "heir" and for the sense of familial and cultural inheritance that is absent from Daphne's life.[2] During their initial phone call, Sheila and Daphne's dissonant understandings of kinship become evident. Sheila assumes they share an automatic familial bond based on shared biology, telling Daphne immediately, "Ooh, goodness, it's you, chile!" (61), in a manner that assumes a previous familiarity that does not exist on Daphne's part. After learning Daphne would like to meet her, she is excited, believing "it means we can really get to know each other" (62), even though Daphne does not request anything beyond initial contact and seeks information about herself rather than a relationship with her birth aunt or a substitute for her adoptive family.

Despite her wariness, Daphne gives in to feelings of excitement as she prepares for their first meeting. This encounter is, significantly, couched in metaphors of travel: "Friday afternoon. Airport anxiety flowed in: that wiry anticipation that accompanies the greeting of passengers, the one that flips the stomach and moistens the palms ... The excitement of coming home" (77). Daphne's nervous optimism speaks to her hope that her aunt and her newfound cultural knowledge will provide the tether she seeks and the cultural and familial continuity that will allow her to map her origins. Yet the vague, agentless phrasing of this passage obscures who exactly is "arriving" – which party is the passenger and which will offer the welcome. When Daphne enters Sheila's home for the first time, their meeting does not give her the sense of arrival she had hoped for: "Daphne sat on the edge of the couch feeling lost in the foreign room" (78). Realizing that Sheila wants more of Daphne than Daphne wants of her, her disillusionment with the meeting is palpable.

As Sheila welcomes her, she says, "I don't get to see too many people from home any more" (78), a comment that confuses and angers Daphne, who has never identified Guyana as "home" and "resent[s] the idea that this woman had anything to do with the things she knew" (78). In their conversation, Sheila asks Daphne little about her life, sharing instead her own "relief of landing" (79) in Canada and her recollections of "back home." Using Daphne as an outlet for her nostalgia, she takes her on "a long sentimental journey" (78) to her birth family's country of origin. She acknowledges Guyana as "a slab of land with mud and jungle [and] too many mosquitoes" (79); her tone then shifts when she talks about her life in Georgetown, the friends who would spontaneously visit, and the strolls along Regent Street and in the Promenade Gardens. She also idealizes the Guyana that existed under colonial rule, arguing that "after independence it all fell apart" (79), although the timing of her arrival in Canada in 1960, the year of Daphne's birth, suggests she has no direct experience of life in the post-colonial state. Sheila speaks of a political framework of which Daphne knows nothing and offers a romanticized image of Guyana in which Daphne cannot participate. In response to Sheila's assumption that Guyana is her "home," Daphne can only say, "I've never been anywhere like that" (79).

The exchange that finally drives Daphne out of Sheila's house occurs when Sheila asks her "what she used to call herself" (81):

> "I mean, what was your hyphenation? I have a friend, a lady from home – she makes me laugh. She says, 'In dis country it's important to have de propa' hyphenation.' Funny, makes it sound like havin' the propa papers, but it's just what you call yourself when someone asks you where you're from. 'Where are you from?' 'I'm a Canadian.' 'No, I mean where are you *from*.' I've heard that so many times in thirty years. Now you know your hyphenation. West Indian Canadian. What did you used to say?"
>
> Daphne's mouth opened slightly. Too fast, too much, all of this. "Nothing, I'd say nothing ..." (81)

The orthography of this passage suggests that Sheila is speaking in more pronounced Creole than at any other point in the novel, using her linguistic performance to underscore her immigrant understanding of ethnicity. Jennifer DeVere Brody argues that such hyphenation can be read "as a productive site of contestation which provides agency to subjects who wish to mark their difference" (153). But for Sheila, hyphenation is not a resistant strategy to rearticulate her place in the Canadian nation-space. For her, the hyphen functions in conservative terms as an important continuity between past and present, the interstitial marker of a linear narrative of migration from one location to another, a direct connection to "back home," and as a way for her to mark her "real" ethnicity in a Canadian context. DeVere Brody also observes that hyphenates are often "miscegenated, grossly hybrid terms" (154), arguing that this creolization offers possibilities through which "othered" subjects "seek to play on the hyphenated divide rather than into it" (157). Sheila's language, which frames hyphenation as "proper" and correlates it to identification papers, positions the hyphen instead as a symbolic instrument of governmentality, the most potent symbolic extension of the Multiculturalism Act, and as a tool for disciplining, containing, and keeping track of the nation's not-quite-citizens. Sheila's oversimplified notion of ethnicity reiterates Daphne's lifelong anxiety and reveals several contradictions in the ways her aunt labels her. On one hand, Sheila appears to be giving Daphne a lesson about cultural marginalization, as though she does not already know this or has never been cast as an outsider to the nation. On the other hand, assuming that Daphne already has an answer to the question of her hyphenation is also to assume that she has somehow inherently "known" she is West Indian all along, despite having just learned about her connection to Guyana. Moreover, Sheila's belief that Daphne too needs some sort of hyphenation attenuates the possibility that Daphne can ever be legitimately Canadian, rehearsing the logic she criticizes in those who ask where she is "really" from.

Sheila's conceptualization of ethnicity relies on simple correlations between identity, geography, and biology. For Daphne, both biological and geographical continuities to a real or imagined homeland have been disrupted by the fact of her adoption and by being raised in circumstances in which she did not know of her ethnic background. Yet Sheila is unable to account for these factors; she assumes that she and Daphne share an identity despite their vastly different experiences. Although the specificities of their mixed-race family are never revealed, Sheila seems to espouse what Stuart Hall has called an "innocent notion of the essential black subject" (1996a: 443). While never identifying herself or Daphne as "black," she does have a similarly essential and innocent understanding of what it might mean to be "West Indian," an identity that should be even more difficult to pin down, given the complex creolized realities and multiple colonial histories of the region. In offering her notion of "proper hyphenation," she tries to give Daphne what Gilroy has called "ethnic absolutisms that have offered quick ethnic fixes and cheap pseudo-solidarities as an adequate salve for real pain" (2000: 6). Sheila truly believes she has alleviated Daphne's lifelong sense of loss and confusion, and she cannot understand why Daphne might not want to assume this newfound label.

For Daphne, born and raised in Canada by Anglo-white parents, there are no simple correlations between identity and place the way there are for Sheila. Nor can she locate herself anywhere in Sheila's immigrant narratives. Because a lifetime of uncertainty has forced her to recognize "identity as a politics rather than an inheritance" (Clifford 1992: 116), she can never be an "heir"/Eyre to Sheila's essentialized West Indianness, and no hyphenation will ever be "proper" for her. But perhaps there are benefits to this refusal. In official liberal discourses of multiculturalism, "ethnic" hyphenation is benevolently constructed as a cultural legacy that immigrant parents pass on to their children, but it is also used as a strategy to contain the contagion of the nation's non-white or non-Anglo presence. Daphne, in rejecting Sheila's offering of the label "West Indian-Canadian," also refuses this limiting discourse.

While Daphne refuses Sheila's gift of "propa' hyphenation," she does accept two leather-bound notebooks, journals that were kept by Gerald Eyre, Sheila's father, during his stay in a psychiatric institution around the time of Daphne's birth. Over the following weeks, as she reads the scrawling, cryptic entries, Daphne discovers horrific details about her birth family that she perhaps would rather not know. But, after hundreds of pages of reading she is no closer to learning the specificities of her "racial" or ethnic make-up than she was before meeting Sheila. In his entries, Gerald believes himself to be a white man who is related to Lord Nelson, but also calls himself a "useless black mulatto" (105). What this label might mean in terms of phenotype remains a mystery, since he is alternately described as being both lighter and darker than those around him. Comparing himself unfavourably to his light-skinned daughter Muriel, Daphne's birth mother, he says, "I am like chocolate beside her" (92); yet when contrasting himself to his fellow patients at the institution, he says, "[M]ost of us here are not white, although I am the closest thing to it" (104). Furthermore, the label "mulatto" might explain the "trace of Africa" (5) Daphne sees in her features, but she still has no explanation for Surefoot's other, more crudely expressed observations: "There's some Indians there look like you, but you also got some Chinese or some slanty shit happenin' in those eyes" (14). Given Guyana's history of slavery and indenture, Indigenous and Asian are possible elements in Daphne's "racial" composition, but neither Sheila nor Gerald ever mentions them.

The journals do reveal many other traumatic details about Daphne's birth family, which send her into an extended state of crisis, a mental breakdown, and a binge of alcoholism. Just as Jane Eyre discovers Bertha, the Creole wife hidden in Rochester's attic, Daphne unearths a frightening familial and colonial legacy. From Sheila she learns that her birth mother, Muriel, committed suicide soon after she was born. From the journals she also learns that she and her mother share the same father as a result of an abusive, incestuous relationship between

Muriel and Gerald. She also discovers that, while institutionalized, her grand/father received electroshock therapy, possibly for engaging in homosexual acts with a co-worker. Upon his release, after the rest of the family has left for Canada, Gerald dies in a bizarre, gothic episode in which he escapes into the Guyanese jungle and cuts off his foot after it becomes infected with gangrene. The violence that has shaped this family, in the form of sexual assaults and incest, physical torture, and the madness of colonialism, can be read as a symbolic microcosm of Guyana's turbulent history and that of the Americas as a whole. In the wake of these discoveries, Daphne's denial and refusal are palpable when she sobbingly confronts Sheila about the journals: "There's nothing of me here. They gave me the wrong file. I want the right file. These have nothing to do with me" (170). The unsettlement she has experienced because she has not known her racial background is now compounded by the trauma of what she does know about her biological family. If turning to her Guyanese history was difficult before, it is now devastating in the wake of these realizations and can only bring her more trauma. In light of the journals, Sheila's nostalgia for Guyana is even more troubling. But while she can reminisce about the family's happier memories, Daphne's tragic discoveries confirm that she can never look back to the past for sustenance. Through Daphne's refusal of Sheila's familial and cultural narratives, McWatt dramatizes the impossibility of a return to lost origins and foregrounds Daphne's need to negotiate a space for herself in the only place she has ever inhabited.

"This Is Mine": Or Is It? Learning Ethical Belonging

As the journal entries become increasingly difficult for her to process, Daphne rejects the possibility that Guyana will ever be a place with which she identifies. Instead, casting aside the journals, and looking out of her apartment window, she claims, "The busy street in front of her was in the present, the here and now, no walls, nothing climbing them. *This is mine,* she thought, then repeated it to convince herself" (111–12). But this assertion, however tentative, is deeply problematic. Daphne cannot possibly claim any North American space as hers when helicopters circle the sky outside her window as a tangible reminder of the bloody events of the Oka Crisis. Before she can turn away from her traumatic past, she must also confront her own complacency about the past and present colonial injustices that have been enacted in the nation-space she currently inhabits. Before she can inhabit the

Canadian nation-space in any kind of ethical way, Daphne must first recognize that there is "no geopolitical or psychic setting, no real or imagined *terra nullius* free from the satisfactions and unsettlements of Indigenous (pre)occupation" (Findlay 368).

The Oka Crisis, one of the most notorious acts of "continuous invasion"[3] of Aboriginal peoples, forces Daphne to confront that Canada, like Guyana, is firmly ensconced in the colonial violences on which the Americas have been built. The novel opens on 11 July 1990, the day the Oka Crisis escalates. Mohawks from the Kanesatake reserve of the Mohawk Nation, who had been guarding an area in the town of Oka known as the Pines since May to protect it from the town's plans to build a condominium development and golf course on a sacred Mohawk burial ground, were raided by the Quebec police, who launched tear gas and opened fire on the protesters.[4] A few hours later, in solidarity, Mohawk from the nearby Kahnawake reserve erected a roadblock on the Mercier Bridge, which connects downtown Montreal to its suburbs on the south shore of the Saint Lawrence River. The ensuing standoff between police, later replaced by the army, and the Mohawk lasted the rest of the summer, the duration of McWatt's novel. The events at Oka were a contemporary manifestation of long-standing land claims disputes and a history of colonial practices by French, British, and then Canadian governments that can be traced back to 1717. Some of these are described in the pamphlet that Daphne's colleague, Joanne, leaves in their manager Daniel's briefcase, whose contents are included in their entirety in the narrative (113–15).[5] Far more than a subplot, Oka provides the contemporary colonial context in which Daphne's struggle to belong occurs. In placing Guyana's and Canada's colonial histories side by side, McWatt dismantles the hegemonic narrative of Canada's benevolence, which relies in part on a contrast to other, supposedly more turbulent or more violent histories in the hemisphere.

The Oka Crisis also revealed fissures in the precarious project of nation-building in the Americas. Amelia Kalant argues that Oka was not merely a local issue, specific only to Montreal or Quebec, but "*a Canadian crisis*" (3, emphasis Kalant's). She reads "the meaning of Oka as a moment in the historical production of Canadianness" (9), arguing that in political and discursive terms, much more was at stake for the nation than the issue of land claims:

> By understanding the complex relationship of appropriation/borrowing through which Canada has become "native"... it becomes evident that

> Oka disrupted a tenuous claim to place, to nativeness and to being "good" to the Indians. Moreover, Oka also disturbed Quebecois pretensions to being native/colonized to English Canada – a status that has been created in part in central Canadian history. In other words, the contest at Oka was partly over who gets to claim native status and how that relates to political right, being colonized, moral and national legitimacy. (22)

Far more than a contest between Native and settler, since in Kalant's conceptualization of Oka both categories are complicated by their various legitimate and illegitimate usages, Daphne's African- and/or Caribbean-descended identity adds another layer of complexity to the discourses of "settlement." She similarly struggles, although on different terms, with her own legitimacy in the nation, her ambivalent presence in both English and French "settler" cultures, and the claims she can and cannot make of Canada in the wake of her rejection of Guyana.

The narrative is structured in a way that draws direct parallels between Daphne's personal crises and the unfolding of the events at Oka, but she is initially unable, or unwilling, to recognize any correlation. The Oka Crisis begins the same morning Daphne goes to the adoption agency and learns that her birth family is from Guyana (McWatt 1998: 8–11). The tensions at the barricades rise around the time Daphne meets Sheila and starts reading Gerald's journals (67–92). And as Daphne discloses the traumatic history of her family to Surefoot in a bar, a news broadcast reveals that the army is being sent in, signalling an imminent end to the crisis (172–3). Daphne's self-discovery and the events at Oka are two intersecting narratives that exist palimpsestically, illuminating multiple legacies of "New World" brutality. Initially too traumatized by her familial crisis, Daphne does not recognize this, and lives in solipsistic avoidance: "She felt the filmy tension in the streets during the day, but slid through it, absorbed by her own riddles. She had bypassed street demonstrations and had flipped past the front-page photos in the *Montreal Sun* ... The Mohawk crisis was like a foreign event; she was seeking something closer" (26). Casting Aboriginal events as outside the Canadian nation, Daphne engages in the same discourse others use to label *her* a foreigner, paradoxically rendering Indigenous peoples, to borrow from Terry Goldie, as the "alien within" (13). Before she can fully articulate her own sense of belonging, Daphne needs to unlearn the dangerous attitudes she has internalized.

She cannot initially identify with the struggles at Oka in part because the participants do not conform to the stereotypical images of gentrified noble savages on which she was raised. The night before she meets Sheila, as the events at Oka are shown on television, "Daphne found it all difficult to watch. It was far-removed, a circus, a fantasy. These weren't the Indians she knew" (69). She appears unable to deal with what Thomas King calls "inconvenient Indians" (2012), and with the complex stories and histories of Indigenous resistance that King has chronicled in his similarly titled book, so she turns instead to her childhood copy of *Hiawatha*, comforted by "the familiarity of the image ... These were the quiet people she knew, not those defiantly boisterous others on the television behind her" (McWatt 1998: 70). Daphne's invocation of the noble savage stereotype reflects an image that, to again borrow from Goldie, "shapes the indigene into a historical artifact, a remnant of a golden age that seems to have little connection to anything akin to contemporary life" (17); images of the indigene as prehistoric "provide a way of avoiding the question of 'indigene as social problem'... Each indigene speaking on television for land rights represents a claim that indigenous peoples are more present politics than prehistoric artefact" (155).

McWatt's depiction of Surefoot's activism offers an important counterpoint to Daphne's initial solipsism. It is also a revisionist response to some of the masculinist biases that circulated within contemporary media depictions of the Oka Crisis. Kalant argues that official discourses often ignored the prominent roles played by Mohawk women, who are regarded as spiritual mothers and leaders within their community.[6] It was largely Mohawk women who began the occupation of the Pines in March 1990, but their presence was obscured as the media increasingly focused on a small male segment of radical neotraditionalists called the "Warrior society" (9).[7] McWatt's novel writes a different narrative, in which the male warriors almost never appear. Instead, readers' views of activism behind the barricades come through the female perspective of Surefoot, who participates extensively at the Mercier Bridge.

In an attempt to politicize her, Surefoot invites Daphne to the bridge, telling her, "You've got a lot to learn ... It'll open your eyes" (99). Although initially reluctant, Daphne eventually agrees. Significantly, it is on her first trip to the barricades that she grasps the shared, albeit not easily equated, colonial processes that have denied both of them access to their familial and cultural histories: "Then she recognized the unnamed something she had sensed, the thing they shared that kept them adrift from others, seeming laden and ridiculous. They were creatures that made sense only in the imagination, that had to be invented like the improbable animals formed by clouds in a childhood game. Animals that floated against all odds. That belonged nowhere else" (149). This painful and fleeting sense of connection that Daphne shares with Surefoot might offer an alternative model for ethical belonging, in which community is imagined on terms other than the exclusionary ones offered by the nation. But in the moment such possibilities might be articulated, state forces immediately render them suspect. Just as Daphne comes to realize the shared colonial histories that have necessitated their acts of cultural invention, Surefoot spots her in the crowd. In a powerful symbolic moment, she tries to reach over the barricades to give Daphne a cup of tea, but the police do not allow it. Her offering can be read in multiple ways: as an assertion of her right to the territory she now fights for – she is the host, and Daphne is the guest receiving her hospitality – and also as an act of solidarity, an acknowledgment in the midst of the Oka Crisis of the ways their colonial histories might intertwine. But the repressive state apparatus immediately attenuates this attempt, underscoring the ways governmental forces often work to contain different racialized and ethnic groups, actively thwarting efforts at coalitional politics and transcultural solidarity in the interest of containing, managing, and disciplining the nation's "others."

Despite the unravelling of her own life, Daphne continues to re-evaluate her assumptions about Aboriginal peoples even as she makes a brief visit to Toronto to confront her adoptive parents, returns to Montreal, experiences a mental breakdown, and goes on an extended drinking binge. These tragic events might be read as both a mental and an emotional unravelling, and also as inaugurating new conditions of possibility for Daphne to relate differently to the people and the world around her. When she wakes up a few days later, one of the first images to enter her mind is of Surefoot at the barricades. Still traumatized by the journals, she realizes, now ironically quoting Longfellow, "*By the shining Big-Sea-Water, stood the lodge of Pau-Puk Keewis.* The words were false. It had all been a ridiculous lie" (175). Significantly, her attempts to come to terms with her own family legacy are accompanied by an acknowledgment of both her complicity and her complacency in the fictions she has attached to herself and others. Just as she refuses to be read through her turbulent Guyanese history, so too does Daphne now confront that Aboriginal identities are far more than the fixed and prehistoric images of noble savagery she once believed. In the final section of the novel, Daphne undergoes a notable shift in perception, reflecting much more critically on her own attitudes. This last section, less than thirty pages long, is divided into three short chapters, two of which are significantly titled "New" (179, 193).

It is not coincidental that Daphne re-evaluates her assumptions about racial identities and her assumptions about Indigenous peoples simultaneously, as she realizes that she cannot read either herself or others through stereotypes or oversimplified racial (or racist) narratives. Daphne's metamorphosis might be read as a shedding, a process of *coming* "out of her skin" to embrace a different understanding of the significance of "race" and phenotype. As a child she searched for a singular "racial" identity to answer the question "what are you," and attempted to contain the complex, messy strains of "race" that marked her body in various and contradictory ways. But by the end of the novel she is no longer interested in naming herself or using easily recognizable labels as a route to belonging. She ultimately rejects the idea that her body is meant to be a repository of racial truth; instead she sees its connection to other, more complex histories.

Whereas she once "kept few mirrors in the house" (4) and painted her stainless steel appliances to keep them "safe from reflection" (4), she now actively works to read other corporeal narratives. As she packs for her weekend at her co-worker Marc's cottage, she sees, for the first, time, the colonial history that marks her body:

> In the bathroom she caught sight of her face, and for the first time in a week she truly saw it. She was ugly. Generations of submission and rebellion still battled for position there. Were hers the eyes of the victors or the vanquished? The ears of slaves or masters? Her hair was born of a cruel passion that sprang up kinky and horny in the moist heat. And her nose was a sculpture: a monument to the history of bones pounding other bones, mixing up dry marrow to unveil the post-historic shape that was displayed like a museum piece in the centre of her face. (186)

Contemplating the ways she has been formed by a history of transatlantic slavery, Daphne reflects on a history of rape and miscegenation that extends far beyond her immediate family. But this difficult moment might also be read for its glimmers of possibility. Her reflections transform her from a passive vessel into an active author of an alternative historical narrative. Her nose, on which she has meditated extensively throughout the narrative, becomes a "monument" to commemorate the enslaved, for whom there are no other memorial sites in the Americas. This moment of corporeal commemoration provides insight into Daphne's initial fascination with Surefoot's photographs of her scars, her own bodily legacy of colonial violence. Both Daphne and Surefoot reconceptualize their bodies as sites of resistance against imposed silences, reading on them alternative narratives that often remain unrecorded in official histories.

Daphne also reflects on the ways her biological family's traumas and the fact of her adoption have disrupted any oversimplified notions of family or kinship relations. As she finally acknowledges her grief, she meditates upon

> [t]he family tree: at the top, Gerald Eyre and his wife, Mary; on a branch below them, Muriel Eyre beside Sheila Eyre. And Daphne? Where was she meant to perch? Parallel, cornered, or off to the side? And a branch for Bill and Jennifer? There seemed no spot she could claim for herself, no offshoot to which she could be grafted, to close the gaping hole in her reality once and for all. So many disrupted nests. (196)

Daphne is devastated by the impossibility of mapping her tangled genealogy or intermingling her birth and adoptive families after her birth mother's immigration and subsequent suicide. Her experiences necessitate a radical re-evaluation of kinship relations based in linear genealogical descent. They also necessitate a reconceptualization of the ways in which familial discourses are used to construct national narratives. If, as Anne McClintock argues in *Imperial Leather*, "nations are symbolically figured as domestic genealogies" (357), then Daphne's family can never provide a model of homogeneity and linear descent on which such mythologies are built. Her tangled family tree will never be seen as a symbolic microcosm of the nation. This points to the fundamental unethicality of narrating nations through genealogical metaphors. This model of an imagined national family cannot make room for "non-normative" families, families that have been disrupted by or bear traces of violence or that descend from colonialism. It is a familial/ national model that writes out both Surefoot and Daphne, as well as other colonial subjects.

"I'm Here": Renegotiating the Canadian Landscape

Daphne's trip to Marc's cottage and her entry into the iconic Canadian wilderness in the final section play a significant role in her shifts towards ethical belonging. At this site, Daphne's awakening culminates and she is forced to question her preconceived understandings of "Canadianness." From the opening pages, Daphne invokes romanticized clichés of the Canadian wilderness. As she and her colleagues plan their trip, Daphne imagines postcard images of forests and loons: "'We could sleep outside on pine needles ... Are there berries you can eat there?'" (29). Upon their long-awaited arrival, "Daphne felt the eminence of cottages – woodland shrines where rites of the seasons were performed year after year. She was an initiate" (188). Kalant argues that such mythologization is a significant aspect of nation formation, claiming that "the search for unity amidst diversity has always led, in Canada, to ... the (native) North, a stand-in for ancient authenticity" (41). But in the wake of Daphne's witnessing the events at Oka, McWatt's portrayal of the trip challenges these hegemonic representations of northern wilderness. The weekend can never be the neutral, depoliticized escape that Sylvie, for example, longs it to be when she asks Marc to turn off the news report about the stand-off on the car radio: "It's been nothing but bad news for weeks. Let's try to have a weekend without it, okay?" (187). The arguments the co-workers have had about Oka continue after they arrive, and the resulting tensions remain as an undercurrent to their visit. In the face of ongoing Aboriginal land claims, the northern landscape is not allowed to be a naturalized, mythical space of "escape."

In the final episode, McWatt engages in a sustained intertextual conversation with Margaret Atwood. Daphne's observation that she goes through life "just below the surface" (200) points to the ways this section resonates with Atwood's *Surfacing* (1972). In Atwood's novel, the unnamed protagonist, her partner, and another couple go to her family's cottage, similarly located near the Ontario–Quebec border, in search of her father, who has disappeared. While McWatt rehearses numerous tropes from this novel, there are also notable differences, the most obvious being her foregrounding of a racialized protagonist, a sharp contrast to Atwood's largely Anglo- and Franco-white narrative.[8] This intertextuality draws attention to the sustained exclusions of race from both hegemonic Canadian cultural production and constructions of the northern landscape. As McKittrick observes, a black presence in Canada is too often presumed to be a surprise, "unexpected [and] shocking, concealed in a landscape of systematic blacklessness" (2006: 93). McKittrick acknowledges that her understanding of "blackness," like mine, is borrowed from Rinaldo Walcott's in *Black Like Who?* Thus, although Daphne's racial indeterminacy is foregrounded in McWatt's novel, I utilize "black" here to invoke her messy and contested histories as well as the fluid understandings of the term posited by Walcott and McKittrick. Juxtaposing McWatt's narrative with Atwood's draws attention to the historical "blacklessness" through which literary and geographical landscapes in Canada have been constructed. Furthermore, while in Atwood's narrative the imperial threat comes from the Americans (who are ultimately revealed to be fellow Canadians), McWatt instead foregrounds the ongoing Canadian colonization of Aboriginal peoples. In so doing, she contests the iconic northern landscape as a site of authentic Canadian identity, depicting it instead as a site of colonial appropriation and racial marginalization. Thus, rather than a rewriting of an earlier literary tradition, it might be more instructive to see McWatt's novel as signifying on Atwood, in Henry Louis Gates's sense of "repetition with a signal difference" (5). These differences show McWatt struggling with some of the questions W.H. New articulates in *Land Sliding* (1997), wherein he queries, "What happens when writers and readers in a society such as Canada's want to acknowledge established traditions yet to resist simply inscribing them, or to parody tradition without necessarily rejecting it, or to devise variant forms of convention in the name of greater accuracy or greater freedom?" (16). McWatt's depiction of the "north" similarly strives to re-evaluate hegemonic Canadian representations of the landscape, particularly in the wake of the Oka stand-off.

Daphne's first immersion into the landscape is powerfully and symbolically illustrative of her metamorphosis:

> Daphne's entry was timid; she waded in from the shore instead of plunging into deeper water from the dock. The soft mud of the lake bottom gushed up through her toes; weeds wrapped around her ankles. The sinking, gooey feeling was unpleasant, so she jumped up and swam awkwardly, breaking the surface now and then with a kick of her feet. Not a graceful swimmer, she gulped for air and swallowed water before deciding just to tread for a while. (191)

Naked, kicking, struggling to breathe, surrounded by water and slime ... the images are resonant of childbirth. But she instead "breaks the surface," experiencing a rebirth as she emerges into her newly conscious self. In this regard, McWatt's revision of Atwood again diverges significantly. Atwood's protagonist regresses into infantile, even animalistic behaviour; by contrast, Daphne's emotional development, her desire to move forward, is reflected in her casting off of some of her emotionally arrested behaviours. Reaching down between her legs, "she felt the tiny pad of hair that had sprouted" (191). No longer infantilizing herself, and developing a new awareness of the spaces she inhabits, she now inhabits her body on different terms as well.

As Daphne canoes with Marc for the first time, she looks at the surrounding landscape and pointedly asks him, "Who owns all this?" (194), thinking immediately of Surefoot. Marc's reply, "Most of it's crown land" (194), invokes a particular aspect of colonial history. As David McNab points out, "[t]he Aboriginal commons are no longer seen as their Territories. They became Crown lands, usually belonging to or owned by the provinces. Then they were taken up as government lands for its exclusive and, frequently, private use" (16). Daphne's query lays bare this process, drawing attention to "the dilemma of geographic enigmas ... including the enigma of what gets forgotten, or hidden, or lost, in the comforts of ordinary space" (Yaeger 4). In struggling to inhabit the Canadian nation-space ethically, Daphne refuses the strategic amnesias that enable ongoing colonial practices, striving instead for a new poetics that considers the underlying violence of spatial appropriation in the Americas. Her interrogations of Marc echo a significant premise on which McKittrick's *Demonic Grounds* is based. As McKittrick argues, invoking Henri Lefebvre and Edouard Glissant: "Insisting that ... the landscape does not simply function as a decorative background, opens up the possibility for thinking about the production of space as unfinished, a poetics of questioning" (xxii–xxiii). These are the poetics that now inform Daphne's relationship to the landscape.

Daphne's question speaks to the challenges she faces in trying to lay claim to a place without being appropriative. How might she try to "root" herself on different terms than those of previous waves of European colonizers? Goldie argues: "In their need to become 'native,' to belong here, whites in Canada ... have adopted a process which I have termed 'indigenization.' A peculiar word, it suggests the impossible necessity of becoming indigenous" (13). Daphne must attempt to "ground" herself without rehearsing this process. Perpetually cast as a racialized outsider, she has never felt herself to be "native" to Canada. Now, she does not seek to make herself an insider or to understand herself as indigenous. Instead, she sets out to establish her own terms for belonging while maintaining some recognition of the histories of Aboriginal displacement.

In the final pages, after Joanne cruelly confronts her about the journals and her mental breakdown, Daphne tearfully escapes the cottage by again taking a canoe out into the lake. She initially struggles, but soon increases her speed, "feeling she had mastered the canoe" (McWatt 1998: 198). This triumph is short-lived, though. She reaches the opposite shore and falls asleep in the sun, and when she awakes, exhausted and sunburnt, she is unable to do more than drag the canoe "clumsily" (201) into the water, "paddling awkwardly" (201); this forces her to relinquish the canoe in search of another route back to the cottage. Her abandoning of the canoe is a symbolic moment in which she refuses the appropriations of white settlers, the same ones in which she once engaged with her acts of imitation. Indigenous scholars point out that the canoe "is a metaphor related to the creation of Turtle Island-North America. In this respect the canoe is depicted in many Aboriginal creation stories" (McNab, Hodgins, and Standen 238–9). If Daphne wants to indigenize herself on different terms than those of earlier waves of white settlers, her narrative cannot be based on the appropriation of Indigenous myths or symbols. In leaving the canoe behind to enter the woods, she is abandoning a borrowed cultural tradition. In finally coming to terms with her own traumatic family history, she must instead construct her own symbols of creation.

For Daphne, this process of (re)creation is not easy, revealing that "both uprooting and regrounding can entail forms of mourning, nostalgia and remembrance as well as physical sickness and experiences of trauma" (Ahmed et al. 9). In an attempt to exorcise the ghosts of her Grand/father, she decides to bury the journals. Repeatedly chanting "Bansimande," which she first heard from Sheila, she places Gerald's journals in the ground "with the ceremony and seriousness of a dignitary's funeral" (McWatt 1998: 203):

> Her performance was personal – primary – as she patted the earth into a small mound. The building of a monument, one she expected to sprout out of the earth like the curly-haired marble head of Zeus atop its shapely carved and muscular body. The beginning of time. The seed of forgiveness. (203)

In this act, Daphne creates her own ritual, invoking language and symbolism from the multiple cultural influences in her life, remaking them to reflect her complex experiences. An act Daphne characterizes as a temporal rupture, this burial allows her both to turn away from her past and to root herself in the Canadian nation-space. Her regrounding is not triumphant; it is traumatic, painful, and difficult work. At this point in the novel Daphne is still upset about her fight with Joanne, hung over, exhausted, stiff, sunburnt and sore, scratched and bruised, and covered in dirt and mosquito bites. She has demonstrated neither the ability nor the desire to dominate the land as previous waves of colonial arrivals have. Instead, her knowledge of the impacts of colonial violence on her own family and history inform her attempts to root herself on different and more ethical terms. Burying her traumatic Guyanese history on "northern," Canadian soil, Daphne further intermingles these spaces and these narratives, planting a new monument that commemorates familial and historical trauma in both these locations, and again grounds Canada in the wider context of the Americas.

In the final three pages, although seemingly lost in the wilderness after burying Gerald's journals, Daphne feels she is "ready to go home" (203), but she still appears unsure of where that might be. Before she leaves for the cottage, she seeks out Michel at the Jean Talon market to ask him for employment selling the vegetables he cultivates on his family's farm. Her newfound interest in agriculture is a powerful symbol of her desire for grounding and her attempt to "root" herself. Unburdening herself of the journals has allowed her to contemplate this possibility. Finding her way onto the side of a highway, she hitchhikes back to Montreal and goes directly to the market to start her new job. To the first truck driver who picks her up, she says, "I'd like to go home" (207), referring to Montreal, a place where she can finally start anew. It is the first time she has uttered the word "home" aloud in the entire novel. Each driver who takes her closer to the city watches her "stare fixedly ahead" (207), purposefully looking only forward, never back. When she gets to the market, she announces to Michel, "I'm here" (208). Now that she has pondered "Who owns all this?," her final utterance in the novel is in sharp contrast to her earlier wish to convince herself that "this is mine." Here she signals a different ethicality, in which she is "placed," but does not invoke the same language of possession she once used. This moment also signals a sense of arrival that is in sharp contrast to her destinationless wandering when she first moved to Montreal. Significantly, it is through the city-space rather than the nation-space that Daphne can finally negotiate a sense of "home," suggesting that national affiliations might well be a difficult, impossible, or undesirable route to belonging. This turning to the city instead of the nation, just as Brand's second-generation characters do, again gestures towards a different, anti-national paradigm for belonging.

In the final section, Daphne also continues to think often about Surefoot, who has been arrested for her participation in the stand-off at the Mercier Bridge. Through Surefoot's insistence that Daphne re-evaluate her perceptions, McWatt may also, like Brand, be looking towards new models for citizenship. "[T]hough belonging does not, *eo ipso*, belong to nationalism, it is nationalism which in our world has appropriated and reconfigured most people's sense of belonging and identity" (Hetedoft and Hjort viii). Surefoot's Indigenous knowledge, however, refuses this model. Kalant points out that "assumptions of 'race' and ethnicity, integral to Western assumptions of national communities, are antithetical to many First Nations practices of making national belonging a matter of behaviour" (225). This alternative conceptualization brings much to bear on Daphne's rejection of ethnic absolutisms and fixed notions of identity. As she meditates on a front-page photo of Surefoot's arrest during the dismantling of the Mercier Bridge barricades, she is struck by her sense of "final triumph" (180). As the police lift her into a truck, "Surefoot's smile wasn't one of nationhood or kinship; it was a simple one of fact" (181). This refusal of both familial and national routes to belonging establishes a model for Daphne as she too struggles to come to terms with her place in the nation. Surefoot's most cogent advice to Daphne – and to herself – is that "belonging is what you give yourself" (98). Her insistence on this powerfully shifts the terms through which belonging is articulated, removing it from the intertwined and exclusionary familial and national discourses. By offering different terms for belonging, Surefoot's statement creates possibilities for chosen, outer-national and outer-biological collectivities that might be based in knowledge, awareness, and ethicality.

In beginning to shift the terms of belonging in such a way, the novel offers no straightforward answers as to what belonging ethically on Indigenous land might look like for the descendants of immigrants. Rather, it suggests that such relationships between the various communities and nations in Canada – both those that have settled and those that have been violently unsettled – require ongoing negotiations, particularly in the face of continuous invasions. This is particularly important in the wake of the "conclusion" in 2015 of the Canadian government's Truth and Reconciliation Commission, which arguably in some ways arbitrarily suggested that some of the issues facing Indigenous communities in Canada have now been resolved. But as Rinaldo

Walcott points out, "[j]ustice is always a work in progress that can only be made sense of by those who understand themselves to be on the receiving end of it, thus making the attempt for its accomplishment always a question or an unfinished project" (2006: 88). I want to suggest that McWatt's novel is a similarly unfinished project. Some of the possibilities it engenders for ethical belonging are facilitated by the novel's decoupling of belonging from the nation, which offers differently articulated geographical and conceptual grounds on which such ongoing negotiations might happen.

Chapter 3

"I Knew This Was England": Myths of "Back Home" in Andrea Levy's *Fruit of the Lemon*

If Englishness doesn't define me, then redefine Englishness.

Andrea Levy, qtd in Maya Jaggi, "Redefining Englishness"

This chapter builds upon my analyses of *Out of My Skin* by extending the discussion of what kinds of attachments the second-generation children of immigrants may – or may not – have to real and imagined elsewheres. My focus shifts from Canada to the UK: Andrea Levy's *Fruit of the Lemon* (1999) focuses on a young black Englishwoman named Faith Jackson, the daughter of Jamaican immigrants who arrived in 1948, and her struggles to situate herself within hegemonic constructions of the nation. The first and last of the novel's three sections are set in England, while the second section centres on her first trip to Jamaica, the country her parents continue to call home.

In this chapter I discuss how, through Faith's travel, Levy tests the myth of "return" to an ancestral familial "homeland" – in this case Jamaica – and finds it an inadequate paradigm through which to frame the experiences of second-generation black Britons. Like McWatt, Levy demythologizes the notion of a Caribbean "back home" and rejects Caribbean attachments as a route to belonging or identity for the children of immigrants. While going "back home" is (sometimes) desirable for Faith's immigrant parents, who invoke this imagined concept in the face of a nation that creates no space for them, Faith herself must negotiate both her relationship with the country of her parents' birth and that of her own as she moves towards "settling up" the ways she locates herself in England. Faith's trip to Jamaica problematizes the notion that the children of immigrants can, should, or are able to attach themselves easily to their parents' birth countries: for Faith, Jamaica will never be "back home" the way it is for her parents. Nonetheless, her trip proves valuable in other ways in that it allows her to situate herself on different terms both within her family and within the country in which she was born. I argue that Faith's trip demonstrates the ways the novel works to "redefine Englishness" for immigrants and their children and also for the nation as a whole. In *Cartographies of Diaspora*, Avtar Brah articulates the UK as a *diaspora space*, arguing that this "foregrounds the entanglement of genealogies of dispersion with those of staying put" (16). Only once Faith acknowledges these messy entanglements can she begin to come to terms with England's colonial legacies and attempt to situate herself within them.

As such, the trajectory of this novel is similar to that of *Out of My Skin*, in that Faith, like Daphne, must learn to challenge dominant national narratives. The novel traces a profound epistemological shift, whereby Faith moves from a false sense of settlement that initially comes by internalizing racism and hegemonic ideologies, such as those espoused by the BBC and disseminated through the mythologization of the English countryside, through a mental and emotional breakdown comparable to Daphne's, and into a new understanding of the ways in which legacies of slavery and colonialism shape the England she eventually calls "home." Like Daphne, Faith must, in the wake of her trip to Jamaica, learn to settle on different terms, and her invocation of "home" comes with a sense of greater awareness and ethicality than she demonstrates at the outset of her physical and emotional journey.

Fruit of the Lemon, Levy's third novel, occupies a significant place in her body of writing. Like her first two novels, *Every Light in the House Burnin'* (1994) and *Never Far From Nowhere* (1996), it focuses on a second-generation female protagonist whose parents migrated to England from Jamaica. But while her first two novels are set almost entirely on council estates, her third novel explores more intensely the ambivalent relationships black Britons may or may not have to Jamaica and its place in the history of transatlantic slavery. As such, it anticipates some of the migratory concerns she takes up in *Small Island* (2004) and the legacies of slavery she explores in her historical novel *The Long Song* (2010). *Fruit of the Lemon* might, in hindsight, also be understood as a historical novel: it offers a glimpse of black life in England in the early to mid-1980s, a period of "rediscovered nationalism" (Golbourne 59) in Britain that drove the conservative Thatcherist politics of the decade and that led to intense racial violence, some of which Levy narrates.

At the outset of the narrative, Faith, a university-educated woman in her early twenties, is living an unquestioningly assimilationist life, naively asserting her Englishness in a highly charged political context wherein blackness is actively written out of the nation. She appears uninterested in her family's Jamaican background and has just moved in with three white flatmates while pursuing a career at the BBC in London. After a brief prologue that narrates the early life of her parents, Wade and Mildred, in Jamaica, and their arrival in England in 1948, Part I opens with Faith's reference to their unusual obsession: "My parents' hobby was collecting empty boxes. They'd been doing it for years" (15). Their unending conversations about the merits of various types of boxes speaks to their sense of unsettlement in London, even after living there for more than thirty years and owning a home for nearly twenty. They are a sharp contrast to Faith's friend and flatmate, Marion, whose entire extended family of "indigenous" white Britons "had all lived in the same street for generations" (93). Marion's family have not always owned their own homes either; even so, they feel a sense of entitlement to their neighbourhood and to the nation that eludes Faith's parents. Moreover, when she spends time with Marion's family, Faith remains silent when they direct blatant racist slurs at various groups, including black people. But while she may not share their racism, at the beginning of the novel, Faith, perhaps surprisingly, shares in this sense of being "settled" in England despite her parents' migratory history.

When her father explains their box collection by announcing, "Your mum and me are thinking of going back home" (44), Faith is confused: "I thought of our old council flat where Carl and me had grown up. Although we had lived in Crouch End for years, it was the crumbling flat in Stoke Newington that I thought of as home" (44). Her inability, or unwillingness, to understand persists: she first believes her parents have lost all their money, then assumes they will go back to Jamaica only for a holiday. When she realizes that they intend a permanent return, Faith is angry and confused by what she perceives to be their sudden nostalgia. She wonders, "Why Jamaica? Why is Jamaica home?" (45). Her anger reflects her rejection of a familial narrative in which she is, by extension, also cast as an outsider to the nation of her birth. But her denial of her family's connection to any place outside of England also indicates her complicity in a national narrative that only understands belonging in singular terms.

Seemingly unaware of the extent to which the nation's colonial history has impacted her life, Faith must learn to question her complacency, just as McWatt's protagonist, Daphne, must challenge the benevolent myth of peaceful Canadian settlement. Faith's understanding of her place in England undergoes a significant shift in the first section of the novel; her employment at the BBC, her visit to her flatmate Simon's country house, and her witnessing of a violent, racially motivated attack on a bookstore, all reveal Faith's increasing distrust of both unofficial and institutionalized narratives of the nation. Together, these events force her to confront dominant constructions of "Englishness" and the ways they both tangibly and symbolically exclude her. As the novel opens she appears to be as "settled" as Marion; but these three episodes work to un-settle her, compelling her to realize that she cannot inhabit the nation on the same terms as her white friends. Paul Gilroy observes in *Small Acts*, "blackness and Englishness are constructed as incompatible, mutually exclusive terms. To speak of the British or English people is to speak of the *white* people" (27). Unable to adjust to this racialization of nationality, Faith must instead work to comprehend it. The rearticulation of national identity has been one of the guiding premises of Levy's corpus. As she argues in "This Is My England," an article she wrote for *The Guardian* in the same month *Fruit of the Lemon* was published, "Englishness must never be allowed to attach itself to ethnicity."

Spaces of Englishness: The British Broadcasting Corporation

When Faith begins working at the BBC, she is unconcerned that she is merely a cog in the wheel of one of the nation's most powerful creative institutions and most public arbiters of British culture. Few other cultural institutions play as significant a role as the BBC in scripting national hegemonies. But as Barnor Hesse observes, "[p]art of the difficulty with dominant cultural formations of Britain is the inability or reluctance of its institutions to accept that European racism was and is a constitutive feature of British nationalism" (2000: 18). This racism, immediately evident in Faith's interaction with colleagues and supervisors, is also a significant aspect of the BBC's history as an ideological tool of Empire. Peter Kalliney observes that the BBC, founded in 1922, "exemplifies the close association between metropolitan modernism and imperial rule" (119), given the ways in which it advocated the consumption of European high culture as a kind of colonial self-discipline.

In the early to mid-twentieth century, "the BBC exported cultural programming to British Africa, India, and the West Indies in an effort to bolster loyalty to the empire among colonial listeners ... not by broadcasting straightforward propaganda, but by advertising the humane spirit and co-operative cultural mission of the empire" (2). In this role as an exporter of British culture, tastes, and values, the BBC, as Dionne Brand recollects in *A Map to the Door of No Return*, was also a way to remind its overseas subjects "that you are living elsewhere" (13); and that, in the Caribbean, "[y]ou are living on an island, banished or uninhabited" (13). Levy comments on the links between the BBC's current practices and the nation's colonial history through the imagery she uses to describe the building and Faith's experiences. The novel's construction of setting and event composes a richly symbolic critique of the BBC's centrality to the cultural processes that marginalize Faith.

The building is portrayed as a microcosm of the nation, a "citadel of entertainment" (30), its borders carefully guarded from outsiders by security guards at the gates. Those who wish to enter must carry a pass or other form of official identification. In her first position as a wardrobe assistant, Faith's supervisor, Henry, makes several references that gesture towards a history of racialized servitude. When Faith arrives on her first day, Henry inquires, "Are you for me?" (34), a question that evokes connotations of ownership – not just of Faith's labour but of her entire person. She is immediately cast as both invisible and hypervisible when Henry promptly forgets she is in the room, then, upon remembering her presence, controls the way she is allowed to occupy space by only allowing her to sit in one specific chair. He also tells her, "We're like a family here, Faith" (36), evoking historical rhetoric of the plantation "family." When she moves to another department to be a dresser, her brother Carl is unimpressed, telling her, "A bit like being a servant – I couldn't do that" (139). These echoes of servitude prey upon Faith, gradually melding into her memories. The images are reminiscent of Faith's first reference to her parents' arrival in Britain, in which her classmates' cruel taunting, "Your mum and dad came on a banana boat" (3), gradually blurs in her mind to "your mum and dad came on a slave ship" (4). In both instances, the references draw attention to legacies of forced migration, slavery, and colonization that have been submerged by mainstream discourses but that nonetheless haunt her daily personal interactions. During the first section of the novel, such historical erasures become increasingly evident to Faith, contributing to her growing unease within the English nation-space.

Faith's job interview invokes crude examples of blatant racial prejudice, yet Faith is initially reluctant to accept that such behaviour can take place at the BBC. She applies for her new position amidst warnings from her colleagues that no black dressers have ever been hired. Her two male interviewers render her ineligible, arguing that she is simultaneously overqualified yet lacking experience. After a ridiculous exchange in which she is told that her job evaluations indicate she walks too slowly, Faith confronts them and is told repeatedly that "[t]here is no discrimination going on in this department" (109). Reluctant to face their complicity in racialized power structures, the two men are more interested in where Faith heard the "rumour" that there are no black dressers than in Faith's concerns. As Gilroy points out in *Postcolonial Melancholia,* racial nationalism too often goes unrecognized in "the anonymous, pin-striped indifference of those who might not profess their commitment to race hierarchy ... but whose actions institutionalize it nonetheless" (124). Despite the disturbing events of her job interview, Faith is awarded the position as dresser. But whereas black female servants historically engaged in extensive corporeal interaction with white women, nursing and dressing them and providing other forms of physical caretaking, Faith instead contends with twentieth-century segregationist attitudes that have maintained spatial distance between black and white bodies. After waiting for weeks, the unspoken assumption that she should not be allowed to dress the white actors culminates in her being awarded a job dressing puppets for a children's program.

Carl's militant black nationalist girlfriend, Ruth, tells Faith she was given the job "just to shut you up. It's tokenism. It's what they do ... [T]hey just employ you and then they can say, yes, we have a black person" (140). Although she offers a significant corrective to Faith's naivety, and to her problematic belief that the events of the interview no longer matter since she got the job in the end, Ruth's black nationalism is not shown to be an empowering politics for Faith. Ruth's oversimplified categorizations and her binaristic belief that "it's black against white" (141) are an inaccurate description of the complexities of British racial politics; furthermore, they cannot account for her own realities as a biracial woman. Ruth's rigid and restrictive attitudes also lead her to tyrannize Carl and Faith's mother, whom she criticizes for cooking roast lamb instead of "black food" (144). She further chastises Mildred with explanations of her false consciousness and her "triple yoke" of oppression as a poor black woman (144). While Ruth ostensibly strives to consider the intersecting dynamics of race, class, and gender, her segregationist attitude, reflected in her comment that Faith needs to "spend some more time among [her] own people" (143), is as problematic as Marion's idealistic second-wave feminist assumptions of universal sisterhood or her Marxist assurances that "all racism would be swept away after the revolution" (94). Ruth's ethnonationalism is shown to be as partial, selective, and exclusionary as the dominant discourses of "Englishness." At no point in the novel does Faith identify with Ruth or her struggles, which suggests that Levy may well be criticizing all forms of political dogmatism, not just those perpetuated in the interest of the nation or the state.

Spaces of Englishness: The Countryside

Overwhelmed by work anxieties, Faith agrees to go away for a weekend with her flatmate, Simon, to his parents' house in the country, where they both hope for "some peace and quiet" (114). This language of restful relaxation reflects their desire for escape; however, their destination in the countryside, the epitome of "true Englishness," renders this impossible for Faith. As Katherine McKittrick points out in *Demonic Grounds,* "the idea that space 'just is,' and that space and place are merely containers for human complexities and social relations, is terribly seductive" (xi). But, following Lefebvre, she goes on to argue that "[g]eography is not ... secure and unwavering; we produce space, we produce its meanings, and we work very hard to make geography what it is" (xi). Levy's portrayal of the English countryside is an examination of the spatial processes through which the landscape of rolling green and meadows has become iconic of a racialized notion of Englishness. The trip, although comprising only one chapter of the novel, is her most extended engagement with dominant constructions of nationhood and what they illuminate, and, more significantly, obfuscate, about English histories and geographies.

Since childhood, Faith has longed to visit "the countryside," but the trip with Simon is the first time she has had access to this landscape. When she recalls the road trips she and Carl took as teenagers, "the country always looked so charming" from his van (56). But, as she further recounts, "[o]ccasionally we used to stop, to get out of the van with the aim of running through a field or paddling in a river. But we were always greeted with fences and gates and barbed wire. And we never knew how to actually get onto 'that green and pleasant land'" (56).[1]

Levy's textual representations of the landscape draw attention to the ways, in Mitchell's terms, "[l]andscape is … a form of ideology. It is a way of carefully selecting and representing the world so as to give it a particular meaning … [and] constructing consent and identity – in organizing a receptive audience – for the projects and desires of powerful social interests" (100). Levy similarly troubles the assumption that space "just is," drawing attention to complex social and economic processes through which it is constructed. Faith's experiences similarly work to historicize the landscape, making visible a legacy of racialized and class-based power dynamics that many of its white inhabitants erase.

Faith is able to gain access to this landscape because she is accompanied by her white, upper-middle-class friend. Simon describes his parents' village as "quintessentially English" (115) – and therefore not urban (i.e., where the immigrants live) – yet it is neither named specifically nor linked to a particular region. Faith only observes that it is "off the main road" (115), suggesting that "the countryside" could be anywhere outside London. This descriptive absence is noteworthy in a realist narrative in which specific London streets and neighbourhoods are named throughout Part I. In this regard, Simon is correct: the village *is* "quintessentially English," represented as an imagined geography, not a literal one. According to Ian Baucom, definitions of Englishness have, particularly since the rise of Empire in the eighteenth century, been closely intertwined with the dynamics of place and geography. He argues that spaces such as the cathedral, the cricket pitch, and – most significantly in the context of Levy's novel – the country house are "locations of identity" (19), places "where an identity-preserving, identity-enchanting, and identity-transforming aura lingers, or is made to appear" (19). Levy explores these formative processes through Faith's visit, during which the country house becomes a metonym for a particular vision of the nation.

Simon's house also exists within an imagined temporality, a vague, indeterminate vision/version of the past. It is introduced without specific architectural descriptors that would allow the house to be linked to a particular period:

> [The house] was made of brick with doors and windows and a roof like most houses. But it was big – a mansion to anyone from a terraced house. And perfectly symmetrical … There were pillars on either side of the door and a large long stained-glass window above it. There were no buildings

> to the left or to the right. Only trees, flowering bushes and variegated shrubs that seemed to cradle the house like a cupped hand. (117)

The wealth of Simon's family is immediately apparent to Faith, but her imprecise description of their home is surprising. While their rented house in London is immediately periodized as "Georgian" (24), this home is more vaguely described through common, undateable architectural features. Its order and mastery over the natural landscape are revealed through the surrounding vegetation, which protectively enables its seamless integration into the surroundings. Its occupants are described in similarly indeterminate gestures to an earlier time. Simon's mother, Margaret, has "grey hair waved into a neat style, reminiscent of WRAFs in Second World War films" (118), while his father, Guy, looks like "he'd just stepped out of the plains of Africa during a hunting trip … He was even wearing a safari jacket" (120). Baucom points out that, particularly since the nineteenth century, "even when it was conceived as something spatially local, or near at hand, Englishness defied its suitors by greeting them across a temporal chasm. Only ever confidently located in the past, it manifested itself in the auratic locale only at the expense of displacing itself in time, rendering itself recollectible, but, finally, ungraspable" (37).

Together, these features of the "quintessentially English" village, with its imagined geography and indeterminate temporality evoking "how England used to be" (116), signal a broader analysis of questions of "heritage" and what, in recent decades, has come to be known as the "Heritage industry" in the UK. As a racialized subject, Faith grapples with some of the issues Stuart Hall raises in his essay, "Whose Heritage? Un-settling 'The Heritage,' Re-imagining the Post-nation." Hall argues that the Heritage industry, which emphasizes the conservation of items, buildings, and historical sites rather than the support of new forms of cultural production, is used to validate "a 'national story' whose terms we already know. The Heritage thus becomes the material embodiment of the spirit of the nation" (3–4). He claims that the Heritage is only "intended for those who 'belong' – a society which is imagined as … culturally homogenous and unified" (6). During her visit, Faith must confront the ways she is written out of these hegemonic visions of the nation, which are largely foreign to her.

The country house is a significant location within Heritage tourism. Baucom points out that "country house fetishism" (21) is "a privileged institution of a discourse of cultural discipline" (167). Such houses are one of the principal means through which the nation constructs its identity, so that complicity in this discourse becomes a necessary element of social citizenship. Robert Hewison argues that "[b]y a mystical process of identification the country house becomes the nation, and love of one's country makes obligatory a love of the country house" (53). This slippage between the domestic and the national is best exemplified in Simon, whose excitement about returning to his childhood home is evident in his repeated assertion that the house and village are "beautiful" (115, 117), and who is convinced that Faith shares his adoration. But she tells him instead, "It doesn't look real" (116). Her mental comparison between Simon's house and one she recalls from a model village in a park near her childhood home suggests that both may well be only deceptive simulacra. Simon reads her comment as a compliment, but actually, her reaction reveals that the national discourse in which they participate is perhaps wholly imaginary.

When they enter the house, Simon and Faith also enter the tradition of the country house tour, which dates back to the late eighteenth century, a time when homeowners became "increasingly interested in displaying [their homes] to a genteel traveling public" (Helsinger 105). Simon displays his parents' home to Faith a similar manner, drawing attention to specific architectural features. Their different class locations are evident in Faith's surprise not at the details, but at the numerous rooms with designated single uses, often for leisure pursuits. The boundary between home and museum is increasingly blurred as Simon points out the portraits of esteemed family members, telling Faith, "[W]e sometimes have to lend the pictures out for exhibitions" (121). Next she learns that "[t]he house was also furnished with antiques. Old furniture passed down from generation to generation. Everything seemed to have been somebody else's once. And most things, Simon would tell me, were 'priceless'" (121). This collection of heritage items is more than a tangible symbol of the Wyndhams' wealth; it provides a material route through which the family can confirm its already well-established genealogy and pass on to succeeding generations the privileges that accompany property ownership. When he and Faith arrive at Simon's old bedroom, the discourses of the domestic, the familial, and the national become explicitly intertwined. Faith is fascinated by the family tree painted on one wall – not of Simon's family, but a meticulous copy of England's royal family. This family tree provides the symbolic context for the Wyndham collection. Simon's ancestry can easily be correlated to the paintings and furniture in the house, whereas his reproduction of the royal family is a means for him to interpolate himself and his ancestors into the national family. His inheritance of the home and its treasured items, and also of a place in the nation, is easily legitimated. By contrast, Faith has neither the material record of her ancestry nor even the most basic knowledge about her family that might provide her with the same sense of security: the prologue opens with only a tiny fragment of her family tree, representing herself, her brother, and her parents. As a result, she cannot make the same correlations between family, place, and nation that Simon does.

When the tour is over, Faith shifts from viewer and spectator to become an active participant in what Hewison calls "the cult of the countryside" (57). Simon and his mother take Faith for a walk, but before they leave, Faith must be appropriately attired in ethnic costume. They find her "a brown anorak," a pair of wellingtons, and "a blue wooly pom-pom hat" (124). She begins her walk optimistically, pleased to have finally reached the site of her lifelong pilgrimage and longing to share this moment with her brother, to show him "that at last [she] had finally found the countryside and that the land was indeed green and pleasant" (125). Her recitation of Romantic poetry suggests that she tries to use this familiar literary discourse to guide her through unfamiliar geographical territory, an act that overdetermines the ways she reads the landscape. At times, Faith is unable to read the landscape at all, and her lack of knowledge prevents her from participating in the experience Simon and Margaret stage for her. As Margaret points to birds in the trees, Faith "would look up to where she was pointing and say, 'Oh, yes,' at nothing at all" (125). Faith's attenuated experience speaks to broader dynamics of power/knowledge in that she is unable to access the cultural codes that would enable her to share in Margaret's enjoyment of the countryside. Elizabeth Helsinger points out that, historically, "[t]he aesthetics of landscape, and the activities of viewing and displaying English places through which it was experienced, created for those who could participate in it a claim on England as their national aesthetic property" (105). Margaret and Simon, in both viewing the landscape and displaying it for Faith's enjoyment, can make such a claim to the nation; Faith clearly cannot. Instead, Margaret puts a flower in Faith's hat and says, "Doesn't she look exotic?" (125). She puts Faith on display, rendering her outsider and other, an object to be seen rather than a knowing subject. Faith's already tenuous access to the landscape is further complicated by this exoticiziation, which entangles her in a series of contradictory discourses. Linda Peake and

Audrey Kobayashi argue that landscapes are sites of "gendered and racialized relations" (239) in which both women and those of "other races" have, through post-Enlightenment binaries, been constructed as closer to nature than to culture. Faith is ambivalently marked as an "exotic" through this readily available ideology, but also because by wearing an *English* flower she has been rendered out of place within the countryside. Margaret's comment, which casts her as simultaneously closer to nature and impossibly distanced from it, leaves Faith with no available subject position to occupy.

The landscape she initially perceived as welcoming soon begins to consume Faith, literally and metaphorically. Unused to the brisk walking, she tires quickly and begins to lag farther behind her hosts:

> I was breathing too heavily to call back but I managed to wave away their concern. But my feet were sinking. With every step the mud seemed to reach further up my wellington boots. I was making very slow progress. The dog had given up on me and decided to stay with the fittest. And Simon and his mother talked while they waited. (126)

As she sinks into the mud, which does not hinder Simon or Margaret, Faith's inability to move reflects the figurative distance between her experience of the countryside and theirs. Their movements are unencumbered, whereas Faith's ability to inhabit this space is substantially compromised, particularly once she is left alone without the benevolent protection of her hosts. Here, the Darwinian language of natural selection evoked in the dog's "staying with the fittest" illuminates the ways in which space is inscribed by cultural power and ideology. Only the "fittest" – the best able to adapt, and to "fit" themselves into the idealized, nostalgic image of the English countryside and the racialized nation it represents – have genuine access to the landscape. As Faith struggles in the mud, she is passed by several other walkers, who neither greet her, as per custom, nor stop to help. Perceived not as a friend but as a threat, Faith is an unwelcome presence whose race marks her as an outsider. As Gilroy argues in *The Black Atlantic*, black settlers to the UK "are perceived ... as an illegitimate intrusion into a vision of authentic British national life that, prior to their arrival, was as stable and peaceful as it was ethnically undifferentiated" (7). Faith's mere presence in the countryside disrupts hegemonic constructions of rural spaces as white spaces, and no matter how she behaves in an attempt to legitimize herself, the other walkers can only perceive her as an interloper; they are directing hostility at a presence that appears as an affront to dominant discourses of rural whiteness.

Faith's marginalization culminates in an encounter with a friend of the Wyndhams', Andrew Bunyan, at a local pub. When Faith, Simon, and his mother enter the pub, Simon gives Faith a tour, as he did with his house, pointing out the photographs taken during various periods. "It's fascinating – the place is absolutely steeped in history. That's what's so great about these old English pubs" (129), he tells her, echoing his comments about his family home. But Faith cannot find herself reflected in the pub's history, nor do the other patrons wish to admit her into its local community. This attitude is epitomized in Andrew Bunyan, whose question, "And whereabouts are you from, Faith?" (130), emphasizes her status as an outsider to both the region and the nation. Learning that her parents are from Jamaica, he tells them of his most recent trip there, during which he encountered a "Winston Bunyan," laughing uproariously at the fact that a black man shares his last name. When he ends with, "What do you think of that, Faith?" (130), she takes the opportunity provided by his rhetorical question to recount a historical narrative that has been forced into silence on this trip: "And because he asked me I said, 'Well, the thing is, that would have been his slave name, you see.' Then before I really knew what I was saying I'd said, 'Your family probably owned his family once'" (131). Her response, which insists on an alternative reading of their immediate exchange and of Bunyan's larger erasure, disrupts the nostalgia of pastoral English gentility. Stunned, Bunyan responds angrily, "No! My family never had connections like that in Jamaica. My family were not in that sort of business. I have no family connections to that part of the world at all" (131). His refusal to entertain a plausible explanation for Winston's last name and his own family's prosperity denies the violent history of an entire region. He must express this denial in order to maintain his family's reputation and a broader image of "civilized" Englishness. Bunyan's strategic amnesia presents a highly selective narrative that disallows the possibility that his family, and the nation, are culpable for past injustices.

Faith's comments, however, force Bunyan to consider this other narrative of slavery. Engaging in what Edward Said in *Culture and Imperialism* calls a "contrapuntal reading" (66), Faith's interpretation of Bunyan's story foregrounds the colonial history of the Caribbean, the constitutive outside of the English history he wishes to both isolate and sanitize. His strategic forgetting, however, is fuelled by an act of speculation; he tells her, "No. You know what it was? A wayward vicar. That's what we all think. We had a lot of vicars in our family. Some vicar just going around sowing his seed. Producing lots of little dark babies. That sort of thing happened all the time" (131). Bunyan prefers to fabricate an explanation of his family's presence in the Caribbean, which immediately belies his insistence that he has no family connections to Jamaica. He also does not specify who the "we" are in his collectivity, again suggesting a slippage between the familial and the national. Both speculations allow him to excuse as an aberration the immoral behaviour of an isolated individual rather than come to terms with the deep-rooted violences of an exploitive system. He does not realize that, like the pub in which they all sit, Jamaica is also "steeped in history." But it is a history that Andrew Bunyan cannot bear to hear, so he must construct other narratives to placate his own, and the national, conscience.

Faith's Breakdown

The disturbing events of her weekend actively trouble Faith's sense of social citizenship. But once she returns to London, the traumatic violence she confronts at the alternative bookstore is a terrifying reminder that English racism is as prevalent in urban settings as in rural ones. Faith and Simon witness the aftermath of a racist attack by the National Front[2] in which a black woman working at the bookstore is struck in the head and left bleeding profusely. When she enters, Faith sees that "[t]he shop had been sprayed with angry red paint. And all over it said NF, NF, NF" (151). The gay and lesbian section has had excrement thrown on it, while "the black and Third World fiction section was spray painted with 'Wog'" (152). This episode precipitates Faith's emotional breakdown, which begins in the store as she tries to help Simon deal with the situation. The episode demonstrates a correlation between extreme acts of racist violence and their supposedly more moderate manifestations. The discrimination she faces at the BBC, her exclusion from the countryside, and this act of vandalism are shown to exist on a continuum – they are not isolated, unrelated incidents. The National Front attacks a leftist bookstore, which disseminates alternative perspectives that make visible the racism, sexism, and homophobia on which all nations are based. This attempt at censorship is not unlike Bunyan's comments in the pub. Under the guise of civility and cordiality, Bunyan too invalidates other narratives that draw attention to the violent processes that are the foundation of England, but that have been strategically erased. Furthermore, the title "National Front" suggests that its members believe the nation can accommodate their attitudes even while publicly denouncing their behaviour as reprehensible.

After the attack, Faith faces the epistemic violence of watching others both deracialize and minimize the episode. When the police arrive, they try to disassociate the perpetrators' actions from the systemic racism they have exhibited, telling Simon and Faith, "They say they're National Front but they're not, they're just a bunch of thugs" (154). Although Simon points out that the two are interchangeable, the police prefer, as Bunyan does with his wayward vicar, to lay blame on a few individuals rather than confront a more pervasive, and organized, structure of power. When she and Simon return to their flat, Faith listens to her flatmates minimize the racial implications of the occurrence, reminding them three times that the victim of the attack was not just a store clerk, but a black woman. Mick is particularly dismissive, repeating the police's claim that "they're just a bunch of thugs" (157). Immediately following this refusal to name the act as racism, Faith begins to self-identify racially: "Mick put four mugs of tea on the table and three white hands and one black stretched forward to take them" (157). In *Welcome to the Jungle,* Kobena Mercer observes that "identity only becomes an issue when it is in crisis, when something assumed to be fixed, coherent and stable is displaced by the experience of doubt and uncertainty" (259). As Faith's experiences in the first half of the novel culminate into a crisis of identity, she confronts the possibility/reality that there is no room for her in the dominant discourses of Englishness.

Faith's breakdown accelerates to the point that she cannot get out of bed, eat, or talk to her flatmates. Her illness might be understood as a Fanonian "nervous condition," one Sartre observes in the preface to *The Wretched of the Earth* as a condition that is "introduced and maintained by the settler among colonized people *with their consent*" (20, emphasis Sartre's). Unable to bear what Fanon in *Black Skin, White Masks* would call the "fact of [her] blackness," Faith realizes she has consented to her own mental colonization in a nation that largely resents her racialized presence. Discovering the extent and profound psychic costs of her internalized racism, she shuts down emotionally and locks herself in her bedroom. She covers all her mirrors, refusing to look at herself because "I didn't want to be black any more" (160). Learning that she is not allowed to be "English" according to dominant paradigms, she also refuses "black" as an identity marker when the two are perceived as incompatible, and when this subject-position means she is "overdetermined from without" (*Black Skin, White Masks,* 116). The narrative does not indicate how long she remains locked in her room, and this temporal indeterminacy signals a significant rupture in Faith's psyche now that she has, to borrow from McKittrick, been "reoriented on strikingly racial terms" (25).

When her parents learn about her condition, they come over immediately with what they perceive to be a solution to her problem. Her mother tells her, "We have been thinking, me and your dad … that what you need is a little holiday … We have been thinking that your auntie in Jamaica would like to know you. And we have been thinking that now might be a good time for you to go and visit with her" (162). Their response is well-meaning but framed in problematic terms. Faith's mother describes this trip as a restful "escape" to the Caribbean, and also as a potential return to her lost familial and cultural origins. Both "escape" and "return" are troubling given that Faith's anxieties are caused by her struggles to find a place for herself *in England*. Removing her from this space will not help either Faith or the nation come to terms with England's postcolonial history or its black citizenry. Her parents' plan positions Faith as both a tourist and a prodigal daughter of Jamaica, but neither role will help her understand what it means to be a black Englishwoman. If she is to be a tourist, destinations are interchangeable; Faith tells her parents, "I don't want to go to Jamaica. It's too far. What's wrong with Spain or somewhere?" (162). Her mother's response, the final line of this first section of the novel, reveals the extent to which their sense of "home" differs from Faith's: "Child, everyone should know where they come from" (162). Her parents assume that Faith should have an attachment to the place where they were born and do not understand that she must negotiate multiple places, both real and imagined, that have shaped her life as a second-generation child. Their insistence that Faith has some inherent connection to "back home" suggests they have dramatically misread their daughter's breakdown.

Jamaica: Testing the Myth of "Back Home"

Part 2 of the novel, titled "Jamaica," begins in the Kingston airport. The first chapter recounts, through recollection and introspection, the process through which Faith has arrived at this destination. Her journey is contextualized through a mental flashback to her stopover at the

Miami airport. The prominence of both airports suggests Levy's interest in exploring this space to understand Faith's shifting identifications. In Miami, she is situated within a substantial collectivity of Jamaicans for the first time in the novel:

> I was halfway through the lounge making my way to the Jamaican Airlines check-in when I saw them. Shabby-looking people ... There were only about twenty of them but they looked so out of place in the plush setting of an American airport. They looked too poor to fly. And they were checking in cardboard boxes onto the airline's weighing scales. Boxes that my parents would have discarded as too flimsy and thin to have been any use. They talked in patois. A language all of its own but with the occasional word that a woman like me who had grown up around the Jamaican accent with its "nah man's" and "cha" and sucking of teeth, could be lulled into thinking I might understand if only I listened harder or they would speak slower. (166–7)

Faith is situated as an outsider to this group, who strike her as out of place in the airport, displaced as they are from what she would expect to be their usual surroundings. Yet it is Faith herself who is out of place beside this microcosm of Jamaican community. Her remark that they look "too poor to fly" suggests her First World perception of airline travel. For her, travel is a choice based on income rather than a necessity people must engage in if they live far from "home." Her marginal understanding of patois highlights her conceptual distance in that she comprehends neither their language nor their mindset. Their boxes, perhaps filled with goods to take to family members or to sell, indicate that they have developed a system in which using every opportunity presented by the baggage allowance is essential, far more than spending money on luggage. Their resourcefulness suggests that despite class differences, they are far more experienced travellers than Faith. As they visually and aurally signal their Caribbean identifications, Faith recognizes a Jamaican collectivity for the first time in the novel, while also realizing her inability and unwillingness to interpolate herself into this community.

Levy's meditation on the airport is significant given that very little critical attention has been paid to this space – a surprising omission within the substantial body of theoretical work on migration, diaspora, transnationalism, and border crossings. One exception is anthropologist and philosopher Marc Augé, who discusses the airport in his book *Non-Places: Introduction to an Anthropology of Supermodernity* (1995). Levy's understanding of the airport is a notable departure from Augé's. Augé argues that in the contemporary conjuncture of "supermodernity," highways, railways, and airports are "non-places" – that is, spaces that exist "in opposition to the sociological notion of place, associated ... with the idea of a culture localized in time and space" (34). Distinguishing between places and non-places, he argues: "If a place can be defined as relational, historical, and concerned with identity, then a space which cannot be defined as relational, or historical, or concerned with identity will be a non-place" (77–8). Because of these absences – of history, relationality, identity – he also claims that "a person entering the space of non-place is relieved of his [*sic*] usual determinants. He becomes no more than what he does or experiences in the role of passenger, customer or driver" (103). The masculinism of Augé's language is perhaps not accidental. The example through which he argues that the airport is a non-place is of a single, upper-middle-class, white male business traveller. His analysis is unable to account for the very different ways this space is occupied by those who fall outside his hegemonic construction.

The people at the gate in Miami, including Faith, experience the airport in ways that negate Augé's postmodern understanding of non-place. A site of arrival and departure, of family reunion or painful separation, of migration, immigration, or deportation, in a diasporic context an airport is not a *non*-place but a highly *overdetermined* place. The airport Levy depicts *is* concerned with identity if Faith can recognize within it a linguistic and sartorial performance of "Jamaican-ness." The determinants through which this recognition happens – language, dress, boxes – become *more* visible to her in the airport setting, wherein a dispersed ethnic collectivity is often reconstituted as they assemble at the gate to their common destination: "back home." To this extent, the airport, rather than being absent of identity, becomes a site of heightened ethnicity in which cultural performances take on greater meaning than they might in other settings. Furthermore, Augé does not address diasporic populations' historical realities of travel when he asserts that the airport, as a non-place, is devoid of history. For Faith and the other Caribbean travellers, a plane trip in the early 1980s cannot be understood in isolation from a five-hundred-year history of forced and voluntary migration. The ship on which Wade and Mildred travel to England, which for Faith evokes the Middle Passage, could not, in Augé's articulation, be considered a non-place. Decades later, the airplane, which has replaced the ship as the predominant mode of travel in Europe and North America, cannot be evacuated of these previous meanings. In Levy's novel, the presence of diasporic bodies in the airport transforms this ostensible "non-place," drawing attention to the turbulent historical realities and exigencies of travel in the Americas. They, and their cardboard boxes, *do* have a history of both roots and routes, and their complex identifications are partly constituted by these places.

As the narrative shifts from Miami to the Kingston airport, Faith is again distanced from her fellow travellers in that she does not share their migratory subjectivity. Her arrival immediately undercuts any ethnonationalist assumptions her parents may have had in sending Faith back to her "roots," as it brings Faith back to the anxious confusion she felt during her breakdown. Her arrival is no glorious return to lost origins, nor is it, as Mark Stein argues, "a sort of birth of Faith's Jamaican self" (71). Faith is never identified, by herself or others, as "Jamaican," and her encounters at the airport confirm her own sense of "Englishness." Worried that she will not survive the ordeal of collecting her luggage and finding her relatives, Faith breaks down again, thinking, "I felt out of place – everything was a little familiar but not quite. Like a dream. Culture shock is how the feeling is described. A name made up by someone with a stiff upper lip who wanted to deny the feelings of panic and terror. The feelings that made me want to run for a corner and cover my head with my arms and scream for my mummy" (169). Her description is laden with British imagery. The stiff upper lip evokes a common English stereotype, while the "mummy" for which Faith longs might be read in multiple ways. Her mother likely possesses the cultural knowledge Faith lacks, but the reference might also be read as a metaphor for the "Mother country," which Faith can easily navigate. When she is hustled by a man who steals her money, she succumbs to this sense of culture shock: "It was then that I cried. In the middle of the arrival lounge at Kingston airport, clutching my open purse and thinking of Mum's words: 'Everyone should know where they come from'" (171). Her mother's aphorism is ironic given that this stranger, who easily identifies Faith as an outsider, has a better sense of where Faith "comes from" than Mildred. Levy thus immediately troubles a narrative of return, rejecting the notion that Faith can seamlessly insert herself into Jamaica simply because of something "in [her] genes" (173).

Faith is never comfortable or "at home" in Jamaica, shifting ambivalently between pleasure, desire, longing, discomfort, and even revulsion.

She experiences Jamaica as simultaneously familiar and unfamiliar; she feels perpetually unsettled. As her Aunt Coral and cousin Vincent drive her from the airport, Faith is struck by the "astonishing strangeness" (178) outside the car window. But when she gets to Coral's she is surprised to find "a bungalow – like something you would retire to in Bexhill-on-Sea" (180). The front room "looked so familiar" (180) that Faith concludes, "[I]t reminded me of home" (180). However, rather than finding comfort in such similarities, she realizes that "[a]ll the familiarities made everything more strange" (181). Now that she has been jarred out of her ignorant First World assumption that her aunt lives in a mud hut and cooks goat in a boiling cauldron, the cultural boundaries between England and Jamaica become indeterminate, providing Faith with no framework through which to read her surroundings. She has a similarly contradictory experience at a wedding she attends. Having struggled to "pass" as Jamaican for two weeks, she briefly succeeds: "No one noticed me. I smiled at anyone who looked in my direction. But no one did. I was blending in. I was just one of the crowd. I was just another guest. It was wonderful" (293). Beginning to contemplate moving to Jamaica with her parents, she enjoys the slow-paced walk to the church, thinking, "Ah my, but you look like a Jamaican now, Faith" (294). The dissonance between "being" a Jamaican and merely looking like one is revealed at the church, where the minister and congregation turn to "get a better look at the foreigner" (295), who wears pants, not a dress as is the custom in some denominations. On her trip to the English countryside, Simon and Margaret's attiring her in suitable dress does not allow her to pass as an English country dweller because her body is racially marked. In Jamaica, marvelling that there are "black people … everywhere" (177), Faith is unable to pass as Jamaican because her sartorial choices mark her body in particular ways.

Notwithstanding the challenges Faith encounters there, her trip to Jamaica inaugurates conditions of possibility for her to renegotiate her understanding of herself within the frameworks of both familial and national collectivities. Most of Part II focuses on Faith's gradual reconstruction of her family tree as gleaned from stories told by family and friends, and her genealogy emerges on separate pages interspersed throughout these chapters. As her family histories are narrated, Faith grows increasingly able to situate herself in a familial context and in the historical context of Empire. The family tree, while largely linear in its generational tracing, must also account for a complex history that includes slavery, as well as multiple liaisons, "outside" children, infidelities, and unknown paternities. Only a few people on the tree are identified by last name, and some entries attempt to account for entire collectives of unknown family members – for example, "Dr. Jackson's wife and family in England" (340). When fathers are not known, particularly during slavery, question marks emphasize this parental ambiguity. Dotted lines account for men's multiple long-term partners. Dates of birth and death are absent, but there are other descriptors, including family members' slave or free status, their geographical origins, their ethnicities, and other details – for example, Muriel "died young" (340). These elements speak to the difficult family history Faith unearths, one that includes the sexual violence of slavery, as well as incest, domestic violence, secrets of paternity, illegitimacy, racial passing, and disappearances. She learns not only that her familial narrative goes back much earlier than 1948, but also that she and her entire family have been shaped by centuries of global forces. Her tracing involves what Catherine Nash calls a "critical genealogy" (188), which "explore[s] the relationships between family history and wider structures of power and patterns of inequality" (188).

Nash argues that genealogies can be counter-discursive in their disruptions of assumed correlations between identity and place: "genealogy is not necessarily tied to political conservatism and cultural defensiveness. Nor does it always foster ideas of simple ancestral roots or pure cultural categories. The empirical imperative of genealogy can create family trees which reflect family connections across ethnic groups" (186). These genealogies "sometimes reproduc[e], sometimes [subvert] the language of cultural purity, fundamentalism and essentialism. Tracing the dynamics of identity and belonging within the practice of genealogy involves considering different spatial imaginations of culture and location – local, national, transnational, global, diasporic – and different ways of imagining human relatedness" (180). These operate in Faith's genealogical project, which offers no simple correlations between place, race, identity, or ethnicity. In this regard, her mother's comment about "knowing where she comes from" becomes increasingly complex. Nothing in her genealogy links Faith specifically or solely to Jamaica, given that it highlights diasporic journeys between various locations in Europe and the Americas. Instead, she is shown to "come from" many different places in Europe and the Americas: her family tree maps a series of migrations and settlements between England, Ireland, Scotland, Cuba, Panama, Martinique, Costa Rica, Canada, and the United States. Even her family's presence in Jamaica cannot be homogenized, since it reflects histories of migration from continental Africa and possibly India, as well as the indigenous Arawak presence. As Faith learns about maternal and paternal connections to England, she confirms that England is also one of the many places she "comes from." Faith's family's experiences have been shaped by arrivals as well as by departures, demonstrating that "roots" in England, as well as "routes" between many other places, are equally important in understanding the complexities of her project.

Faith's genealogical (de/re)construction compels her to reconsider her assumption that "[t]here was no 'oral tradition' in [her] family" (4). This oral tradition, which she discovers while listening to Coral and other relatives, and which reveals the complex genealogical entanglements of the Caribbean, allows her to piece together the various confusing fragments she heard growing up and to fill in many of the ellipses in her parents' meagre narratives. These oral traditions are shown to be at least as important as gaining familiarity with the physical geographies of Jamaica, as a means to understand more clearly "where she comes from." Faith's newfound ability to locate herself on a broader and much longer line of ancestry might be directly comparable to Simon's in that she now has a familial record through which to contextualize her life in England, just as he does. But Faith's oral diasporic history makes a very different commentary on hegemonic historical processes than Simon's material record of family inheritance. In "The Local and the Global," Stuart Hall argues that marginalized subjects "can only come into representation by ... recovering their own hidden histories. They have to try to retell the story from the bottom up, instead of from the top down. And this moment has been of such profound significance in the post-war world that you could not describe the post-war world without it" (35). Thus, Faith's are not simple acts of discovery; they are not part of a search for the "facts" of her family's lives; rather, they are a rearticulation which suggests that all narratives are partial, provisional, and positioned. Faith also learns many family stories from women whose knowledge of domestic intricacies informs their perspectives. She realizes that family members only have partial narratives: some know of details or events that others do not, and some of their information is gleaned through gossip or rumour. These historically feminized modes of communication extend Hall's argument regarding "histories from below." Levy does not merely validate them as legitimate sources of knowledge in Faith's search for familial information; she also makes an important commentary on the role that female perspectives play in sustaining and developing diasporic histories and in rearticulating diasporic spaces.

Levy's novel recognizes the radical potential in this historical reinscription, as Faith's family's story illustrates the colonial narratives England refuses to acknowledge. These narratives "from below," which are repeatedly traced back to England, Ireland, and Scotland, deny Andrew Bunyan's assertion that wealthy British families had "no connections" to "that part of the world." Tracing family history in this manner also speaks to an exigency resulting from Faith's family connections to the Americas. As Levy points out, "[i]t is hard for anyone to research their genealogy, but it is even harder ... for someone with my background. Most of the records are incomplete or unavailable at best; destroyed or nonexistent at worst" ("This Is My England"). Given that other documentation may not be available to her, particularly about her enslaved descendants, Faith has no alternative but to turn to this oral history from below to reconstruct her family.

Faith's genealogical project does not draw simple correlations between identity and place, nor is it a route to pedigree or social legitimacy, as is the case for Simon. Instead, Faith recognizes, ultimately, her own illegitimacy, and the possibilities therein, when she claims proudly, "I am the bastard child of Empire and I will have my day" (327).[3] For her, this illegitimate status is not a source of shame but a new lens through which she can understand her place in England as the child of immigrants. "Bastards" disrupt linear genealogies of descent and challenge the notion that families are ordered and enclosed, with neatly defined boundaries. As the bastard child of Empire, Faith can similarly destabilize a national narrative of homogeneity. She may not have access to the material inheritance that Simon does, but her multiple cultural inheritances reimagine the boundaries of "Englishness" and enable her to lay claim to the nation on different terms than she did during previous encounters in the English countryside. When she struggles for admittance on the terms established by the nation, she is perceived as an "illegitimate intrusion." Now that she has refused to be an outsider and embraced her "bastard" status, she establishes her own terms for admittance into the national family. As she prepares for her return, Faith only identifies with her birthplace: "I was going home to England" (320). Her understanding of England in the wake of this trip, however, is very different from the perception she had before she came. Newly critical of those who are "unaware of our shared past" (326) – as she was only a short time ago – Faith now articulates a different narrative in which the nation is situated globally, inextricably linked to its former colonies. She can now articulate, in Stuart Hall's words from "Old and New Identities, Old and New Ethnicities," "the outside history that is inside the history of the English [as] [t]here is no English history without that other history" (49).

Part III of the novel, like Part I, is again titled "England," and while it is only half a page long, the section resituates Faith, preventing the novel from being read as an oversimplified narrative of return to lost Caribbean origins. The section is a rehearsal of her parents' arrival in 1948, but with some notable differences that ensure that Faith is not cast as an immigrant or an outsider like they were. Perhaps the most significant difference is that Faith is "placed" in this section through its title, which situates her within a specific geography. By contrast, Wade and Mildred are not "placed" anywhere in the opening section, which has no title or referent. Their arrival in England is narrated in the unlabelled section following the title page of the novel, which appears before Part I, "England." Is this opening section meant to be a preface? A prologue? Some liminal space? The section's lack of geographical determinant emphasizes Wade and Mildred's sense of psychological unsettlement.

The final section of the novel repeats some key lines, nearly verbatim, with alterations that highlight Faith's newfound sense of awareness. When the *Empire Windrush* arrives on Guy Fawkes' night, Wade and Mildred see fireworks lighting up the sky. Mildred explains, "At first we didn't know what it was for. In Jamaica you only get fireworks at Christmas. Your dad thought it might have been a welcome for us, having come so far and England needing us. But I didn't think he could be right. And he wasn't" (8). On the last page, after her plane lands, Faith also sees fireworks, and her remarks echo those of her parents: "I thought it may be a welcome for me having traveled so far and England needing me ... I knew I couldn't be right and I wasn't ... No. I knew this was England, November the fifth. There are always fireworks on November the fifth. It was Guy Fawkes' night and I was coming home" (339). For Faith, the epistemological nexus of power/knowledge has now shifted. She "knows" England in a way that her parents did not, in a way the Wyndhams or Andrew Bunyan do not, and in a way she herself did not before her journey to Jamaica. Her return home on a nationalist holiday is rearticulated through Faith's newfound understanding of the nation's impurity and creolization. Thus, Faith does learn the lesson her parents set out to teach her when they sent her to

Jamaica: "everyone should know where they come from." But Faith learns that lesson in a very different way, and about a very different geography, than her parents perhaps intended. Now she also knows that she "comes from" England. But she also knows England to be a place that is situated in a wider diaspora and that it has been shaped by its role in a centuries-long process of global expansion.

Armed with this understanding of colonial history, Faith returns to England on more informed and more politically engaged terms. As a child she had struggled to keep her parents' immigrant status a secret; now, in the last line of the novel, she states that she is ready "to tell everyone ... [m]y mum and dad came to England on a banana boat" (339, ellipses Levy's). In the opening line of the novel, bullies ignorantly hurl this phrase as an insult; now, Faith reclaims the fact of her parents' arrival as a starting point for a different narrative. The enunciatory act with which the novel ends enables Levy to self-reflexively comment on the importance of fiction and its strategic use as a tool through which she can redefine Englishness. Just as Faith now longs to tell her story, so too does Levy move beyond hegemonic discourses to articulate a different conceptualization of the nation and a different place in it for the children of immigrants.

More broadly, the novel also illustrates that, for immigrant families and their children, "home" is a very complicated concept, constantly shifting and in need of persistent renegotiation, based on one's context and surroundings and the familial or social communities in which one is situated. The shifts in power/knowledge articulated in the novel illustrate that settling in and naming a place as "home" might appear to be a local act, but an act of settlement on different terms often involves situating that locality both globally and historically. The novel suggests that such attempts made by the children of immigrants to settle in the UK on different terms will simultaneously unsettle dominant and bounded understandings of nationhood. The ways in which Levy both intertwines and complicates the notion of "home" for England and for immigrant communities extend the notion of diaspora-space and offer a different narrative of what "knowing Englishness" might look like for both its white and its non-white citizens.

Chapter 4

"The Abuses of Settlement": Esi Edugyan's *The Second Life of Samuel Tyne*

> [T]he racialized terms of nationhood, belonging, geography, and citizenship – those discourses and experiences which attach identity to place and vice versa – are terms which are not fully experienced by several communities. Black narratives of un-belonging, non-citizenship, and elsewhere not only rupture the homogeneity of nation-space by asserting blackness and/in Canada, they also stretch and reconfigure the meaning of unsatisfactory racial, geographical boundaries.
>
> Katherine McKittrick, "'Their Blood Is There, and They Can't Throw It Out': Honouring Black Canadian Geographies"

This chapter focuses on Esi Edugyan's *The Second Life of Samuel Tyne* (2004) and shifts from the UK back to the Canadian context. I build on my examinations of Levy's novel by again considering the need for different epistemological frameworks than those offered by hegemonizing national discourses – frameworks through which we might better understand the ways the second-generation children of immigrants struggle to negotiate belonging. Edugyan's novel is an important one in this study given the ways it complicates and unsettles various geographies and assumptions about "race" in Canada. In setting the novel mainly in the small town of Aster – which is based on the historical black settlement of Amber Valley, Alberta – and tracing the Porter family's early-twentieth-century migration north from Oklahoma, Edugyan disrupts the mythos of the Prairies as a space built solely by the labours of European-descended peoples. The novel further complicates the black presence in Aster through the arrival of Maud and Samuel Tyne, post–Second World War immigrants from the Gold Coast, and their twin daughters, Yvette and Chloe, second-generation Canadians born in Calgary. This focus on early-twentieth-century African American migration to Canada, and on a continental African family that arrives in the immediate postwar period, also unsettles the commonly held assumptions that blackness in Canada is recent, largely Caribbean-descended, and/or restricted to large urban centres. These various textual interventions provide the framework within which the geographies represented in the novel offer possibilities through which racial, spatial, and familial boundaries might be stretched and reconfigured.

The Second Life of Samuel Tyne also offers a more extended look at the direct interactions between immigrant parents and their Canadian-born children than any in my study thus far. Chloe and Yvette are only twelve years old during the summer in which most of the events in the novel take place; as a result, Maud and Samuel's parenting processes and decisions, as well as those of other parents and townspeople, are given considerably more prominence in the novel than those of the adult-aged second-generation children in the previous texts examined. Unlike the protagonists in Brand's and Levy's novels, who are in their twenties, and unlike McWatt's thirty-year-old protagonist, Chloe and Yvette are situated more distinctively within a family unit than within a peer group – which is largely non-existent for them except for Ama Ouillet, the twins' schoolmate, who spends the summer with the Tyne family in Aster. The biological and outer-biological family dynamics that play out in their interactions are often richly symbolic of the broader political and social concerns with which this study engages.

In Edugyan's novel, the intersecting, multiscalar geographies of the Canadian nation, the Canadian prairie-space, and the home enable us to think further about the family as a symbolic, micropolitical realm in which social citizenship is negotiated for immigrants and their children. In particular, *The Second Life of Samuel Tyne* offers a profoundly detailed look at the hostilities faced by non-white immigrant families, particularly before the Points System was inaugurated in 1967, thus laying bare the myths of Canada as a nation of racial tolerance and confronting long-held assumptions that Canada has always welcomed new immigrants. Specifically, the novel depicts in detail the challenges faced by immigrant women in mothering their Canadian-born children. It also offers a more extensive examination than any novel in this study of the deep psychic costs of trying to belong for the second generation, particularly within geographic spaces like the Prairies, wherein marginalizations and erasures of blackness are so endemic. The novel reveals that nationhood, belonging, geography, and citizenship are, as McKittrick suggests in the epigraph above, incredibly precarious for black families like the Tynes, and particularly so for second-generation children like Chloe and Yvette, who do not conform to either the racial or the gendered expectations established for them by the dominant society. Nonetheless, through their persistent presence, and by reimagining familial and kinship boundaries, the novel offers some alternative possibilities for what "settling up" might look like for both non-white and white citizens who have experienced hegemonic marginalizations.

My analysis begins with a look at the novel's publication history and at the ways in which that history engaged, in troubling ways, in acts of erasure by initially foregrounding and then later removing indigenous presences in various editions of the text. Those actions leave me as a literary critic unsettled as I strive nonetheless to build an argument around the ethicality of the novel. The analysis in this chapter is based on the novel's first edition, published in Canada in 2004 by A.A. Knopf. A subsequent edition was published in 2005 under the Vintage imprint, but with significant revisions to the text.[1] The second edition includes numerous and seemingly minor changes in detail that do not alter the outcome of the story but that do result in a very different politics of racial representation. For example, in the first edition, there is a scene in which Maud first learns of the family's inheritance of the home in Aster; in the second edition that scene has been replaced by a meeting with Yvette and Chloe's teacher in which Maud must remind the teacher that her daughters were born in Canada and consequently do not have accents. In the second edition the narration of the twins' destructive behaviours in Aster has also been changed to suggest, in less ambivalent terms, that they are responsible for the fires in the town.[2]

What has been omitted from the second edition is perhaps more surprising than what has been changed. First, at the town meeting to discuss the fires, the first edition includes an extended debate among the townspeople regarding "Article 9," a bylaw related to architectural and historical preservation that provides an ironic commentary on the ways Aster has erased its black origins. This debate is omitted from the second edition. Also absent in the second edition is the backstory of Ama Ouillet. In the second edition, there are almost no details offered of the Ouillet family history and there are no references to her Aboriginal grandfather. Even the French ancestry of her paternal grandmother remains largely unexplored. Finally, the second edition does not offer any details of the process through which the twins are institutionalized, nor is there any specific diagnosis made of their "psychosis." In the first edition, in the scene where the twins are committed, an Aboriginal couple sits silently in the waiting room with Maud and Samuel. They do not appear in the second edition, which eliminates this scene entirely. The result of these omissions is that in the second edition, the Prairies are represented as a less heterogeneous and less contested space than they are in the first edition. Furthermore, by excising the Aboriginal presence, Edugyan also, problematically, marginalizes the complex dynamics of settler colonialism on which the Canadian prairies are built. My analysis in this chapter, based on the first edition, takes up some aspects of the text that have been eliminated from the second edition, for I feel it is important to engage with Edugyan's original references to Aboriginal characters. I also offer analysis of the symbolic implications of Article 9 in order to consider the ways in which black histories are erased from regional and national narratives. I focus on the first edition of Edugyan's novel in order to examine the various processes whereby settler colonialism disciplines both Indigenous and black presences in Canada. I appreciate the ways in which these conversations are staged in the first edition, but I am also deeply troubled by what has gone missing from the novel in subsequent editions as it is shaped by market forces and publication decisions that are partly within but also partly beyond Edugyan's control.[3]

The temporal setting of the novel is also significant in the context of a discussion about immigrants and their Canadian-born children. The principal narrative is set in 1968, described as "an age characterized by its atrocities" (1), through global references to Polish anti-Semitism, American race riots, the Vietnam War, and numerous political assassinations. Benedict Anderson has insisted that 1968 must be seen as an "1848-style annus mirabilis" (1996: 6), given the rapid increase in European political activism and the ongoing decolonization movements in Africa and the Caribbean. Michel Foucault has similarly emphasized the significance of 1968, claiming that the activism of that period enabled particular discussions about power in his own writing. Speaking about his early work, he argues that "[t]o put it very simply, psychiatric internment, the mental normalization of individuals, and penal institutions have no doubt a fairly limited importance if one is only looking for their economic significance" (116). But the politicization of 1968 confirmed for him that these issues "are undoubtedly essential to the general functioning of the wheels of power" (116). Edugyan's narrative likewise takes up issues of psychiatric institutionalization and the mental (ab)normalization of the second-generation twins, exploring the ways these discourses are used to construct and police a particular type of nation with specific regulations for entry and citizenship. In her novel, personal and familial interactions are consistently informed by broader questions of power and ideology, and her emphasis on 1968 establishes an insistently politicized framework through which to understand and critique these issues.

The temporal periodization of the novel is also significant in a Canadian context. This time period saw wide-ranging changes to the country's immigration regulations with the introduction of the Points System in 1967, less than a year before the main events in the novel take place. For much of the previous century, state policy encouraged immigration from Britain, the United States, and northern Europe – in that order – while actively discouraging most immigrants, who were categorized as "undesirable" based on their assumed inability to assimilate into Canadian culture. The narrative describes Samuel and his uncle Jacob arriving "on a wave of immigration" that included "war brides, Holocaust survivors [and] refugees of every skin" (8), but historical statistics suggest that few of those arriving in Canada would have been African. As recently as 1952, Canada's Immigration Act prohibited or limited the admission of people based on "such factors as nationality, ethnic group, occupation, lifestyle, unsuitability with regard to Canada's climate, and perceived inability to become readily assimilated into Canadian society" (qtd in Knowles 137). Not until 1962 did new regulations begin to dismantle the inherent racism of the nation's immigration policies. The Points System, which assigned points for measurable factors such as age, education, employment potential, and ability to speak English or French, supposedly heralded a new era in Canadian history in which ethnic or racial discrimination would end. Nonetheless, as it turned out, certain groups continued to be favoured over others, given that fifteen of a total of one hundred points could be granted subjectively, based on "the immigration officer's assessment of the applicant's adaptability, motivation, initiative, and other similar qualities" (qtd in Hawkins 405). The Points System reignited debates about the desirability of immigration for Canada, debates that play out in the novel through conversations between the Tynes and their first acquaintances in Aster, Ray and Eudora Frank.

E/Racing the Canadian Prairies

As characters, the Franks demonstrate the extent to which Anglo-whiteness is normalized on the Prairies and point to the ways in which other presences are actively erased. Their interactions with the Tynes often play out in symbolic terms, in that they represent a kind of hypocritical white liberalism that demands particular types of obedient nationalism from Samuel, Maud and the twins. Ray and Eudora's conservative political beliefs reflect dominant Canadian anxieties about the new immigration system and provide insight into the exclusionary nature of the nation and the region in which Maud, Samuel, and the twins attempt to settle. While they initially appear helpful and supportive of Maud and Samuel, who are "model" and therefore perceived as exceptional, their political values reveal the dissonances between their individual treatment of the family and their beliefs about immigrants more generally. During a dinner party, Ray laments, "I tell you, we've got a policy to change in this country if we don't want to see another depression. Year after year, rules of entry just get laxer, and if we keep on like this, we don't risk just our culture, but bankrupting ourselves" (159). He catalogues a list of ethnicities, including "Chinese who came up for the railroad ... Mormons ... Russians, Hungarians, French Catholics, Jews ... ex-slaves" (159), asking, "Now tell me, where is there to put all these people?" (159). His reference to space is both literal and symbolic, suggesting that Canada can make no room for "others," many of whom would have arrived in Alberta decades before he did. Even the "two founding nations" narrative is marginalized in favour of a rhetoric of singular white and English origins, or what Daniel Coleman in *White Civility* has called the construction of Anglo-whiteness as Canada's "fictive ethnicity."

Ray's racist references are among the most pervasive in the novel. He insinuates repeatedly to Samuel and Maud that they should "know their place" and that their family should be grateful for every opportunity in their new country. For example, he chastises Samuel for quitting his job as an economist in the federal civil service, claiming, "It can't look good for you to go throwing away good jobs just like that ... These highfalutin office jobs are hard for *any* man to come by" (69). He also repeatedly refers to Samuel as "you guys," an indeterminate collectivity that is variously used to mean "black," "African," and "immigrant" but that always assumes that Ray and his kind are the "real" Canadians, unmarked citizens who need not be categorized by difference. His comments are an expression of what Linda Peake and Brian Ray call "normalized racism" (181), which is "manifest not only in extreme epithets, but in insinuations and suggestions, in reasoning and representations, in short, in the microexpressions of daily life" (181).

Peake and Ray wonder, "Can our geographical imaginations be usefully employed to dismantle whiteness?" (181). Edugyan's creative imaginings speak to their query. Throughout the novel, the Franks are represented in a manner that destabilizes their normativity; they are not allowed to be the invisible "Canadian" standard against which all "others" are measured. As Iain Chambers emphasizes, "[e]thnicity does not simply belong to the 'other,' but is also a part of being white" (1994: 39). And as Coleman elaborates, in Canada the privilege of white normativity "operates paradoxically as being so obvious that it remains unexamined" (3). Edugyan's novel, however, insistently examines these racialized discourses. Ray and Eudora are constructed in ways that emphasize their Anglo-Canadian ethnicity and that draw attention to their cultural and racial markers. Readers first encounter the Franks when they arrive at the Tynes' door to welcome them to Aster: "A couple stood on the porch. Their skin, and indeed their clothes, were so uniformly white they might have climbed from a salt mine" (59). The Franks are not just introduced as white characters, they are portrayed as *hyper*-white, a description that challenges their racial normalization through its hyperbole. In her sustained critique of Canadian multiculturalism and nationalism, Himani Bannerjee points out that "to be a 'white man'… is not a simple physical fact; it is a moral imperative and an ideology" (73). Through Ray in particular, Edugyan demonstrates the ideological underpinnings that inform his restrictive understanding of Anglo-Canadian "whiteness," as well as the extent to which he constructs himself and "Canadianness" according to these narrow paradigms.

Edugyan similarly complicates the racial geographies of the town of Aster, drawing attention to its construction as a space of normalized whiteness. While the narrator immediately makes ironic reference to the fact that the town's "most noted relic was the fellowship between its men" (1), Ray and Eudora repeatedly insist that Aster is a "close-knit" community (287). Their deep investment in this small-town narrative is closely intertwined with the ways Aster is racialized. According to Coleman, historical constructions of Canada's Anglo-whiteness have been formulated upon "a British model of civility. By means of this conflation of whiteness with civility, whiteness has been naturalized as the norm for English and Canadian cultural identity" (5). Thus, Aster can only be "close-knit" for those who are considered to be a part of its social fabric. As the Franks also point out, it is a town where "not too many outsiders come in" (114). When Samuel asks Ray where Saul Porter is from, he replies, "anywhere but here" (139), although he immediately contradicts himself by acknowledging that Porter was one of Aster's founders and has a longer presence in the town than he himself does. At the town meeting, Tara Chodzicki, who must spell out her name and by extension her Eastern European origins to the townspeople, is similarly ostracized. Ray's anti-immigrant circumlocutions also suggest that the boundaries of his Aster cannot be stretched enough to include people of French Canadian ancestry. Nonetheless, Aster is not the homogenous small town some believe it to be. When the Tynes first arrive, Samuel comments, "What an inspiring mix of people this town has, isn't it? The reports all praise the city's diversity" (58). In contrast to Ray and Eudora's belief that there are few outsiders, Samuel observes "the Greeks, the Italians, the Dutch, the Portuguese, even these few third-worlders" (59), who have, like the Tynes, left Calgary or Edmonton to make their home in Aster. The dissonance between Samuel and the Franks' characterizations of the town reveals the lengths to which Ray and Eudora go to create their fiction of the town's cultural purity. The Franks demonstrate that a hegemonic and normalized whiteness is in fact a complex ideological narrative, one that writes out racialized "others," even white people who are not of British descent.

The construction of Aster as a space of normalized whiteness also relies on the erasure of its history as one of the first black settlements in Alberta. Through the townspeople's active disavowal of the town's black origins, Edugyan narrates broader historical concerns. She has said that excavating such lost Prairie histories was one of her main motivations in writing the novel.[4] Writing about the persistent marginalization of blackness in Canada, Rinaldo Walcott argues that black Canadian histories and geographies "occup[y] the place of the repressed" (2000: 35):

> The long and now broken silence in St. Armand, Quebec, concerning the slave cemetery that was almost ploughed over – called "nigger rock" by the locals; the destruction of Africville in Nova Scotia in the sixties; the demolition of Hogan's Alley in Vancouver in the sixties; the changing of the name of Negro Creek Road to Moggie Road in Ontario in 1996 – all are random examples of a willful attempt to make a Black presence in Canada absent. (35)

Prairie settlements like Amber Valley – the inspiration for Edugyan's Aster – can easily be added to this catalogue of erasures. Her novel offers extensive historiographic interventions that explain the history of the town, the Porter family's motivations for migrating from Oklahoma, and the obstacles they faced during their first decade in Canada[5] as part of the first wave of black migrants, who experienced "the abuses of settlement" (199). In addition, through the contemporary townspeople's discussions about "historical preservation," Edugyan lays bare the processes whereby such histories are willfully absented.

These erasures are revealed during the town hall debate about Article 9, "which restrict[s] people from making changes to any town property without consulting an elected board for Historical Preservation" (117). Those in favour of the bill argue it is about "preserving what's best in our town" (118); those against it claim it is "unfeasible ... border[ing] on immoral" (117), even "intolerant" (118). One man who rejects the bill metatextually points out that "[o]ne building went from being a regular cake to a wedding cake when it added a turret – this later turned up in an Alex Colville painting. That moment in art history never would have happened if this bylaw had existed back then" (117). It seems that the town's appearance in a painting by a Canadian cultural icon is a historical event worth promoting; yet the committee ostensibly in favour of preserving the town's heritage does not even mention Aster's origins as an all-black settlement. The "history" they prefer to preserve is Aster's more recent self-incarnation as a largely white enclave, which is now apparently "what's best" about their town. The absurdity of the debate becomes clear when one considers that both sides ultimately strive to entrench Aster as a space of normalized whiteness; as such, one townsperson's suggestion that Article 9 would "[help] the town retain its integrity" (118) becomes deeply ironic.

Yet the physical landscape surrounding the town is indelibly marked by traces of Aster's black origins. Edugyan's narrator offers a four-page history of the founding of the town, a story couched in rumour and "myth" (41) that comments indirectly on the limited discursive spaces to which black histories are often relegated. "Myth told of the town's birth as the first black hamlet in Alberta, one not so welcome in those days" (41). The local people, "folk who had themselves migrated little earlier" (41), are vehemently opposed to the arrival of these "strange pilgrims" (42) and work to discourage further migration by building a stone wall to separate their homesteads from the town:[6] "Each man took his hand in the construction, and before long every layer read like a patch in a stone quilt, with a detailed square from each family" (42). The simile of quilting suggests that this troubling moment provided the foundation on which later Asterians would weave their narrative of a "close-knit" community. But this attempt at spatial containment became too great an effort for the white settlers, and "the wall remained ten inches high for several decades. The passing years saw it kicked down, eroded by constant rain. Now it rises scarcely two inches, a skirt of parched rock at the river's edge. So the myth goes" (42).

Edugyan's narrative offers racial antagonism as the explanation for the existence of Stone Road, but "few people actually believed the myth" (42), and the town prefers to speculate about its origins, and no more: "Truth is, no one knows how Stone Road came to be. Too mathematically perfect to seem natural, its mystery is the theme of an annual town contest" (42). Contemporary Aster's rejection of this tangible evidence of exclusion is both an erasure of black presences from the geographic landscape and part of the process through which English Canadian whiteness is constructed. As Coleman observes, constructing whiteness involves "activities of self-invention, reinvention, self-maintenance, and adaptation, even as they try to avoid observation and detection as anything but fixed" (10). Thus the white townspeople's manipulation of both physical space and the narratives that surround it evidence the contradictory processes of this management. Coleman further observes "the structural contradiction of civility itself, with its vigilant policing of the borders, even when those borders are being … expanded" (22). Seen in this light, the town contest to solve the "mystery" of Stone Road becomes a second act of containment, a discursive act of garrisoning the town's whiteness that echoes its earlier, literal attempts. The contest also illuminates what white townspeople cannot bear to hear about their ancestors. The "myth" of the wall's origins, bearing witness to blatant racism, offers a different and much more ominous interpretation of Ray's loud insistence that "not too many outsiders come in."

Decades later, "outsiders" like the Tynes are disciplined by much more insidious forms of social surveillance, and Maud, Samuel, and their daughters are expected to conform if they hope to gain even provisional admittance to Aster or to the nation. Ray suggests that, particularly for immigrants,

> [i]f they're going to be here, they've got to accept not only the benefits but the responsibilities of being Canadian. A country's not just a piece of land. What makes a nation a nation is when a group of like-minded people decide to work towards common causes, common goals …

> People who aren't interested in the concerns of language, religion, politics, all that, can't rightly call themselves *active* citizens. Really, now, think about it. (160)

Maud and Samuel are in fact engaged with all of the issues Ray lists, as are Yvette and Chloe. Maud and Samuel have put significant thought into the language spoken in their household, Maud is involved in a Christian church community, and the twins' daily banter, with its references to the Vietnam War and the Diefenbaker government (25), demonstrates that they are intelligently and actively engaged in politics. But this engagement does not occur under the hegemonic terms established by Ray, for whom the "greater good" and "common goals" are defined by a very restrictive and homogenizing understanding of "community" that does little to include the Tynes' perspectives.

I have offered this extensive meditation on racial/spatial containment as a backdrop to my subsequent analyses of both generations of the Tyne family. As Coleman argues, "white civility operates as a mode of internal management: the subjects of the civil order discipline their conduct in order to participate in the civil realm, and they themselves gain or lose legitimacy in an internally striated civil society depending on the degree to which they conform to its ideals" (11). The Tyne family, both black and immigrant or immigrant-descended, and therefore far outside the bounds of the hegemonic white settler narrative, face profound acts of discipline and management during their processes of settlement. Their challenges provoke a number of questions for me: What does it mean to belong to a place that engages in such blatant acts of racial marginalization, erasure, and dissembling? How does one belong when one is being actively erased from the nation? And is belonging or settlement even possible under these un/settling terms? How can racialized immigrants and their children construct an identity for themselves when regional and national narratives, as Edugyan's novel demonstrates, are such active and concerted constructions of whiteness? The Tyne family must struggle to find a way through these various contradictory discourses. I argue that in many ways the novel sets up belonging as an unattainable goal.

Mothering the Second Generation

The Tyne home in Aster is an important site through which to think about the ways the family attempts to negotiate a place for themselves.

For Samuel, and for other male characters, questions of social citizenship play out in the realm of property ownership, which is a symbolic route to belonging in Aster and in the nation. The challenges Samuel faces regarding the legitimate ownership of his house and land – challenges launched by both Saul Porter and Ray – play out in microcosm the debates around legitimacy, belonging, and the tenuousness of black claims to space and place that I discussed in the previous section. But while the male characters' symbolic citizenship struggles take place over land and home ownership, the women in the novel engage in these debates within the domestic realm and through their childrearing activities. As Linda McDowell reminds us, "a focus on the social relations within a domestic space crosses the boundary between the private and the public, between the particular and the general, and is not, as is often incorrectly asserted, a focus on the 'merely' domestic or the private sphere" (72–3). Anne McClintock puts it more directly: "the domestic is political, the political is gendered" (1995: 32). She also stresses that "[d]omesticity denotes both a *space* (a geographical and architectural alignment) and a *social relation to power*" (34, emphasis McClintock's).

Seen in this light, Eudora, Maud, and Akosua's debates about their housekeeping and mothering stage a wider conversation about the relationships between domesticity, gender, citizenship, and nationhood, revealing a complicated power dynamic inflected by issues of class and race. If, in some strains of nationalist rhetoric, the maintenance of the home stands in for the maintenance of the nation, then improper housekeeping and poor childrearing reflect poor citizenship: "If familial and national identity mutually attest one another ... then the right or wrong working of families and the proper relationships among family members variously signify the stabilities and instabilities of the nation-state. The calls for a potent nation-state are often metaphorized as the call for stable bourgeois families, families in which individuals fill their proper roles for the good of the state" (Smith and Brinkler-Gabler 13). Edugyan explores these correlations at length. Long sections of the novel take place within the women's homes; except at the town hall meeting, readers rarely encounter these characters in the public sphere. Edugyan's extensive use of domestic settings suggests the importance of this space as a site through which to examine the intersections between the macro- and the micro-political.

Maud, Eudora, and Akosua's debates about housekeeping, and especially childrearing, suggest that the parenting of the children of immigrants is a poignant site through which to police the boundaries of the nation and articulate models of "ideal" female domestic citizenship. Eudora's exemplary performance of domestic duties, coupled with her Anglo-white heritage, mark her as the most desirable of female citizens, one who "knows her place" within hegemonic narratives of the nation. Eudora believes that "a house is the direct reflection of its owner" (221) and takes great pride in maintaining hers in the most rigorous and societally conventional manner. When Maud, Ama, and the twins visit Eudora for the first time, Maud is flustered by the seeming perfection of the home, which is decorated in "surprising good taste. Most of the furniture was beige, with the occasional coloured chair, and Eudora hung only paintings, not prints, each chosen with a refined eye" (99). Appliances are new, the home is immaculate, and a fresh-baked plate of cookies awaits the unexpected guests. When she knows in advance that company is coming, Eudora hosts spectacular dinner parties. Despite her domesticity, she still has time for organized feminist activism, but even these activities reveal her collusion with, rather than opposition to, traditional gender roles. She espouses the maternal, domestic values promoted by first-wave feminist organizations like the Women's Christian Temperance Union. Eudora "agreed with a woman's right to vote, but believed this was extent to which women should be involved in politics. She maintained that all women should have the right to higher education, but if pressed hard enough she would admit it was unnatural ... She was vice-president of the National Association for the Advancement of Women (NAAW), and yet she knew a woman's true duty was to her home" (60).

Eudora is, however, unable to participate in one of the most important activities in the maintenance of the nation: being one of the "biological reproducers of the members of national collectivities" (Anthias and Yuval-Davis 7). Eudora's inability to have children qualifies her access to social citizenship and sheds light on her interactions with Maud and Akosua. Unable to reproduce normalized whiteness herself, Eudora keeps a careful watch on these two "outsiders" in order to moderate their potential contamination of the nation. Homi Bhabha, in *The Location of Culture* (1994), argues that to be a racialized subject is "to be amongst those whose very presence is ... 'overlooked' – in the double sense of social surveillance and psychic disavowal" (236). Eudora's desire to "overlook" Maud is evident from their first meeting, during which the Franks brazenly enter the Tyne home uninvited, armed with one of Eudora's tortes as a welcoming gift and means to entry. Eudora enters the kitchen, behaving "as though her presence were the most natural thing in the world" (61), and criticizes every aspect of Maud's domesticity. Although the family is finishing a home-cooked Ghanaian meal, Eudora says, "Poor dears. Been cleaning so hard you haven't had a chance to go shopping" (61), the insinuation being that Maud is not feeding her family properly. She then roots through their cupboards in search of a knife, complaining that Maud "obviously [hasn't] done the drawers yet" (62). Every comment she makes is a veiled suggestion that Maud's housekeeping abilities are inferior to hers. Despite having no children of her own, she also interferes in Maud's parenting decisions, even after their relationship has soured. For example, when Chloe and Yvette turn thirteen, Maud plans a modest celebration, but her event is "undermined by tactless guests" (244) when Eudora again appears on their doorstep uninvited, with a lavish cake and gifts for the twins, despite her increasing suspicion of their behaviour. Eudora's anxiety about the twins, and her interference in Maud's domestic decisions, reflect a desire to police the boundaries of her community through the only means available to her.

Within Eudora's hegemonic perception, Akosua Porter needs even more social surveillance than Maud. After Eudora has entered Maud's home uninvited, the two of them pay an unexpected visit to the Porter home, where Maud demonstrates her complicity in Eudora's construction of domestic hierarchies. In contrast to Eudora's excessive performances of hospitality, Akosua invites the women "grudgingly inside" (144), where they survey her "dignified poverty" (144). The kitchen floor is overlaid with a carpet "that shamelessly displayed its stains" (144), and Maud and Eudora are overwhelmed with "the heat, the rancid scent of cooking oil and incense" (144). The house shows visible traces of the Porters' class status, as well as racial markers: "Over the deep freezer hung a print of the Last Supper, Jesus and his black disciples robed in kente cloaks" (144). Of greater concern is the sheer size of the Porter family: "The children seemed to multiply before Maud's eyes" (144), and she and Eudora react negatively to what they perceive is her inability to contain them. Maud's observation demonstrates her internalization of readily available stereotypes about African women, which many continental African feminists have negated. Ghanaian feminist Ama Ata Aidoo argues that "the image of the African woman in the mind of the world has been set. She is breeding too many children she cannot take care of, and for whom she should not expect others to pick up the tab. She is hungry and so are her children" (39). Readers later learn that some of Akosua's children are from Porter's first marriage, further underscoring her family's lack of conformity to the image of the small, patriarchal, nuclear family unit. Thus, in symbolic terms, Akosua's children demonstrate multiple possibilities for contaminating the nation.

The debates between Maud and Akosua about how to raise their Canadian-born children enact in microcosm the two positionalities available to immigrant families within dominant discourses: cultural assimilation versus long-distance ethnonationalism. Between the mid-nineteenth century and the mid-twentieth, Canadian immigration laws were repeatedly amended so as to deny entry to various groups of racialized immigrants on the grounds that they were unassimilable.[7] Thus Maud, knowing she has come to "a country that had no need of her" (24), rejects nearly all of her Ghanaian customs. She and Samuel, who have transformed themselves from "Maud Yaaba Adu Darko" and "Samuel Kwabena" into the innocuous Tynes, are repeatedly held up as a positive example. In Ray's words: "You two are *model*. Look at someone like Porter. No steady job, a wife who doesn't work, and look at his brood. She's barely off the boat before she pops out ten kids" (161). Maud is consistently labelled a "model" because of how hard she has worked to obliterate her West African cultural traditions. Soon after arriving in Canada, she refuses to speak anything but English; and using homemaker magazines and a Bible – the missionary's historical tools of racial and spiritual "uplift" – she practises reading aloud in order to "shave her origins from her voice" (24). Even Samuel, who demonstrates assimilationist tendencies himself, is alarmed by Maud's behaviour: "in lapses that betrayed just how deeply this new country had altered her thought, she bragged about having 'good genes.' She was even thinner than before they had married, when just the sight of her awkward bones made him mournful for the destitute child she'd been. Now Samuel felt uneasy near that body" (21). Maud also wears make-up to cover her tribal markings, even though they are "still visible under face powder" (24). Uninterested in what Charles Taylor calls the multicultural "politics of recognition" (25), Maud seeks *not* to be recognized by her ethnicity. Instead she strives for an invisibility that is impossible given her racially marked body.

Maud's specific Fante ethnicity is not even revealed until she encounters Akosua, a "bad immigrant" whose Ghanaian ethnonationalism emphasizes her refusal to assimilate. Unlike Maud, who attends the town hall meeting in a Western-style dress, Akosua wears "a kente headdress" (115), an act that actually results in a *mis*recognition when Eudora incorrectly labels her "Indian." After many years in Canada, Akosua continues to express her Ghanaian identity in the present rather than past tense. When Maud asks her, "Which part of Gold Coast were you from?" (145), she indignantly retorts: "*Eih,* what is this Gold Coast business? 'Which part of Gold coast?' she asks. Ahein ... Did we not see independence? Must we still go by that name? Are we not ourselves? *Sth.* And what do you mean by 'were?' I *am* from Winneba. I *am* from Ghana. I am *not* from *Gold Coast*. You sign the paper and like that you forget your heritage, isn't it?" (145).

Maud and Akosua's differing beliefs about Canadian assimilation and Ghanaian ethnonationalism inform the ways in which they raise their children. If, as Anthias and Yuval-Davis argue, women's domestic roles in the nation-state include being "active transmitters and producers of national culture" (7), Maud and Akosua have different visions about which national cultures are to be re/produced by their children. Within minutes of Maud's first entry into Akosua's home, she criticizes her mothering abilities, and she is disdainful of Akosua's many children, whom she views as ill-mannered, uncontained, and, like their mother, uncivil: "eyeing the strangers, they lingered in corners, sat on counters, one even busied herself at the stove" (144). Upon her first visit to the Tyne home, Akosua makes the same claim about Maud's children, complaining that they have "no discipline" (195) when they do not address her with the age-specific respect that would be expected of them in Ghana. She is also critical of Maud's refusal to teach her children Fante or Twi, accusing her of trying to "kill her heritage" (202) at her family's expense. But while both women feel that they have chosen the best route for their families, neither of their positions is a plausible option for their second-generation Canadian children, whose complex processes of identity formation extend far beyond the assimilation–ethnonationalism binary. Although their positions are vastly different, both Maud and Akosua embrace a rigid and singular understanding of ethnicity that cannot account for the multiple and conflicting influences in their children's lives.

Maud internalizes her assimilationist attitudes to such an extent that she becomes her society's ideal self-policing subject, disciplining her domestic practices to fit within hegemonic Canadian expectations. Once she begins a relationship with Akosua she polices her household behaviour as well: "Maud's greatest coup was doing for Akosua Porter what she wished someone had done for her on her arrival to Canada.

Every day Maud could be found talking to Akosua in the Tyne kitchen, pontificating on the workings of western society. She told Akosua what to shop for, and donated some of her best clothes to the Porter cause" (208). Teaching her "things both already knew" (228), Maud attempts to "domesticate" Akosua just as she has domesticated herself. Her lessons invoke both the domesticity of home life and the processes of making herself "domestic" instead of "foreign." McClintock observes that "[e]tymologically, the verb domesticate is akin to dominate, which derives from *dominus*, lord of the *domum*, the home. Until 1964, however, the verb to domesticate also carried as one of its meanings the action 'to civilize'" (1995: 35). Maud internalizes this colonial mentality throughout the novel, directing it first towards herself and then towards Akosua in behaviours that reveal the dangerous extent to which she has embraced Eudora and Ray's notions that she and other immigrants should "know their place."

The Second Generation and the Costs of (Un)Belonging

Issues of community play out in very different ways for Chloe and Yvette. As the first generation of characters born in Canada, they face different questions around belonging than their parents. Maud and Samuel work to assimilate, yet they also identify with their Gold Coast origins in ways their children never can, and they still have ties to the country of their birth that are revealed in culinary habits and linguistic practices such as riddles and proverbs. Chloe and Yvette's ethnicity can only centre on their use of the more fluid label "black," potentially the only one available to them given Maud's efforts to erase West Africa from familial memory. As Rinaldo Walcott asks: "What are the terms which make one a Black Canadian? When does one cross the imaginary border between immigrant and national? Does the crossing of that boundary only happen for Black people when they are born in this land, and if so, why?" (1999: 16). These questions inform the twins' interactions with others and their efforts to negotiate a space for themselves, within their family, within Aster, and within the nation. Chloe and Yvette face both a generational gap and a cultural gap between themselves and their parents, and Maud and Samuel often cite these factors to explain their inability to understand their daughters. As their erratic behaviour becomes, to them, increasingly confusing, Maud and Samuel find themselves at a loss as to how to deal with them. Maud's ultimate acknowledgment that "[y]our dad and I, we, we don't know what to do" (295), speaks to the ways Canadian-born children are so often perceived as utterly incomprehensible by their immigrant parents.

It is noteworthy that mental breakdown has been a recurrent theme in the present book. McWatt, Levy, and Edugyan all depict female characters who have faced manifestations of mental illness and psychic rupture as they struggle to understand themselves and their place within oppressive and marginalizing spaces and discursive regimes. How, then, might we read these breakdowns, and their significance, collectively and symbolically? What might they reveal about the profound costs of trying to belong for racialized second-generation children, especially on the restrictive terms established by the Canadian or the English nation? And how might these costs be especially steep for women, who also face gendered forms of marginalization, surveillance, and corporeal and psychic discipline? In the case of Chloe and Yvette, whose mental illness is the most severe and sustained of any of the characters in this study, their "madness" might be read as a response to a recurrent trope in English Canadian literature: the isolation, alienation, and madness provoked by a hostile Canadian landscape. I am thinking in particular about Sinclair Ross's prairie literature, as well as short stories like Joyce Marshall's "The Old Woman" and Susana Moodie's famous sketch "Brian the Still-Hunter" in *Roughing It in the Bush.* Edugyan's novel racializes this trope and provokes for me a different kind of question: How might the twins be driven mad, literally and symbolically, by a context and a landscape that nullifies them, that disavows their very presence as black girls, despite their being born and raised in Canada? According to Andrea Davis, "Edugyan uses the twins to mark the degree of trauma that results from the (dis)location of African diasporic families in the Americas, permanently estranged from space and place, from history and memory" (42). The twins' experiences might, I argue, also point to the kinds of traumas faced by racialized subjects in a Canadian and specifically a Prairie context.

Both within and beyond the narrative exist multiple interpretations or routes through which to think about the twins' "madness," suggesting that it cannot be read or understood through any single symbolic or cultural narrative. Edugyan bases Chloe and Yvette on two historical examples of twin girls who spoke their own invented languages to each other: "Poto and Cabengo," born Grace and Virginia Kennedy in the United States in 1970, and June and Jennifer Gibbons, who were raised in Wales by Barbadian immigrant parents in the 1960s and 70s.

According to Davis, the experiences of the Gibbons twins, some of which are mirrored in Edguyan's novel, "are proof of the kinds of trauma that afflicts women and girls in deeply classist, sexist and racist societies of the (over)developed world" (43). In a Ghanaian cultural context, there are several potential "explanations" for Chloe and Yvette's behaviours. First, when Maud runs away from her family's compound near Accra to escape her father's physical abuse, he curses her womb to barrenness, bidding her a lifetime of unhappiness if she leaves him. When, despite his malevolent wishes, Yvette and Chloe are born, "[b]oth Samuel and Maud were embarrassed to admit that not even an ocean could distance them from their superstitions. For twins were a kind of misfortune" (24). As adolescents, when the question of their setting the town's fires arises, Eudora relates Akosua's theory, according to which the family has been cursed because of Samuel's cultural negligence in not performing the forty days' libation after Jacob dies: "She says you never had a proper burial for your uncle … She says he's causing madness in your children because of it" (275). These intersecting narratives suggest that the novel is not meant to be a diasporic reimagining of any one Ghanaian cultural belief in a Canadian context. Edugyan presents multiple psychological, cultural, symbolic, and mythical possibilities through which to interpret the twins' mental illness, working both within and against all of these discourses to represent Chloe and Yvette in complex and multilayered ways.

The twins' "madness" might also be read as part of an intertextual conversation with various postcolonial and continental African texts and contexts. In *Black Skin, White Masks*, Frantz Fanon insists that "beside phylogeny and ontogeny stand sociogeny" (11), arguing that colonial alienation is a result of complex social processes. Maud's worries that the twins don't fit in suggest that she too draws correlations between their mental instability and their social marginalization. Yvette in particular expresses a race-based sense of alienation that is noteworthy in a text in which questions of racialization, while prominent, are rarely articulated. Maud overhears a conversation "in which Yvette had said that she 'got tired of being black.' Tired of the sugary way she had to behave to get people to play with her. Tired of being asked where she was *really* from, tired of being talked to as though she didn't speak English and tired, above all, of feeling incapable of great things" (34). Later, Yvette and Ama enter a diner, which they quickly leave after Yvette states: "I hate that … Even though this town used to be all black, everywhere you go they stare at you" (106). These insights into Yvette's psyche provide a different framework through which to understand the twins' descent into madness.

Double Crossings (2001), McClintock's analysis of mental illness in the nineteenth century – how it was represented during the era of high imperialism, and how it was racialized and sexualized – offers insight into the social dimension of the twins' condition. McClintock invokes a warning given by a missionary to South African writer Bessie Head, which Head recounts in *A Question of Power* (1974): "You must be very careful. Your mother was insane. If you're not careful, you'll get insane just like your mother" (16). McClintock argues that this warning

> captures in miniature ... a founding conflict that has animated Western notions of mental illness ... On the one hand, the warning ("you'll get insane just like your mother") presents madness as a taint in the blood, a degenerate flaw passed relentlessly from mother to child. Mental illness here belongs in the inexorable and unanswerable domain of blood and biology ... At the same time, the warning ("you must be very careful") presents madness as a *behavioural* flaw. Here mental illness belongs in the domain of discipline and punishment: "If you're not careful ..." Mental illness, here, is presented as a behavioural condition, subject to a carceral and punitive regime. (10)

This contradiction, which constructs madness as simultaneously inherent and socially produced, plays out in the twins. Because their clinical diagnosis cannot account for the dimensions of their behaviour that appear to be social responses to their marginalization, these behaviours are articulated as behavioural flaws.

Yet the third-person omniscient narration of Edugyan's novel allows no glimpse of the twins' world view or of their own perceptions of their rapid mental disintegration. Their perspectives can only be inferred from their increasingly abnormal behaviours. Some of their actions cannot be explained, rationalized, or defended. Others, however, suggest a manifestation of a genuine struggle to belong, both within their multiethnic family and within dominant white society. After one of their earliest stretches of several days in which neither twin speaks aloud to anyone, Samuel eavesdrops at the first sign of voices from their room: "The rapid-fire staccato words sound like a tape run backwards, rushed and guttural. Perhaps, Samuel thought, in their cleverness they have gone and learned another language. But despite his polyglot repertoire, Samuel couldn't discern it. Strangely inflected, they had both acquired enough to talk quite rigorously" (252–3). The twins' invention of their own language is perhaps not a random act, for it comes in the wake of their meeting Akosua, during which she had criticized them for not speaking Twi, Fante, or any Ghanaian language. Iain Chambers argues that "language is not primarily a means of communication; it is, above all, a means of cultural construction in which our very selves and sense are constituted" (1994: 22). The twins' attempt to remedy their imposed monolingualism, which divides them from both their cultural origins and their multilingual parents, might be read as a response to Akosua's accusations. Ama hears their incomprehensible whispering as well, shortly before finding under Chloe's bed "two dozen hairbrushes, some brass, some wooden, some of a plastic fashioned after gold. All lay with their handles at an exacting forty-five degree angle" (254). Ama also finds in Chloe's pillowcase "a small bale of coarse, black hair" (255). These behaviours gesture to West African animist religious traditions, in which the hair taken from a person can be used to cast a spell on him or her. The twins' made-up language, and their obsession with hair, historically an important racial marker, suggest that their new fetishes might be read not as random acts but as a complex effort to work through their racialized identities. Further, that Ama is the target of some of the twins' hostility is, while not justifiable, perhaps not surprising, given that she is consistently described by both Maud and Samuel as feminine and beautiful in ways they are not.

Unable to deal with them in any meaningful way, Maud and Samuel resign themselves to sending the twins to a residence for distressed children. Their psychiatric evaluation and institutionalization, a momentous decision for the family, is described in a rushed episode of less than two pages, in which Maud and Samuel, without understanding the details of the paperwork thrust upon them, sign the twins over to be wards of the state. This instant termination of their parent–child relationship reveals the extent to which the state can invade kinship relations, particularly among racialized communities. At the institution, where Maud and Samuel sit in the waiting room for the results of the twins' tests, "There was a second couple there, two Natives in formal but stained clothes who leaned against each other sleeping" (296). Their silent presence for the duration of Maud and Samuel's visit provides a ghostly backdrop for the scene, drawing attention to the unspoken subtext of residential schools, forced adoptions, and other traumas that Aboriginal peoples have experienced as a result of the state's failure to acknowledge their languages, cultures, and systems of kinship. Their entry into the mental health system, coupled with the Tynes', demonstrates that certain families – specifically, racialized families – are far more susceptible to governmental practices and state intervention than others.

Reconceptualizing Kinship and Ethicality

Ama suffers perhaps the most at the hands of the twins, and despite Samuel's efforts to involve her in their lives she has little impact on Chloe and Yvette's troubled myopia. Yet although her anxieties manifest themselves in far less harmful ways, Ama faces similar issues around cultural marginalization. In her first introduction to Samuel she is described as racially indeterminate, "with skin the colour of oats and almond-shaped eyes of a nameless hue" (35). The backstory of her French grandmother, Geneviève Ouillet, reveals that her paternal grandfather was an Aboriginal man who assumed Geneviève's French name when they married (183) and that her father is Métis. Just as the twins know little about their parents' background in Gold Coast, Ama's family, particularly her domineering grandmother, is conspicuously silent about its mixed-race make-up. In *Circles of Time* (1999), David McNab observes that in the nineteenth century, Métis people were highly regarded because of their mixed ancestry. Intermarriage was heralded as bringing about "the development, through a sharing of cultures, a new society. The Métis were to be the harbingers of social change. They had created a new and distinctive society" (23). Gradually, however, "this cultural view of race changed substantially ... By the early twentieth century Métis people would, it was hoped, assimilate, and nothing further would have to be done" (23). Ama's father appears to have gone this route. Having married a white woman, he works to ensure that his family associates with "pious and monied families" (36) from their church. Ama takes Catholicism as her "birthright" (35) but seems to know almost nothing about her Aboriginal grandfather or his cultural or spiritual traditions. Even her access to her French Canadian background is tenuous. When her grandmother picks her up from the Tyne home after the twins leave her to drown in the Athabasca River, Ama can only communicate with her in a muddled and heavily anglicized French: "Grandmère, *voulez* stay for *thé*?" (182). When her grandmother admonishes her in rapid and fluent French, her only response is a tearful *"Je ne comprends pas"* (182). Like the twins, she cannot speak the language of her family, and this causes her stress and anguish.

Ama also, perhaps surprisingly, shares some common experiences with Samuel despite their differences in age, gender, and ethnicity. Initially uneasy about his attentions, she soon realizes that "his attraction to her had nothing sexual in it; it had cleaner, sadder roots: estranged from his family, he was a deeply lonely man" (57). Ama too is deeply lonely. She has no friends and, abandoned to the care of the Tynes for the summer while her parents go to Paris in search of a cure for her mother's multiple sclerosis, Ama spends much of her time alone, unable to form relationships with Chloe or Yvette. But during her summer in Aster, Ama and Samuel develop considerable affection for each other, displaying the only moments of genuine connection in a household in which members are otherwise profoundly alienated. Despite Samuel's "reticence to enter family life at all" (107), he expresses love for Ama, although he "wondered, not without some guilt, why affection for Ama came so much more easily to him than it ever had for his twins" (169). His attitude is very different from Maud's. While she too cares for Ama, "for her, nothing could overcome blood ties" (175), and she favours her own daughters even when they are trying to inflict bodily harm on her or Samuel. Samuel's disregard for blood, one of the sacred fluids of familial continuity, speaks to his willingness to conceptualize relationality on more malleable terms.

If the workings of families symbolically reflect the workings of the nation, then Samuel's ability to look beyond blood – which serves as a metaphorical signifier of national purity as well – reflects significant potential for reconceptualizing nation-space in similarly flexible ways. After Maud's death, Saul Porter also passes away, and Akosua, true to her ethnonationalist beliefs, returns to Ghana. When Ama learns of Samuel's illness and utter isolation, she does not hesitate to return to Aster to care for him in the final months of his life. Entering the house, she is "astounded ... it had remained unchanged these thirty years right down to the bowl of false oranges at the entrance. Clothes had stiffened on hangers, and the muddy children's tracks on the Venetian carpet could easily have been hers" (321). Although the house itself is represented as a space of stasis, the relationship that is newly articulated between Ama and Samuel points towards different conditions of possibility for constituting kinship bonds across boundaries of race, ethnicity, and biology.

The Tyne house has succumbed to the pervasive rot and filth that Maud and the family fought against from their first arrival. This rot is a significant recurring trope in the novel. Maud and Samuel's first encounter with the house immediately reveals its decay: "Bramble roamed the halls on some unfelt draft. The dust-grey sills had collected the fat, petrified bodies of insects, scattered like droppings. In the front room, sheets, probably blown from the covered couches, sank in hog-ties around the furniture's ankles. There was a heavy odour in the air" (51). No matter how much they clean they are unable to restore the house to any reasonable state. Porter's house is no better: "The house was run-down, its weathered paint like some gruesome human rash. One could almost hear the decay" (142). Aster's town hall, although recently restored, is similarly decaying: "The paint flaked away. The wood creaked. Woodlice devoured the foundations. Anthills rose like piles of sawdust around it" (111). Even on Ray's farm, otherwise better maintained than most of the buildings, "the smell of rot wafted from the distance" (128). But nothing compares to Genevieve Ouillet's home, which Ama refers to as "that great house of rot" (37), full of filth and mould that reveals "an outer decay that barely reflected the decay within" (221).

Edugyan's use of these images might be read as an intertextual dialogue with Ghanaian writer Ayi Kwei Armah, whose writing also includes extensive descriptions of filth and decay. I make this connection not to suggest any simple or literal correlation between the political and social context of the Canadian prairies and that of post-colonial Ghana, but to suggest that placing these two literary and physical geographies in conversation with each other *matters*. Understanding Edugyan's work as being in dialogue with Armah points to the ways in which her writing engages with multiple literary traditions, including the Canadian prairie writing I mentioned earlier, as well as with some significant continental African authors. In engaging with these multiple literary traditions, Edugyan's novel speaks to and across various diasporic locations and in so doing un/settles a conceptualization of the Canadian prairies as a bounded or contained geographic space.

In Armah's *The Beautyful Ones Are Not Yet Born* (1969), the unnamed protagonist contemplates a politically corrupt post-colonial Ghana through recurrent images of a rotting Accra. In a passage that continues for two pages he reflects on a banister in a government building:

> [I]t was barely possible to see the banister, and the sight was like that of a very long piece of diseased skin ... They were no longer sharp, the cracks, but all rounded out and smoothed, consumed by some soft, gentle process of decay. In places the wood seemed to have been painted over, but that

> must have been a long time ago indeed. For a long time only polish … had been used … The polish, it was supposed, would catch the rot. But of course in the end it was the rot which imprisoned everything in its effortless embrace. (14–15)

Edugyan's text invokes this passage when Ama tries to clean and restore order to the Tyne home. She quickly discovers the difficulty of the task: "She whitewashed the cellar, with its stink of rotting tuber and its larvae, and she poisoned the woodlice from the undersides of tables and banisters. The decay kept reclaiming its territory, but she refused to give in, recleaning what had been scrubbed an hour earlier" (324). Ama soon gives up the futile endeavour, focusing instead on caring for Samuel in his dying days.

In this regard, Edugyan's novel again gestures to Armah's, for despite their sustained images of filth and rot, both texts also suggest, symbolically, that decay might provide the fertile soil out of which renewal or rebirth can emerge. In Armah's novel the final chapter opens with the protagonist awakening to a hopeful new day: "already the sun was up over the sea, its rays coming very clean and clear on the water; and the sky above all open and beautiful" (211). The cleanliness of this imagery is striking when read against the previous chapters, which provide a detailed sensory description of a corrupt government official climbing through a filthy, feces-filled latrine in order to escape prosecution. The final pages of Edugyan's novel similarly resonate, as Samuel, for the brief period in which Ama returns to care for him, experiences his "second life." For in spite of the decay that surrounds them, they both realize that "[a] new life begins, the past can never be recovered" (324).

In their second life together, Samuel and Ama create a reconstituted, trans-ethnic family, one that provides them with a newfound sense of kinship. Ama unflinchingly performs the most intimate tasks and cleans up as Samuel's body slowly fails him. When Samuel dies, she performs the final duty of bathing his body and preparing it for the funeral, and makes the arrangements for his burial. Ama and Samuel's relationship bears witness to a powerful form of chosen, outer-biological kinship that speaks to the exigency Donna Haraway expresses for thinking beyond the limits of the biological. Recall that Haraway longs for "models of solidarity and human unity and difference rooted in friendship, work, partially shared purposes, intractable collective pain, inescapable mortality, and persistent hope" (265). Samuel and Ama demonstrate these forms of solidarity, forming a relationship based on shared pain and on their willingness to confront their own mortality as Samuel dies. Although resulting from different circumstances, Ama and Samuel's reconstituted family echoes that of the four friends in *What We All Long For,* who also insistently look beyond blood ties to form their most meaningful connections. Ama and Samuel's bond of non-hierarchical kinship looks beyond patriarchal or gendered power dynamics and instead relies on an economy of caregiving, in which Samuel for his part provides belonging and emotional sustenance for Ama as she looks after his daily needs. Their relationship creates possibilities for rearticulating familial bonds and also, symbolically, for reconceptualizing citizenship.

In a symbolic sense, this chosen family may also reflect other possibilities for rethinking the nation in similarly egalitarian, creolized, and plural terms. In its lack of emphasis on blood, birthplace, or ethnicity, the grounds on which imagined communities are most often formed, Ama and Samuel's relationship might provide alternative, more flexible, and also more ethical models for citizenship than those promoted by Ray, Eudora, and the other inhabitants of Aster. While their models of belonging are based on rigidity, exclusion, and singularity in the interest of constructing artificial homogeneities, Ama and Samuel instead emphasize malleable, chosen collectivities that cross ethnic and "racial" boundaries. Ama and Samuel model other possibilities for belonging that might also extend to the political realm. If, as McClintock reminds us, the domestic is political, then this reconstituted family is an example of a collectivity established on different terms, one that potentially enables other, more ethical forms of belonging.

But the most radical reimaginings of ethicality, and the most profound conditions of possibility in the novel, are rendered through the unnamed twin who returns to reclaim the house in the final paragraph. The narrative voice shifts from past to present tense as it articulates the twin's first fleeting attempts at her own "second life" and her hope that she is "strong enough to begin again" (328). She returns to a house that immediately begins to emerge from its stagnant decay upon her arrival: "she walks the weed-strewn path to the old house to find it so identical to her memory of it that already it is changing" (328). As she faces her first night of freedom in decades, she, like Armah's protagonist, looks for "the sight of dawn" (328) and, in the final words of the novel, contemplates the life she hopes to lead:

> Devastated to have outlived everything, to have outgrown even her own madness, her solitude is only one of many new struggles she will have to

> overcome, the worst of which is knowing this. It will not be an easy road, but many have worse, and her only obligation amidst all the pain and occasional pleasure is to live in the best way she is capable of. That is all we have. (328)

The twin's final recognition that her only obligation is to lead an ethical life might be the most powerful articulation of social citizenship in the novel. The absence of a specific party to whom she might bear an obligation proposes an ethical relationality that looks beyond the limiting scope of familial, regional, ethnic, racial, or national collectivities. In the final line Edugyan turns outward to the reader through her use of the first-person plural. The "we" to whom she speaks might be comparable to the community Brand invokes in the title of her novel: a trans-ethnic, trans-cultural collectivity that similarly longs for outer-national and outer-familial possibilities through which to live "in the best way we are capable of."

This important invocation of morality and ethicality is dramatically different from the kinds of state-sanctioned ethicality propagated by the Canadian nation. The narrative that has circulated for the last several decades regarding Canadian immigration policy is that this nation will provide a safe haven for immigrants, who supposedly will be able to live according to their beliefs and practices in "the best ways they are capable of." This was the guiding premise of the Points System, which rewarded middle-class values such as the importance of education and stable employment. These things reflected a key premise of the multiculturalism that emerged in the first Trudeau era, and they continue to underpin the narrative promoted today in the second Trudeau era as the nation continues to craft an international image of itself as place that welcomes those fleeing global crises. Edugyan's novel as it circulates in this contemporary context asks us to reflect on the long history of "abuses of settlement" – the exclusions and erasures that are necessary to articulate this national image. But more importantly, the novel asks us to look towards a different kind of ethical communalism that might transcend such divisions, and in so doing to write a different kind of national/familial narrative that acknowledges and bears witness to these acts of erasure.

Chapter 5

"When Roots Won't Matter Any More": Zadie Smith's *White Teeth*

I've been puzzled by the fact that young black people in London today are marginalized, fragmented, unenfranchised, disadvantaged and dispersed. And yet, they look as if they own the territory. Somehow, they ... in spite of everything, are centred, in place: without much material support, it's true, but nevertheless, they occupy a new kind of space at the center ... I do feel a sense of – dare I say – envy surrounding them.

Stuart Hall, "Minimal Selves"

[T]he terms of debate in contemporary English racial politics – race, culture, ethnicity, nation – are made intelligible by a disavowal of their gender address.

Ranu Samantrai, *AlterNatives: Black Feminism in the Postimperial Nation*

The final chapter in this study returns again to the British context to consider Zadie Smith's *White Teeth* (2000). Just as Brand's *What We All Long For* is significant in the ways it rewrites the city-space of Toronto through the lens of a second generation, Smith's novel narrates a creolized, immigrant, and post-immigrant London in which British muliticulturalism is neither new nor noteworthy, but simply a "tired, inevitable fact" (440).[1] In this multigenerational narrative, second-generation Britons Irie Jones and twin brothers Magid and Millat Iqbal explore processes through which they and their immigrant families might lay claim to the nation. The trope of rooting – as opposed to routing – pervades the novel, and while Smith's narrative considers their families' wide-ranging histories of transnational migration, the second-generation children are better understood through their efforts to ground themselves than through their families' diasporic scattering. Born in London's suburbs, Irie, Magid, and Millat have rooted themselves in England, reasonably confident, as Hall states above in "Minimal Selves," of their place in the nation, even when that nation is far less certain about the terms of their presence and continues to marginalize and disenfranchise them. Smith recognizes that the centre does need to be made anew in order to account for these "stubbornly non-colonial descendants" (Gilroy 1999; 60) of Empire. The novel illustrates that first-generation immigration and second-generation settlement are ongoing, complex, and often messy processes, which are not neatly resolved or "concluded" by virtue of British birth. This notion of messiness will become increasingly important as the chapter proceeds.

In *White Teeth*, reconceptualizing the nation, and thinking differently about Britain's contemporary racial politics, must (as Samantrai suggests in the epigraph above) pay attention as well to the ways in which gender politics are intertwined in these discussions. In Smith's novel, such reconceptualization is in many cases facilitated largely by the female characters. While Smith's novel is not an exclusively feminist project, the text explores significant possibilities for thinking beyond national parameters and their attendant racial paradigms in specifically gendered terms. Critics have thus far been conspicuously silent about the feminist implications of Smith's work,[2] focusing largely on the novel's treatment of British multiculturalism at the turn of the millennium. While this chapter contributes to those conversations, I will extend them by examining the ways in which the public and domestic spaces of London are (re)shaped in particular ways by female characters. I will also consider the ways in which Irie's reproductive body destabilizes the very premise of generational descent, as she looks towards a time and place "when roots won't matter any more" (527).

Smith's first novel is an unruly and uncontainable book that transcends straightforward categorizations. I begin my discussion by considering the implications of the novel's popular appeal, given that it is by far the bestselling book among those examined in this project. Smith has been nominated for and awarded a multitude of prestigious British and international literary prizes, but none of her subsequent novels have surpassed *White Teeth* in popularity. Her first novel was a national and international bestseller, selling over 600,000 copies in its first year. Since then, it has sold well over a million copies worldwide, and in 2002 it was made into a BBC television miniseries, which was rebroadcast in the US on *Masterpiece Theatre*. *White Teeth* thus occupies an interesting and sometimes productively contradictory space at the intersection of the literary and the popular, one that might enable an alternative conceptual space through which to think differently about nationhood and the roles played by literary production in its maintenance.

In his analyses of popular literature and the imagining of Englishness, James Donald wonders: "[H]ow might popular fictions shape our perceptions and experience of identity and difference?" (166). Exploring the relationship between canon-formation and nation-formation, he reminds us that historically "'Literature' became institutionalized simultaneously as both an academic discipline and a formative tool of the national culture" (169), claiming that "[f]rom the start, the tensions inherent in the concepts of 'the nation,' 'the people,' and 'culture' were built into the institution Literature. It exists to give them form, to contain them. Retrospectively, it provides the criteria for selecting certain texts as 'the canon' of English literature, as the history of 'England' given imaginative expression" (169). But he continues by asking: "So where does 'popular literature' fit in? Sometimes the term implies a residue left over after true Literature has been defined. Sometimes it refers to the writing that people actually choose to read ... But the idea of popular literature as a failed Literature still seems to dominate, and limit, analysis" (169).

Although most of the reviews of Smith's novel were decidedly positive, sometimes overwhelmingly so, at least one critic characterized it as "failed literature." James Wood, in a now-infamous article in *The New Republic*, offered an extended and often vitriolic critique of "the big contemporary novel" (41), taking aim at Smith as well as other writers like Salman Rushdie, comparing them unfavourably to "truly" great authors like Tolstoy, Chekhov, and Dickens. Wood complains that many contemporary novels are implausible, sloppy, overworked, and "congested" (41) in their "pursuit of vitality at all costs" (41). About *White Teeth* specifically, he writes that its failure results from "an excess of storytelling" (42) and that Smith's storylines "develop wildly, but her characters do not develop at all" (45). He also faults the ways in which she engages with the novel as a genre, claiming that "[f]ormally, her book lacks moral seriousness" (43). While Wood's arguments have since been negated in popular circles by the commercial success of Smith's novel and the commentary of other reviewers, and also in academic contexts by the literary criticism of several scholars, there has been little comment about the inherent misogyny in Wood's review. In his concern that *White Teeth* too greatly defies generic conventions, he derisively refers to it as "hysterical realism" (41), invoking the gendered language of mental aberration used to discipline and contain women in the nineteenth century. Citing the implausibility of Irie having sex with both Magid and Millat on the same day, Wood complains that this is an example of "Smith's hot plot which has had its way with her" (42). Dismissively viewing Irie's act only through the lens of sensationalized romance fiction – again a popular genre negatively attached to women – Wood appears unable to read this plot line counter-discursively, as Smith's refusal to contain female bodies or female sexualities, for example. As I argue below, Irie's sexual acts, and the child that results, have profound personal and political implications for thinking differently about gender, race, ethnicity, and generational descent – possibilities that Wood attenuates though his misogynistic dismissal.

Throughout his review, Wood repeatedly declares *White Teeth* to be a messy and unmanageable novel. I want to argue otherwise: that the novel's most fruitful potential for disrupting dominant British national narratives lies in its very messiness, both stylistically/generically and in the uncontainable ways it crosses the boundaries between the literary and the popular. If one purpose of "capital-L" Literature is to reproduce the nation, then what kind of Britain does Smith's novel reflect? She does not offer an imaginative expression of a unified and coherent national culture and instead portrays a nation perpetually destabilized by its own confusion about the shifting and increasingly racialized parameters of both British and English identity. Smith's novel reflects Barnor Hesse's argument in *Un/Settled Multiculturalisms* that contemporary Britain needs to be understood as a space of "cultural entanglements" (2); these "commonplace forms of *creolization, hybridity, syncretism,* represent a profound challenge to the idea that national and social forms are logically coherent, unitary, or tidy" (2, emphasis Hesse's). Smith similarly recognizes these entanglements as complicated and messy. Her articulations of British multiculture reflect this sense of tumultuousness, as in, for example, her description of the second generation as "children with first and last names on a direct collision course" (326). But her observation that "we have finally slipped into each other's lives with reasonable comfort" (327) also suggests a willingness to live with this untidy sense of entanglement rather than a desire to create order out of the fractured cultural narratives that have resulted from centuries of colonial rule. In this regard, Smith takes as her starting point a conclusion to which Levy's protagonist Faith comes in *Fruit of the Lemon*: the "shared past" (325) of the English nation and its "bastard child[ren] of Empire" need to be recognized (326).

The ways in which *White Teeth* can also be understood as popular literature facilitate this disruption of singular and homogenizing British national narratives. As Daniel Coleman has observed of the Canadian context, "popular literature is what allows us to see a contest between representations of the nation" (35). Smith is writing a similarly contested narrative. She gives voice to Britain's ongoing need to understand itself as a multiculture, but she does so in a way that both writes and writes *against* the nation, challenging the hegemonic discourses through which this multiplicity has been marginalized for centuries. Moreover, the implications of the messy cultural entanglements she represents extend beyond the literary realm. As Richard Iton reminds us, there are many ways "a deep engagement with popular culture might enhance our understanding of developments in the formal political arena [which suggests] that greater attention to a fuller range of deliberative practices and spaces might compel a revision of our notions of the political" (29).

Space, Place, and Generational Difference

Feminist geographer Dorreen Massey argues that "the spatial organization of society … is integral to the production of the social, and not merely its result. It is fully implicated in both history and politics" (4). Smith's novel focuses on this spatial organization and the ways it has gendered and racialized London by disciplining female and non-white bodies. One significant aspect of spatial and racial contestation is housing, and the immigrant characters' uneven attempts to transform their homes into safe, comfortable domestic spaces for their families. Their housing choices gesture towards the racial tensions that dictated migrants' patterns of movement and dwelling in postwar London. James Procter argues that during these years, "[t]he dwelling place was … the site at which the regulation, policing and deferral of black settlement were most effectively played out. It was around housing that the national panic surrounding black immigration tended to accumulate and stage itself" (22). Smith's novel similarly plays out these moments, framing the confidence of the second generation in a context that draws attention to their parents' and grandparents' much more tenuous access to space. One of the first homes described is that of Hortense Bowden, Irie's maternal grandmother, who emigrated from

Jamaica with Clara, Irie's mother. Their first home is a small, dark basement apartment: "The Bowden living room sat just below street level, and had bars on its window, so all views were partial" (29). Decades later, Hortense still lives in this flat, and when Irie moves in with her temporarily she realizes the home is "still dark, still dank, still underground" (382). Procter observes that basements are one of the "recurrent locations within black literary discourse of the last fifty years" (1), citing postwar diasporic writing by authors such as George Lamming and Sam Selvon.[3] Smith's description of Hortense's flat harks back to narratives such as Selvon's *The Lonely Londoners* (1956), or Lamming's *The Emigrants* (1954), drawing attention to the social conflicts and housing shortages that prevented Caribbean migrants from renting certain homes and moving into certain neighbourhoods.

The Iqbals' motivation for moving to the ethnically diverse suburb of Willesden is more explicitly discussed: "Samad was moving out of East London (where one couldn't bring up children, indeed, one couldn't, not if one didn't wish them to come to bodily harm, he agreed), from East London with its NF gangs, to North London, north-west, where things were more … more … Liberal" (59, ellipses Smith's). Samad's desire to move comes in the wake of Alsana's pregnancy and their desire to protect their unborn twins. John McLeod points out that "[r]epresentations of postcolonial London bear witness to modes of authority which attempt to trap London's newcomers and their families in a particular mapping of the city (if not erasing them from the map entirely), regulating their movements and placing their activities under surveillance" (9). In this case, the modes of authority are explicitly represented by the National Front, whose violence is a literal manifestation of the discourses of regulation and containment that characterized Powellian and later Thatcherite attitudes towards migrants and their children.

These discourses are explored further in Alsana's reflections on her new neighbourhood:

> Alsana had a deep-seated belief that living near green spaces was morally beneficial to the young, and there to her right was Gladstone Park, a sweeping horizon of green named after the Liberal Prime Minister … and in the Liberal tradition it was a park without fences, unlike the more affluent Queen's Park (Victoria's), with its pointed metal railings. Willesden was not as pretty as Queen's Park, but it was a nice area. No denying it. Not like Whitechapel, where that madman E-knock someoneoranother gave a speech that forced them into the basement while kids broke the windows

> with their steel-capped boots. Rivers of blood silly-billy nonsense. Now she was pregnant she needed a little bit of peace and quiet. (62–3)[4]

Alsana seeks escape from Powell's rhetoric of domestic invasion and his belief that she is among those whose true place is in "another country, and whose home will continue to be elsewhere for successive generations" (140). She strives to make Willesden her home, and her longing for "peace and quiet" must be read literally in the wake of racist violence. She also hopes the city can be home for her future children; thus she chooses the space to which she believes they will have greatest access. Just as the steel-tipped boots of the National Front drive the Iqbals out of Whitechapel, the pointed metal railings serve as a symbol of restricted entry into Queen's Park. Alsana's hope for her unborn children is encompassed in the image of Gladstone Park. A space with no barriers, it is a poignant representation of the ways she envisions the city and the nation for them. A decade later, her children come to appreciate the value of green spaces as an escape from their own painful experiences of discrimination, describing parks as "the lungs of the city, some place where free breathing was possible" (174).

Ball claims that for many second-generation black British writers, "while young protagonists are shown on the move and on the make in the metropolitan cityscape – dynamically interacting in the public spaces of streets, clubs, schools, or workplaces – the parents are often ... relegated to private, domestic space as the comparatively static representatives of cultural tradition" (224). In Smith's novel, these binaries do not always hold true, as they are further mediated on the basis of gender. Particularly among the first generation, Alsana and Clara occupy the urban streetscape in very different ways than their husbands, Samad and Archie. Cultural geographer Don Mitchell has observed the traditional coding of "the public spaces of the city as 'masculine'" (209), arguing that "urban public space itself is predicated on the exclusion of women – both physically and psychologically" (210). The women in Smith's novel disrupt these assumptions, spending a great deal of time in public spheres in a way their husbands do not, offering a critique of the ways urban spaces are gendered and racialized.

Disconnected from their families, Archie and Samad spend most of their spare time together, yet they are rarely in public places. Instead, they are shown almost exclusively in three spaces: their homes, their workplaces, and O'Connell's, an Irish pub with Iraqi proprietors. O'Connell's in particular is represented as an atavistic space filled with pathetic, aging men reliving the past. That no women are allowed suggests the pub can be read as a site of failed masculinity. Nonetheless, Archie and Samad are comfortable there, and their ongoing reminiscences of the Second World War pervade their conversations, even fifty years after the fact, and despite their marginal participation as part of a maintenance battalion populated by "the rejects of war" (89). Although Archie recognizes that "no one wanted to talk about *that* any more" (14), he and Samad perpetually relive their war years. Joe Kerr describes London as a city "fully immersed in the culture of war" (74), a culture that is palpable in the many monuments and the attitudes of those who continue to tout the Blitz as the city's predominant historical event. Archie and Samad participate actively in this culture. In *Postcolonial Melancholia,* Gilroy pathologizes this ongoing obsession, claiming that "there is something neurotic about Britain's continued citation of the anti-Nazi war" (89), and wondering why it is still "a privileged point of entry into national identity and self-understanding" (89).

Alsana and Clara, by contrast, are more interested in the times and places they currently inhabit. Unlike their husbands, who restrict their movements to only a few locations, Alsana and Clara are not tied to the private, domestic realm of their homes. Their friendship develops on the sidewalk between their two houses and is cultivated through numerous picnics with Alsana's niece, Neena, in the same parks they have sought out as nurturing atmospheres for their children. On these occasions, Alsana and Clara talk and worry about the kinds of access their children will have to the society into which they have been born, considering these issues far more often than their husbands do. They support each other through the challenges of raising children who are culturally different from them, while Neena tries with varying degrees of success to help them understand their children and spouses. They also share intimate conversations about sex, sexuality, feminism, the drawbacks and virtues of arranged marriage, and their husbands, who, so they recognize, have "one leg in the present, one leg in the past" (80). These outings provide them with a vibrant sense of female community, and their willingness to discuss the intimate details of their domestic and sexual lives dismantles the conventional binaries through which the public and the private are gendered as mutually exclusionary realms.

While their fathers remain in only a few spaces, and their mothers travel largely in their own suburb, Irie, Millat and Magid are comfortable in many parts of London, and they move through different neighbourhoods with ease. As the narrative remarks, "the children knew the city" (174). Viewing their place in the city as unworthy of comment, they repeatedly refuse the Powellian discourse that marks them as outsiders. When Joyce Chalfen asks Millat and Irie the tired question, "Where are you from?" they simultaneously and automatically respond, "Willesden" (319). When Joyce probes about where they are from "originally," Millat wryly replies, "Whitechapel ... via the Royal London hospital and the 207 bus" (319). The second-generation children also know that they will encounter hostility from those who resent their confident presence. Riding the bus in Harlesden, they behave in an exuberant, unruly manner typical of nine-year-olds. A disgruntled white passenger begins to say, *"If you ask me ... they should all go back to their own ..."* (163), correlating their behaviour to "race" rather than to the fact of their being children. Magid, Millat and Irie respond with the only weapon they have at their disposal: their physical presence: "But this, the oldest sentence in the world, found itself stifled by the ringing of bells and the stamping of feet, until it retreated under the seats with the chewing gum" (163). Millat calls, "Shame, shame, know your name" (164), as they disembark. The children use their bodies and their voices to shout down this racist comment and to underscore their right to be on the bus and to live peacefully in their own country. Still stung by the incident a few blocks later, Irie "wanted a rematch" (167), so she initiates a game of "Tax that!": "Magid and Millat jumped into action. The practice of 'taxing' something, whereby one lays claims, like a newly arrived colonizer, to items in a street that do not belong to you, was well known and beloved to both of them" (167). Unable to respond directly to the man's racist belief that they should "go back to where they came from," they instead engage in an exercise of "colonization in reverse" through which they claim the streets of the city. They "tax" the items they desire but that are out of their families' reach, such as expensive bicycles and BMWs. But the game also highlights their ability to inhabit the various spaces of the city. As in Stuart Hall's opening epigraph, they literally act as if they own the territory.

As they become teenagers, the children lose some of this confidence in the face of a society that depicts them as simultaneously hypervisible and invisible. Magid has been removed from the city, sent by Samad to Bangladesh in the hope that he will learn to become "a real Bengali, a proper Muslim" (215). Irie and Millat remain in London, where their experiences teach them to be wary of those who would depict their lives as one-dimensional. Millat learns that "he had no face in this country" (234) beyond the crudest stereotypes: "he smelt of curry; had no sexual identity; took other people's jobs; or had no job and bummed off the state; or gave all the jobs to his relatives; that he could be a dentist or a shop-owner or a curry-shifter, but not a footballer or a filmmaker; that he should go back to his own country" (234). Irie learns to hate her hair and her body and is taught by her English teacher to ignore representations of blackness in literature even when they are glaringly obvious: "Irie didn't know she was fine. There was England, a gigantic mirror, and there was Irie, without reflection. A stranger in a stranger land" (266).

Their parents try in various ways to help their children deal with their alienation, encouraging approaches that range from assimilation to traditionalism. With the Iqbal family in particular, Smith again disrupts gendered discourses through which women are constructed as the cultural arbiters of the family. As Anthias and Yuval-Davis remind us, within nationalist discourse, women are traditionally seen as the "reproducers of the boundaries of national groups (through restrictions on sexual or marital relations)" and "as active transmitters and producers of the national culture" (7). Alsana refuses these tasks, and instead it is Samad who plays the most active role in policing his sons' cultural boundaries. Against Alsana's wishes, he sends Magid "back home" to Bangladesh. Alsana also chastises Samad for the ways he dictates Millat's life in London. Instead of insisting that Millat uphold cultural tradition, she tells Samad, "You say we have no control, yet you always try to control everything! Let *go*, Samad Miah. Let the boy go. He is second generation – he was born here – naturally he will do things differently" (289). Anne McClintock, in *Imperial Leather*, argues that within discourses of cultural nationalism, "women are presented as the atavistic and authentic body of national tradition (inert, backward-looking and natural) ... Men, by contrast, represent the progressive agent of national modernity (forward-thrusting, potent, and historic)" (359). In the Iqbal family, this gender dynamic is reversed. Samad is presented as inert and backward-looking, while Alsana's more progressive cultural attitudes allow her to recognize that her sons' needs as second-generation Britons differ from hers and Samad's.

Magid and Millat: Assimilation and Ethnonationalism

Partly as a result of their father's interventions, Magid and Millat pursue very different strategies through which to understand their place in the city and the nation. Neither son is is entirely successful. Magid's approach is consistently assimilationist, and he abandons South Asian cultural markers so as to fit in with his peers. His parents are shocked when a group of white children appear on their doorstep looking for their son, "Mark Smith," but this is only one sign of "a far deeper malaise" (151). Rather than wishing for trendy toys or brand-name clothes like his brother, Magid "wanted to have a trellis of flowers growing up one side of the house instead of the ever-growing pile of people's rubbish; he wanted a piano in the hallway in place of the broken door off cousin Kurshed's car; ... he wanted the floor of his room to be shiny wood, not the orange and green swirled carpet left over from the restaurant" (151). Recalling Baucom's claim that "notions of location have been ... consistently vital to the diverse constructions of English identity" (221) sheds light on Magid's wishes. Magid does not simply long for class mobility; he desires an image of Englishness, one that he expresses in specifically spatial and architectural terms. Samad's decision to send Magid to Bangladesh is a response to these attitudes and is similarly expressed through spatial rhetoric. To pay for Magid's plane ticket, "he remortgaged the house, he risked his land, the greatest mistake an immigrant can make" (194). Yet after eight years away from the country of his birth, Magid returns as an intensified version of the younger "Mark Smith." Having become "more English than the English," he is now an atheist rather than a Muslim, with a penchant for white linen suits, colonial literature, and affected speech patterns. He is also incapable of thinking for himself or making decisions on his own, even relying on a coin toss to determine whether he should meet with his estranged twin brother. Having become one-dimensional, and now unable to communicate beyond clichés, he claims that he is so drawn to Marcus Chalfen because "[y]ou put it so well and speak my thoughts better than I ever could" (366). A true colonial mimic man, Magid no longer has a voice of his own and has obliterated any sense of his own subjectivity.

Unlike his brother, who has a clear, if misguided, understanding of his English identity, Millat is confused by his multiple cultural influences: "Millat didn't need to go back home: he stood schizophrenic, one foot in Bengal and one in Willesden. In his mind he was as much here as he was there. He did not require a passport to live in two places at once" (219). He seeks out other young, second-generation males of various ethnicities, and rebels by attempting to put literal and emotional space between himself and his immigrant parents: "A distance was establishing itself, not simply between *fathersons, oldyoung, bornthereborhnhere,* but between those who stayed indoors and those who ran riot outside" (219). Dissatisfied with his father's ethnonationalism and rejecting his brother's project of assimilation, he turns to his friends, with whom he forms "a new breed" (231) they call "Raggastanis." Described as "a cultural mongrel" (231), the gang draws on a hybrid of ethnic, linguistic, and religious influences, including South Asian, Caribbean, African American, and Chinese. However, the promise of this new, creolized collectivity is undercut by an often misdirected rage and by their inability to question their own political positions. The Raggastani uniform revolves around oversized Nike clothing, much of which is made in sweatshops in the countries their families are from, a hypocrisy that seems to be lost on the young men. Misguidedly, they also participate in protests during which they burn copies of *The Satanic Verses* and support the *fatwah* against Salman Rushdie even though they have never read the book. They view their participation as a response to societal prejudices, unaware that their actions are directed at an author who shares their concerns about the marginalization of postcolonial migrants and their children in Britain. Their views are often expressed as a response to having been "fucked with" (232) by peers or teachers for wearing traditional clothing or challenging the racism directed at them. But while their anger is understandable, their behaviours are often misdirected responses to the discrimination they face.

Millat gradually moves away from the Raggastanis and into the circles of KEVIN, "the Keepers of the Eternal and Victorious Islamic Nation" (295), a group of young Muslim fundamentalists described as "an extremist faction dedicated to direct, often violent action, a splinter group frowned upon by the rest of the Islamic community" (470). In a nation that has been unsettled by the 7 July 2005 London subway bombings and the intensification of religious extremism across Western Europe since the publication of Smith's novel, this group sheds light on the ways terrorism can be a native, home-grown phenomenon that often results from a profound sense of alienation and marginalization from the dominant culture. Millat joins the group believing he has become a better Muslim than his father, whom he chastises for drinking alcohol and not having Muslim friends. Yet his own hypocrisy is lost on him given that he continues to sleep with multiple women and smoke marijuana despite KEVIN's prohibitions. His commitment to their restrictive tenets is both selective and half-hearted. Proselytizing to a young Indian woman about the group's belief in feminine modesty and purity, he tells her, parroting the words of a pamphlet, "'That's what we think,' uncertain if that was what he thought. 'That's our opinion,' he said, uncertain whether it was his opinion" (374). Millat's attempts to force himself to fit the narrow, restrictive parameters of a KEVIN Muslim are not unlike his brother's efforts to embody a narrow, oversimplified version of Englishness. The group's dissonances, moreover, do not easily facilitate conformity to Islamic beliefs. Despite their invocations of religious purity, they "[take] freely from Garveyism, the American civil rights movement and the thought of Elijah Muhammed" (470), blurring the boundaries between the religious and the political. A mongrelized, hybrid group like the Raggastanis, their beliefs speak to the ways all fundamentalisms are partial and selective.

Thus, while Magid goes to Bangladesh and learns to be an Englishman, Millat stays in England and becomes a Muslim fundamentalist. This reversal, one of many in the novel, rejects easy correlations between identity and place and challenges the idea that Englishness correlates to whiteness. Magid and Millat's experiences draw attention to the messiness of contemporary cultural processes, in which "late modern western and western-influenced 'non-western' societies can no longer be thought of as either discrete or unitary national formations" (Hesse 2000: 20–1). But while the twins complicate assumed correlations between religion, "race," ethnicity, and geography, it turns out that embracing either British assimilation or Islamic fundamentalism remains a limiting avenue through which to negotiate their place in the nation. The cost of either, both social and psychological, is too great.

By contrast, Irie Jones's complicated struggles to belong reflect an attempt to establish different terms for thinking about questions of identity. As with the first-generation immigrant parents, the second generation's spatial and cultural negotiations diverge on the basis of gender. While the twins in various ways debate whether the beliefs of "back home" can – or should – be accepted in their contemporary British context, Irie extends the debate by calling into question the very notion of "back home," particularly as a viable option for the second generation. When she moves in with her grandmother, Irie turns to the unread books about Jamaica on Hortense's bookshelf. In them, she discovers a nation that makes her temporarily turn away from her own, and she quickly embraces all things Jamaican: "So *this* was where she came from. This all *belonged* to her, her birthright, like a pair of pearl earrings or a post office bond. X marks the spot, and Irie put an X on everything she found ... birth certificates, maps, army reports, news articles" (400). Believing she has found her "roots," she actively disengages from the place and the culture in which she has grown up. When she angrily turns off Joyce Chalfen's radio gardening program, her remarks can be read as a literal rejection of the Chalfen family's influence on her, and also as a symbolic recognition of the painful and difficult work she has faced in her attempts to belong: "It just seemed tired and unnecessary all of a sudden, that struggle to force something out of the recalcitrant English soil. Why bother when there was now this other place?" (402). Just as Irie begins to entertain this possibility, however, the narrative immediately undercuts the notion that Jamaica, or any other place, can be the idealized, simplified answer to the problems she faces in England, or a site of return, "[b]ecause *homeland* is one of the magical fantasy words like *unicorn* and *soul* and *infinity* that have now passed into the language" (402). Irie very quickly realizes that going "back to the source of the river, to the start of the story, to the homeland ... was as useless as chasing your own shadow" (407). In this regard, Smith's novel is comparable to Levy's. But, while *Fruit of the Lemon*, through Faith's visit, tests the hypothesis of Jamaica as homeland and finds it lacking, Smith truncates this possibility within a few pages of Irie having contemplated it.

The Chalfen Family: Spaces of Britishness

Irie's cultural anxieties are exacerbated by Joshua Chalfen and his parents, Joyce and Marcus, who have been assigned to tutor her and Millat. Just as the Franks "overlook" the Tynes in Edugyan's novel, so too do the Chalfens engage in the social surveillance of their wards. White and bourgeois, the Chalfens are unlike any other family Irie has experienced. Gilroy reminds us that "'[r]ace' differences are displayed in culture which is reproduced in educational institutions and, above all, in family life. Families are therefore not only the nation in microcosm, its key components, but act as the means to turn social processes into natural, instinctive ones" (1987: 43). This metaphor is sustained by the image of Marcus feeling he has "strayed abroad" (416) when outside the realm of his immediate family, and by Irie's feeling like "she [is] crossing borders, sneaking into England" (328), when entering the Chalfen house. The family's racism, sexism, and homophobia are invisible its members, who even even have their own little Enoch Powell in their son, Oscar, who says, "I hate brown strangers" (326). They interact only with extended family members who have "good genes" (314), a reference that invokes the social Darwinism that has historically informed extreme versions of nationalist discourse. Moreover, the relationship between the Chalfens and Irie and Millat is repeatedly phrased in terms of a colonial encounter. The Chalfen home is described as a "missionary vessel" (323), and Joyce takes seriously her job of enlightening the children. She invests so much in the "improvement" of Irie and Millat because "she needed to be needed" (315). This desire speaks to the need Britain has historically had for its colonies, for the raw materials and labour that sustained its wealth; it has also perpetuated its image as a global imperial power. Joyce "pined for the golden age when she was the linchpin of the Chalfen family" (314), just as a melancholic post-colonial Britain pines for the golden age when it was the linchpin of the commonwealth and when its national narrative rested on myths of its pure, homogenous whiteness.

Irie is fascinated by the family's private spaces, particularly Marcus's study and what it tells her about his life and that of her own family:

> Marcus's room was like no place Irie had ever seen. It had no communal utility, no other purpose in the house apart from being Marcus's room; it stored no toys, bric-a-brac, broken things, spare ironing boards; no one ate in it, slept in it or made love in it. It wasn't like Clara's attic space, a Xanadu of crap, all carefully stored in boxes and labeled just in case she should ever need to flee this land for another one. It wasn't like the spare room of immigrants – packed to the rafters with all that they have ever possessed, no matter how defective or damaged, mountains of odds and ends – that stand testament to the fact that they *have* things now, where before they had nothing.) Marcus's room was purely devoted to Marcus and Marcus's work. (335–6)

The spatial differences between their homes are partly class-based: Marcus can afford a house large enough to accommodate the private retreats necessary for his and Joyce's white collar work, and no functions of basic sustenance – eating, sleeping, sex – take place in them. The notion of domestic privacy, a late-eighteenth-century bourgeois development, was closely intertwined with Enlightenment understandings of individual subjectivity, both of which are evident in Marcus's study. It is a marked contrast to the inevitable communalism that results from the close quarters of Irie's parents' much smaller house, in which most rooms are used by multiple family members for multiple purposes, none of which are intellectual labour. Of greater significance are the spatial differences that reveal that Marcus is settled to a degree that Irie's mother can never achieve. Note that nearly two decades after Clara moves into the home in which she plans "to settle down for life" (47), the packed boxes – a recurrent image that echoes the boxes of Faith's parents in *Fruit of the Lemon* – suggest that her home continues to be inscribed with the markers of transience. The clutter of items Irie describes in the "typical" immigrant space also rearticulates understandings of use-value, in that they offer immigrants not functionality but security as reifications of their potential for commodity ownership (having something as opposed to having nothing). This space, filled with damaged items they insistently hang on to, echoes Brand's representation of Oku's and Tuyen's parents' homes in *What We All Long For*, which are similarly filled with things they can't let go of, literally or metaphorically. Brand's and Smith's images evoke the ways many immigrants are unable to move beyond their traumatic experiences. Irie's realization that her mother and other immigrants are "damaged people" (379) is the catalyst that causes her to move out of the Jones home, just as Tuyen seeks escape from her parents' emotional baggage.

By contrast, Marcus's study bears no evidence of trauma, and he instead surrounds himself with markers of domestic contentment: smoking accoutrements and family photos. Also, one wall displays a meticulously mapped family genealogy, with which Irie is similarly amazed:

> The differences between the Chalfens and the Jones/Bowdens were immediately plain. For starters, in the Chalfen family everybody seemed to have a normal number of children. More to the point, everybody knew whose children were whose. The men lived longer than the women. The marriages were singular and long lasting. Dates of birth and death were concrete. And the Chalfens actually *knew* who they were in 1675. (337)

Another marker of the family's class status, the family tree is a tool for Marcus to emphasize his pedigree and middle-class respectability. However, as Wytold Rybczinski emphasizes, genealogy is an invented tradition, often used in a "process of cultural authentification" (10); he observes that in the United States, nineteenth-century interest in genealogical mapping developed "partly [as] efforts by the established middle class to distance itself from the increasing number of new, predominantly non-British immigrants" (10). The Chalfen family tree similarly strives to articulate the family as legitimately British. However, unknown to Irie, who is envious of their "purity" (328), they are "after a fashion, immigrants too (third generation, by way of Germany and Poland, née Chalfenovsky)" (328).

Given that genealogy is often "personally symbolic but politically significant" (Nash 182), Marcus's efforts to indigenize himself and his family can be read as an effort to establish his connection to both a literal geography and an imagined community. Anne McClintock in *Imperial Leather* reminds us that "nations are symbolically figured as domestic genealogies" (357), while conversely Nash points out that that, in attempting to replicate discourses of cultural purity, "[g]enealogy is both shaped by and supports the ways in which cultural difference, 'race' and ethnicity feature in discourses of the nation-state" (182). Again, the Chalfen family tree is intertwined with a particular image of English nationhood, which it both symbolically represents and literally reproduces. Its ordered symmetry reflects the image of a nation that is ideally assumed to be composed, according to Gilroy, of "even, symmetrical family units" (1993: 27). Its long-lasting heterosexual pairings and "normal" number of children together suggest families that are easily contained to produce a legitimate citizenry, and its reliance on the patriarchal line echoes the state's gendering of power. Moreover, its ostensible ethnic homogeneity is both a means to embrace, and a reflection of, assumed notions of English racial purity.

Irie's genealogy, by contrast, is a messy, impure tangle of descent. Feeling deeply inadequate in the face of the Chalfens' familial order, she imagines what her own family tree might look like, based not on archival research but, like Faith's in *Fruit of the Lemon*, on "rumour, folk tale and myth" (328). In the absence of birth, death, and marriage dates, Irie uses phrases like "Way back when – Lord knows" (338), and where there are no legal marriages she states: "copulated with" or "paternity unsure" (338). She also marks illegitimate relationships such as "Great Uncle P." and "god knows how many women," who produce a substantial "34 children," some of whom are named while others are not (338). The only branch of the family tree to include surnames is her own, and these can only be traced back to her great-grandparents. On other branches, even first names are not available, and these are marked with question marks or "unknown issue" (338). A genealogy based on nonlinearity and uncertainty, it is best characterized, in Deleuzean terms, as rhizomatic rather than arborescent.[5] Such a rearticulation demonstrates that immigrant communities may need different constructions of kinship to reflect their realities than those offered by patriarchal

European models of descent, which have historically been used to verify property inheritance.[6] As Nash further observes of hegemonic genealogical work, "in family histories which are seldom characterized by marriage within only one ethnic group, and in a genealogical tradition in which kinship and ethnicity can be reckoned through both paternal and maternal descent, doing genealogy involves choices about which line or lines to follow and which ancestors matter" (183). While there is no textual evidence to tell us whether the Chalfens have been selective in their mapping, their belief in purity and good genes suggests this possibility. Irie, conversely, has not been selective. She traces her family largely through maternal lines of descent, and none of her ancestors are shown to "matter" more than others. Irie's family tree reveals that tracing a genealogy provides evidence of hybridity and impurity, and reflects the untidy and entangled realities of all national formations.

The trope of mapping, so important to genealogical research, arises as well in Marcus's scientific research and his work on genetic mapping. Brand's observations in *A Map to the Door of No Return* regarding the selective and interpretive nature of cartography bring much to bear on genetic mapping, which, despite assumptions of scientific objectivity, engages in similar processes. Donna Haraway explains the origin of the cartographic language used in genetic projects like Marcus's, observing that such discourse results from a scientific methodology that records only partial information:

> Conventionally, the genome refers only to the nucleic acid that "codes" for something and not to the dynamic, multipart structures and processes that constitute functional, reproducing cells and organisms … Embodied information with a complex time structure is reduced to a linear code in an archive outside time. This reduction gives rise to the curious, ubiquitous mixed metaphor of "mapping the code" applied to projects to represent all the information on the genome. (245)

Haraway is critical of such metaphors, arguing that this representational practice "constitute[s] a kind of artificial life research" (245) that "bears no necessary relationship to messy, thick organisms" (246). In this regard, cartographic mapping, genetic mapping, and genealogical mapping all operate according to similar principles. Just as a genome map does not necessarily represent the entirety of a complex, multifaceted biological creature, a genealogical map or family tree does not necessarily bear any relation to the messy complexities of kinship relations. These forms of mapping are partial and potentially selective, yet they are often used to construct objectivity. As Haraway states, in a conclusion that echoes Brand's, no type of mapping is ever neutral: "Cartographic practice inherently is learning to make projections that shape worlds in particular ways for various purposes" (132). In characterizing the practice of mapping as a *projection* rather than a *reflection*, she draws attention to the subjective intentions that colour ostensibly unbiased familial or scientific research.

Marcus's most controversial project is his development of FutureMouse (based on the actual and notorious Oncomouse project), in which he genetically engineers a lab mouse to develop certain types of cancer in the interest of scientific research. He is undeterred by the ubiquitous criticism he faces and clings to the myth of scientific objectivity, refusing to see the racist, Darwinist implications of his project, in which the mouse is engineered for inexplicable reasons to turn from brown to white in the third year of its life. In *Against Race*, Gilroy argues that recent scientific developments, such as genetic engineering and DNA research, "impact upon how 'race' is understood" (20), and that "[t]he new racisms that code biology in cultural terms have been alloyed with still newer variants that conscript the body into disciplinary service and encode cultural particularity in and understanding of bodily practices and attributes determined by genes" (127). Marcus's attitudes suggest that these new dimensions of racism are invisible to him as he blindly insists on the neutrality of his research.

FutureMouse becomes the locus at which the Chalfen, Iqbal, and Jones families converge, as the narrative builds to its public unveiling and the three families' affairs become increasingly intertwined. In this last section of the novel, Smith develops a recurrent trope, the (impossible) search for a "neutral space."[7] Joyce Chalfen, inappropriately meddling in the affairs of the Iqbals, wants desperately for Magid and Millat to meet after their long estrangement, telling Alsana, "If we could find some neutral place, some ground where they both felt no pressures or outside influence …" (443). Alsana echoes a Lefebvrean axiom when she retorts, "But there are no neutral places any more!" (443). Joyce's answer to a "neutral space" is a study room in a nearby university; apparently she is unaware of the colonial discourses that have historically shaped educational institutions (consider, by way of contrast, Smith's narration of the history of Glenard Oak, the high school Joshua, Irie, and the twins attend). The narrative elaborates on the impossibility of Joyce's mission: "A neutral place.

The chances of finding one these days are slim ... The sheer *quantity* of shit that must be wiped off the slate if we are to start again as new. Race. Land. Ownership. Faith. Theft. Blood. And more blood. And more" (457).

Irie similarly longs for a "neutral space" in which she can distance herself from her family's emotional turmoil. As they ride the bus to the FutureMouse launch, she uses spatial metaphor to again compare her family to those of indigenous middle-class Britons:

> What a *joy* their lives must be. They open a door and all they've got behind it is a bathroom or a lounge. Just neutral spaces. And not this endless maze of present rooms and past rooms and the things said in them years ago and everybody's old historical shit all over the place ... And every single fucking day is not this huge battle between who they are and who they should be, what they were and what they will be ... No attics. No shit in attics. No skeletons in cupboards. (514–15)

The geographies she invokes echo her earlier comparison between her mother's attic room and Marcus Chalfen's study. She again articulates the temporal difference between immigrant families, who dwell in the past, and "native" families, whom she believes live in the present, in specifically spatial terms. But as Lefebvre points out, no spaces are free of historical inscription: "the past leaves its traces; time has its own script" (37). Irie's quest for a neutral space in England is just as elusive as her search for a Jamaican "homeland," which she also believes should be "fresh and untainted and without past or dictated future – a place where things simply *were*" (402). Katherine McKittrick argues that it is deeply problematic to assume a "discursive attachment to stasis and physicality, [to] the idea that space 'just is'" (xi). Thus Irie must recognize that, just as homeland is an "imaginary" concept, so too is the idea of "neutrality" in spatial discourse.

Marcus and his research team believe they have found a "neutral space" in which to unveil their FutureMouse project. They have chosen a room at the Perrett Institute in the heart of downtown London; however, that building's urban, imperial, and global centrality immediately puts paid to its neutrality. It is hegemonically perceived as

> [t]he final space ... [A] corporate place, a clean slate; white/chrome/pure/plain (this was the design brief) used for the meetings of people who want to meet somewhere neutral at the end of the twentieth century;

> a virtual place where their business ... can be done in an emptiness, an uncontaminated cavity; the logical endpoint of a thousand years of spaces too crowded and bloody. This one is pared down, sterilized, made new every day by a Nigerian cleaning lady with an industrial Hoover and guarded through the night by Mr. De Winter, a Polish nightwatchman. (517–18)

The imaginary designers through which this passage is focalized construct a troubling correlation between neutrality and capitalism, as though to suggest that contemporary global capitalism can be disconnected from centuries of colonialist exploitation. However, as Iain Borden and colleagues argue, "while urban professionals such as planners and architects might believe themselves to be in turn democratic negotiators, community advocators, [and] neutral social scientists ... they act as part of much broader, much deeper systems of power, economics and signification" (5). These systems of power are evident in the Nigerian cleaning lady and Polish watchman, whose presence in and maintenance of the space draw attention to unequal class, race, and gender relations. In this "neutral" space, domestic work is still relegated to women, Eastern Europeans, and black people. The room is constructed, in Lefebvrean terms, as "transparent space." Lefebvre argues that transparent space conceals the social processes that create space as a social product, claiming that "the illusion of transparency goes hand in hand with a view of space as innocent, as free of traps and secret places" (28). The white, chromed plainness of this room, however, cannot conceal the ways hegemonic power systems use it to promote the illusion of their own neutrality.

This room, designed with the assistance of public feedback, highlights the ways space is used to formulate national identity:

> [F]ortunately, after years of corporate synaesthesia ... people can finally give the answers required when a space is being designed, or when something is being rebranded, a room/furniture/Britain (that was the brief: a new British room, a space for Britain, Britishness, space of Britain, British industrial space cultural space space); they know what is meant when asked how matt chrome makes them feel; and they know what is meant by national identity? symbols? paintings? maps? music? air-conditioning? smiling black children or smiling Chinese children or [tick the box]? world music? shag or pile? tile or floorboards? plants? running water? (518)

This passage, beginning with grammatically correct sentence structure, disintegrates into linguistic and stylistic confusion. Its form echoes the emotional trajectory Britain faces, from its supposed certainty in its "rebranding," to its confusion about its "unresolved postcolonial condition" (Hesse 11), or what Gilroy calls its postcolonial melancholia. The "people" are described as unraced and ungendered, impossibly "neutral," like the space their opinions inform. But the numerous question marks suggest they are *not* clear about how national markers such as maps, music, or symbols should be read; nor do they understand at all "what is meant by national identity." The passive, agentless construction of these questions also makes invisible the political, economic, social, and corporate forces that have shaped this supposedly singular and unified construction. Gilroy has observed "the collapse of English cultural confidence that has fed the development of anxious and insecure local and national identities" (1999: 67), and this anxiety plays out in Smith's discussion of "rebranding Britain." The nation is uncertain of how to rebrand itself, and the impossible searches for "neutral space" in the novel suggest that Britain was never "branded" as clearly as it believed.

Irie's Genetic Experiment: A Third Generation and Beyond

By the end of the novel, Irie, recognizing her own and the nation's inability to transcend the messiness of history and its inscriptions on geography, strives to look towards the future and to articulate creolized, post-immigrant forms of identification. Again her perspective diverges radically from Magid and Millat's. After the fight that occurs at their reunion, the narrative predicts that they "will race towards the future only to find they more and more eloquently express their past, that place where they have just *been.* Because this is the … thing about immigrants … they cannot escape their history any more than you yourself can lose your own shadow" (466). In a seemingly deliberate slippage, Smith casts the British-born brothers as immigrants for the first time in the novel. Arguably, this move is not meant to suggest that Magid and Millat do not belong in the nation; rather, it illuminates another recurrent trope in the novel: the notion that immigrants look towards the past and to elsewhere, while the second generation dwells in the present and in the place they are currently situated. But this binary of immigrant/post-immigrant is not as simple as it appears, nor does it divide neatly along generational lines, Instead, gender is the line along which characters are differentiated. The male characters in the novel – Magid and Millat, Archie, and Samad – are shown repeatedly looking towards the past, often maintaining and policing rigid gender and cultural boundaries. By contrast, the female characters – Alsana, Clara, Neena, and, most importantly, Irie – are the ones who transgress or dismantle these boundaries, in part by insistently looking towards the future.

The reconceptualization of space, place, and belonging that Irie longs for is expressed in her contrast to Samad. In a tearful breakdown about his unrecognizable, wayward sons and his sense of feeling caught between two countries, Samad tells Irie, "And then you begin to give up the *very idea* of belonging. Suddenly this thing, this *belonging*, it seems like some long, dirty lie … and I begin to believe that birthplaces are accidents, that everything is an *accident*" (407). He sees this state of affairs as a "dystopia" (408), but Irie realizes in this moment that it would instead be a utopia for her, a condition of possibility: "the land of accidents sounded like *paradise* to her. Sounded like freedom" (408). Irie's desire for the "land of accidents" is noteworthy in light of an "accident" of her own: her pregnancy, which is revealed to readers in the final pages of the narrative. Despite critical interest in the intergenerational aspects of Smith's novel, there has been very little discussion of this unborn baby and the possibilities it engenders for imagining a nation of the third generation and beyond.[8]

Irie's pregnant body is the site at which the messiness and uncontainability of Smith's novel culminates and the site at which multiple geographic scales converge. According to McDowell, "Questions of the sexed body – its differential construction, regulation, and representation – are absolutely central to an understanding of gender relations at every spatial scale. Attitudes about the body and its place run through the meaning of the nation as much as the meaning of the home, as well as ideas about community and open spaces such as the street and the city" (68). A biological experiment that is potentially far more interesting than Marcus's, Irie's baby is conceived after she has sex with both Millat and Magid within an hour, an act that ensures she will never be certain of its paternity, given that as twins they will have identical DNA. The ways in which Irie understands the significance of this child provide a notable commentary on the conceptual possibilities which might be engendered through the third generation. Initially anxious about never knowing who the father is, Irie wonders, "If it was not somebody's child, could it be that it was nobody's child? … That is how her child seemed. A perfectly plotted thing with no real coordinates. A map to an imaginary fatherland" (516). This worry is immediately negated by Irie's recognition that it is *her* child; that its legitimacy does not have to be derived from the patronymic. This rejection of patriarchal lineage articulates an alternative model of kinship, one more akin to that reflected in her imagined family tree, given that this child will also be marked with "paternity unsure" or "lord knows." Moreover, this creolized baby will never be understood through "the easy, lazy options that reduce race politics to the simple binary code of black and white" (Gilroy 1993: 5). Irie and her baby can also be understood metaphorically, for if the family is a microcosm of the nation, then this is a microcosm of a very different type of nation than that represented by the Chalfens. Creolized, impure, and matri-rhizomatic, this alternative vision of the nation speaks to the potential inherent in Irie's familial experiment.

This unborn baby also provides a commentary on the revisions to British citizenship laws that occurred just before and during Irie's lifetime. The 1981 British Nationality Act altered the nine-century-old law of *jus soli*, or law of the soil, through which citizenship was based on the principle of territory (traditionally derived from one's place of birth), replacing it with the practice of *jus sanguinis*, or law of blood descent, which dictates that only those whose parents were born in the United Kingdom can themselves be British subjects. As Harry Goulbourne points out, "Children of Commonwealth citizens resident in the UK do not become British citizens by virtue of being born in the country. Such individuals can apply for citizenship after ten years' continuous residence in the country" (54).[9] According to Baucom, "whereas through the entire preceding history of the British Empire, Britishness had been affirmatively grounded in the law of place, the 1981 Nationality Act codified a theory of identity that sought to defend the 'native' inhabitants of the island against the claims of their former subjects by defining Britishness as an inheritance of race" (8). The act was an attempt to block post-colonial "others" from becoming legal British citizens. Irie's baby draws attention to the ridiculousness of this law, which has merely delayed the inevitable by one decade. This racially mixed baby will have immediate access to British citizenship since both of its parents were born in England, belying the notion that Britishness will be a white racial inheritance. Moreover, through Irie's father, Archie, this baby would have even qualified for full citizenship under the earlier – and equally notorious – 1971 Immigration Act, which created differential citizenship rights for those born in various parts of the Commonwealth, but which only conferred the full rights of British subjects on those who had at least one grandfather born on British soil. Irie's baby thus calls into question the very purpose of *jus sanguinis*, demonstrating that, if its goal truly is to racialize British identity in particular ways, the nation's willingness to alter a nearly millennium-long tradition has been an exercise in futility.

Irie's baby also provides her with a tangible reason to look towards the future, to imagine the details of the vision she begins to articulate in her discussion with Samad. Having come to accept the child's undeterminable paternity, she now recognizes the potential in this: "Irie's child can never be mapped exactly nor spoken of with any certainty. Some secrets are permanent. In a vision, Irie has seen a time, a time not far from now, when roots won't matter any more because they can't because they mustn't because they're too long and they're too torturous and they're just buried too damn deep. She looks forward to it" (527). Again the reference to mapping has multiple resonances. This baby, given its uncertain paternity, cannot be mapped genetically or biologically; it cannot be mapped genealogically onto a conventional patriarchal family tree; and it cannot be mapped geographically because it is not traceable to a single "homeland." The hopes Irie expresses for the child are expressed in the religious rhetoric of visions, an apt comparison to a phenomenon perceived by some as inspirational and by others as irrational. But her vision is also an admission that she and her generation have not yet achieved such an undisputable place in the nation, despite doing considerably better than their immigrant parents. She articulates this ideal state as an aspiration for her child, and her language of "looking forward" encompasses both an anticipatory optimism and a refusal to dwell in the past. However, in looking towards a time in which "roots" no longer matter because they are tangled and untraceable, Irie also looks towards a world in which her offspring no longer *need* to, are no longer *required* to, trace their lines of descent to other places. In such a circumstance, the very concept of immigrant-descended "generations" will cease to matter. Just as "native" Britons are not described in generational terms, she hopes for a time when her child need not be seen as "third generation" and when identifying in this way has become irrelevant. In this regard, Irie's vision is a radical re-evaluation of the presumed correlation between identity, genealogy, and geography.

Irie, and also Alsana and Clara, are constructed throughout the novel as post-immigrant social and political subjects whose actions necessitate a different conceptualization of spatial relations; as Lefebvre argues, "new social relationships call for a new space" (1996: 59). Recognizing the relationship between physical geographies and social identities suggests also the need to rearticulate existing understandings of British nationhood to make room for Irie's vision. Smith's novel, in these ways, supports and advances the arguments made by Hall and Gilroy, who advocate a re-evaluation of contemporary British discourses of multiculturalism as a means of thinking differently about the nation. Hall wonders, "What are the premises behind a radically distinctive form of British multiculturalism? It would need to be grounded not in some abstract notion of nation and community, but in the analysis of what 'community' actually means and how the different communities which now compose the nation actually interact on the ground" (2000: 231–2). This everyday multiculturalism would have to be used for particular purposes: "rather than a strategy for improving the lot of the so-called 'ethnic' or racialized minorities alone, it would have to be a strategy which broke with ... majoritarian logic and attempted to reconfigure or reimagine the nation as a whole" (232). The notion of conviviality on which Gilroy's *Postcolonial Melancholia* is based similarly calls for "a reworked and politicized multiculturalism" (6). Smith's novel is fuelled by these same questions, but she extends Hall and Gilroy's arguments by offering a vision of what this distinctive and reworked multicultural nation might look like by focusing on everyday exchanges and "on the ground" interactions of the sort to which Hall refers. The novel, like Brand's, presents everyday practices as a strategy through which to revise national narratives from the "bottom up" rather than from the "top down." Smith's willingness to articulate hopeful and optimistic visions for the future, through her female characters in particular, speaks to the potential that is engendered by these post-immigrant reimaginings.

In these ways, Smith's novel in many ways ultimately – and productively – interrogates the very premise of generationality on which this project rests. Specifically, both Irie's unborn, unmappable "third generation" baby, and more broadly the novel's push towards substantively and constitutively different understandings of what constitutes marginality, nationhood, and multiculturalism, suggest that generationality may perhaps also have limitations as a paradigm through which to make sense of difference, belonging, or settlement in either Canada or the UK. Speaking of the Canadian context, Robertson Davies, in a linearly assimilationist fashion, argues that "we know that the blackest and most turbaned newcomer to our country will have descendants who will, within three generations, be Canadian in spirit" (180). Smith's novel, and the other novels in this study, suggest otherwise, illustrating that the processes through which the children of immigrants, and their descendants, negotiate social citizenship are considerably more complex than Davies assumes. These processes are ongoing rather than easily resolved within a finite number of generations. Moreover, these processes are also very often vexed and inevitably messy. It is this messiness that Smith's novel encapsulates so well, pointing us to the fact that part of what constitutes conditions of possibility is their very unpredictability.

Conclusion

"Conditions of Possibility"

The generic skeleton of the novel is still far from having hardened, and we cannot foresee all its plastic possibilities.

Mikhail Bakhtin, *The Dialogic Imagination*

This study of second-generation children of immigrants in black Canadian and black British women's writing has, above all, considered possibilities – the possibilities that are enabled by the creative but too often attenuated within theoretical or state-based political realms. I have aimed to think about the ways cultural productions articulate possibilities: while political policy and public debate are often limited in the kinds of discursive moves they can make, cultural producers can move anywhere in their creative reimaginings. In this project I have aspired to demonstrate that literature can be used to open spaces in which, and through which, to rethink bodies, families, towns, regions, cities, and nations. In various ways, Brand, McWatt, Levy, Edugyan, and Smith bear witness to the wide range of colonial and global violences, and to the various traumatic histories of migration, that have shaped and sometimes overdetermined these spaces. But in their writing, and in their *act* of writing, these authors also look towards possibilities, even while maintaining an awareness of the difficult, painful circumstances in which they try to speak them. Nonetheless, these writers are not prematurely celebratory. Their novels recognize the continuities between transatlantic slavery, colonial domination, and the contemporary injustices of the current global capitalist conjuncture, and explore the discursive violences that erase these histories from national narratives. They also recognize that, for both first-generation migrants and their second-generation children, marginalizations are often intensified along the axis of gender. Both Angie's suicide and Cam's recurrent insomnia in Brand's novel and Maud's nervous breakdown in Edugyan's are related to their perceived inadequacies as mothers, and they often blame themselves for familial instabilities that have resulted from state interventions into their domestic realms. Similarly, the twins' mental illness in Edugyan's novel, Daphne's descent into an eating disorder, alcoholism, and a breakdown in McWatt's novel, and Faith's dramatic epistemological crisis in Levy's novel speak to the ways in which second-generation attempts at re/settlement are particularly painful and difficult work for women.

But in looking towards alternative paradigms for citizenship and belonging, these writers also recognize that thinking about possibilities may well be an ethical responsibility in any transformative project. Instead of offering concrete solutions or specific political prescriptions, these texts create discursive openings by enabling what I have, via Michel de Certeau, been calling "conditions of possibility." Their commitment is not to providing answers, but to establishing different terms in which to ask questions of and about the nation. These writers' use of – and disruption of – the novel form is not incidental to this transformative project. Just as they seek to reimagine national paradigms, so too do these texts reimagine the potential uses of literature in constituting and reconstituting national collectivities (as well as other terms for thinking about communities). Benedict Anderson, in *Imagined Communities*, has explored at length the coterminous rise of the novel and the nation in the late eighteenth and early nineteenth centuries, and the functions the novel has played in "provid[ing] the technical means for 're-presenting' the *kind* of imagined community that is the nation" (25), arguing that the emergence of the novel engendered particular forms of consciousness or modes of apprehension that "made it possible to think the nation" (22). My project has sought to interrogate the relationship between national and novelistic discourse, and my arguments in this book come to rest on the premise that if historically the novel and the nation have been so closely intertwined, then un-settling one will inevitably involve un-settling the other. My project has also sought to highlight the urgencies of such reconceptualizations, given the inherently racialized characteristics of both the novel and the nation, despite their presumptions of hegemonic whiteness rarely being named as such.

According to Richard Iton, "[i]t might be argued that the nation itself, as a modern emergence, cannot sustain nonwhite aspirations for emancipation" (196). "The nation state as an organizational mechanism" he continues, "from this vantage point, might be best understood as intrinsically anti-black" (197). By extension, then, the novel as a genre, emerging from the same epistemological moment, might be similarly articulated as anti-black. Sylvia Wynter, in "On Disenchanting Discourse," suggests this. She argues that as the novel underwent significant epistemic, typological, and tropological transformations from the seventeenth to the nineteenth centuries to reflect a particular kind of ostensibly "universal" humanism (the "figure of man"), these changes came to include "the topos of 'sensory nature,' [which] would now become that of a projected 'primal nature' encoded, at the global level, in the *native* (with its zero degree signifier form as the *nigger*), whose ideologic was to be disseminated by the mode of the novel and by its founding discourse of biological idealism" (215). Given these profound discursive limitations, how, then, might the novel be used to imagine a different kind of epistemological order? It would seem that novel writers face the proverbial challenge of using the master's tools to dismantle the master's house, to borrow Audre Lorde's famous articulation. How are racialized writers to work within a literary genre that has emerged out of, and is embedded in, epistemological frameworks that render blackness as anti-human, as ontologically other, and as inherently marginal? Brand, having pondered these questions, points out that "[n]arrative is, to my mind, almost always implicated in the colonial/imperial/racist project" (2017: 60), and that within this genre, character and landscape are "weighted with whiteness as a fundamental/originary category" (60). Taking Brand's and Wynter's concerns seriously thus necessitates a profound and radical rearticulation of the epistemic boundaries of the novel to account for other, more liberatory possibilities.

Some of the novel's possibilities lie in its continual evolution; as Mikhail Bakhtin argues in the opening paragraph of *The Dialogic Imagination*, "the novel is the sole genre that continues to develop, that is as yet uncompleted" (3). And, as countless literary scholars have pointed out, it has been developed in particular ways by black and racialized writers, such as those examined in this study, in the interest of articulating different kinds of literary and epistemic narratives. Arguably, the novel's greatest potential lies in its ability to imagine what does not currently exist, on terms other than those currently offered by existing literary, political, and/or epistemic orders. Iton cites Ralph Ellison, who contends that "the novel at its best demands a sort of complexity of vision which politics doesn't like" (Ellison qtd in Iton 11). As Iton elaborates, "While intentions are not always easily known, the effects of a vote or decision can be more clearly ascertained. The inclination in formal politics toward the quantifiable and the bordered, the structured, ordered, policeable and disciplined is in fundamental tension with popular culture's willingness to embrace disturbance, to engage the apparently mad and maddening" (11). This sense of messiness, unmanageability, and unfinalizability pervades every novel in this study, and each, in its own way, expresses a desire to move beyond the political and discursive moves that limit our understanding of the second generation to a contest between assimilation and long-distance ethnonationalism, or oversimplified political binaries that assume either engagement with or refusal of the nation-state. The novels in this study have expressed different ways of being-in, and being-of, the nation that are, arguably, not yet available within the formal political realm. In so doing, they offer spaces through which to begin to engage in important reimaginings of citizenship and belonging.

For these reasons, I have understood the works in this study as notable examples of what Sylvia Wynter calls the "counter-novel." Wynter calls for "the construction of new conceptual tools and theoretical paradigms [that] move beyond the hegemonic paradigms of literary criticism" (207), in order to enact an epistemic shift and create a discursive space for issues and concerns that do not have a space in other forms of writing and that cannot be articulated within existing epistemological orders. She writes that counter-novels look beyond the oppositional to instead engage in constitutive projects that rethink masculinist, Eurocentric nineteenth-century ontologies. Pointing out that both women and racialized minorities have historically been constructed as subcategories, subordinated to the category of "the majority," she argues that counter-novels refuse to position either of these groups as "negative ontological others" (217). In other words, for Wynter, counter-novels don't "write back," they merely "write," and in so doing they play an important role in articulating a different kind of episteme through which to render "new objects of knowledge" (207). The five counter-novels in this study, in establishing different paradigms for conversations about the second generation, about citizenship, and about a reimagined multiculturalism, enable similar possibilities, encouraging different conceptual moves than those available in legal state discourses around citizenship, multiculturalism, "race" relations, and immigration policy.

Brand, McWatt, Levy, Edugyan, and Smith all ponder these possibilities at different moments in their texts. The second generation's invocation of their "borderlessness" in Brand's *What We All Long For* is what enables them to begin conceptualizing new possibilities for citizenship, friendship, and political engagement. McWatt's novel offers a different kind of Canadian "settlement narrative," one that accounts for a history of settler colonialism and indigenous displacement in the face of recent waves of immigrant arrival, to consider what ethical belonging might look like for their descendants. Levy's novel ends with a significant shift in relations of power/knowledge. Faith's last line anticipates the conditions through which her enunciatory acts might speak a different type of nation and a more engaged relationality. In Edugyan's novel, the final request, both of the unnamed twin and of the reader, to live "in the best way we are capable of," establishes a different moral and ethical code than the exclusionary and selective one offered by national paradigms. In *White Teeth*, Samad's dystopia, in which he "gives up on the very idea of belonging," is Irie's ideal state, from which she might perhaps look to a place in which there need not be any correlations between ethnicity, identity, and geography. The geographic and discursive spaces gestured to in each of these novels do not simply reflect an abandonment of nationhood. Instead of merely writing against exclusion and hegemonic narratives of ethnic, cultural, or "racial" homogeneity, they envision alternative spaces from which citizens can make ethical demands of nations in the interest of looking towards different futures, new heterogeneities, and other possibilities.

The notion of second and subsequent generations is a recurrent historical trope in any nation with a substantial history of immigration. But I believe it is also necessary to think about the uniqueness of this most recent second generation and to see their assertions of transethnic conviviality as an expression of the possibilities to which I have been referring. This is why, in this study, I have insisted that the "second generation" is something more than either a label of identity or a marker of temporal or genealogical chronology. Too often, the question asked in multigenerational contexts of migration has been the one I cited from Robertson Davies in the previous chapter: How many generations does it take to achieve belonging, to "legitimately" lay claim to a nation? Perhaps this is the wrong question to be asking: Is two generations "enough"? Three? Four? It would seem that any recourse to generational descent as a marker of belonging in fact leads down a path of *im*possibility. In this regard, it is perhaps necessary to look beyond the periodizing or chronological notion of generation altogether, as Irie tries to do in the final pages of *White Teeth* when she longs for a time "when roots won't matter any more." This statement would seem to be a recognition that as long as she and subsequent descendants invoke lines of descent – no matter how long – they are casting themselves outside of the nation at the very moment when they are trying to interpolate themselves within it by invoking "elsewhere" as a site of origins.

The post-immigrant paradigm through which I have framed this project seeks a more enabling conceptual place. To that end, I have contemplated a second generation not through discourses of identity, genealogy, or chronology, but rather as the embodiment of a "condition of possibility" in itself. As this second generation looks beyond binaries of "here" versus "elsewhere," "migrancy" versus "settlement," and assimilation versus ethnonationalism, they have considered both the joys and the struggles of inhabiting nation-space in a manner that is "celebratory even with the horrible." They have celebrated, embraced, and facilitated possibilities while also recognizing, and refusing, the often restrictive conditions in which they can be attenuated. Assimilation compels an amnesia of the horrible by necessitating a forced forgetting of the potentially traumatic legacies of migration; ethnonationalism, rather than being understood as a cultural celebration, reflects the despair of being unable to "get over" what has been left behind. A second generation, in refusing both of these, seeks other routes through which to negotiate their place within the nation. These reimaginings are not merely resistant, they are transformative as well. For in attempting to create inhabitable spaces for themselves, a second generation also insists that nations be "more" than they currently are.

Notes

Introduction. "Settling Down and Settling Up"

1 A recent exception is Marc Matera's in-depth cultural history, *Black London: The Imperial Metropolis and Decolonization in the Twentieth Century* (2015). Matera argues that too much scholarship has reduced anticolonial political struggles "to a nationalist teleology" (3) that does not pay sufficient attention to black internationalism. He claims that "[t]he political possibilities envisioned by black intellectuals and activists in late imperial London challenge this conflation of resistance to imperialism with the pursuit of independent nation-states" (3); this necessitates a reconceptualization of their attendant understandings of freedom, nationality, and citizenship. He suggests instead that anticolonial resistance nationalism needs to be considered both within and alongside "the multiplicity of black internationalisms" (18), which were being articulated in London by activists, intellectuals, and artists during this period.

2 The genealogical language of inheritance is of particular significance in the context of this project for reasons that will be elaborated below.

3 Hesse, Ed., *Un/Settled Multiculturalisms.*

4 Feminist geographers in particular have challenged the assumption that an attachment to space or place is informed by a politics of stasis or exclusion. As Doreen Massey questions in *Space, Place, and Gender* (1994), "Why is it that settlement or place *is* so frequently characterized as bounded, as enclosure, and as directly counterposed to spaces and flows?" (7, emphasis Massey's). She also wonders, "Can't we rethink our sense of place? Is it not possible for a sense of place to be progressive; not self-enclosing and defensive, but outward-looking?" (147). Massey

suggests that a progressive sense of place might enable other grounds, both literal and discursive, on which political struggles might be engaged. Linda McDowell similarly acknowledges: "It is important to recognize that localism does not necessarily imply a narrow view of the world, nor travel a broad one" (208). Both Massey and McDowell call into question a premise that has worked its way into certain aspects of cultural theory in the last decade: the idea that migration is inherently more "progressive" than localism or settlement, which are assumed to be conservative and reactionary.

5 *The Canadian Oxford Dictionary*, Ed. Katherine Barber (Toronto: Oxford UP, 1998).

6 I will elaborate on this concept of "settling up" below.

7 Paul Gilroy, in *There Ain't No Black in the Union Jack* (1987), points out that "[f]amilies are ... not only the nation in microcosm, its key components, but act as the means to turn social processes into natural, instinctive ones" (44). Anne McClintock, in *Imperial Leather* (1995), bases much of her gendered analysis of the colonial project on the obverse observation, that "[n]ations are frequently figured through the iconography of familial and domestic space" (357). See also Nira Yuval-Davis, *Gender and Nation* (London: Sage, 1997).

8 For a detailed summary of Glissant's articulations of root identity and relational identity see *Poetics of Relation* (1997), 143–4.

9 In addition to Stuart Hall, see for example James Donald, who argues that the concept of Englishness "has neither substance nor stability" (171). Similarly, Iain Chambers observes "two perspectives and two versions of 'Britishness.' One is Anglo-centric, frequently conservative, backward-looking, and increasingly located in a frozen and largely stereotyped idea of the national culture. The other is ex-centric, open-ended and multi-ethnic" ("Narratives of Nationalism," 153). Seen in this light, it might be apt to suggest that, just as Englishness is, according to Coleman, Canada's "fictive ethnicity," so too has Englishness become the fictive ethnicity of Great Britain.

10 Coleman borrows this term from Balibar, "The Nation Form."

11 Ashley Dawson points out that notwithstanding a sustained narrative of racial and national purity that many Britons have clung to since the Second World War, this reified model of national identity has little historical accuracy, observing that "as long ago as 1700, Daniel Defoe described the English as a 'Mongrel Half Bred Race'" (6).

12 For more extended analyses of Canadian multiculturalism see Bannerji's *The Dark Side of the Nation* (1–12, 15–55, 87–120); Rinaldo Walcott's *Black Like Who* (29–30, 77–81); and Thobani's *Exalted Subjects* (139–75).

13 To offer one example, the 1981 British Nationality Act does not grant British-born children of Commonwealth citizens automatic British citizenship. These children can only apply for British citizenship after ten years' continuous residence in the country. The British Nationality Act will be discussed further in chapter 5, in conjunction with Zadie Smith's *White Teeth*.

14 McWatt made this statement at York University on 30 March 2006, during a public reading and talk for the *Canadian Writers in Person* series. She reiterated this point over a decade later during the Toronto launch of her co-edited book, *Luminous Ink: Writers on Writing in Canada* (2018), on 2 May 2018.

1. "A Kind of New Vocabulary"

1 Notably, one other critic has challenged the celebratory notion of global citizenship and cosmopolitanism through which some scholars read *What We All Long For*. Joanne Leow, focusing on Quy rather than the second-generation protagonists, thinks about "the complex implications behind the idea of Toronto as a globalized space" (193). She argues that through Quy's multiple displacements as an undocumented migrant, the novel also offers "a sustained examination of how multicultural Toronto is implicated in a distinctly unequal form of globalization" (193).

2 This argument is inspired by visual artist Jamelie Hassan's presentation of her billboard installation, "Because there was and there wasn't a city of Baghdad" (first mounted 1990), at the inaugural TransCanada conference in Vancouver in June 2006. In her discussion, Hassan pointed out that "There was and there wasn't …" is a common opening line in Arabic oral stories and folk tales and is used as a means of embedding both truth and fiction into a narrative. Reading the first line of Brand's novel through this lens provides interesting interpretive opportunities, as well as a means of understanding her conceptualization of space. Similarly, in Brand's opening paragraph, there both "is" and "there isn't" a city of Toronto.

3 I read Brand's "un-mapping" here via her explorations in *A Map to the Door of No Return*. In her memoir, Brand reflects on the mapping practices of different historical periods, observing their sometimes substantial variations even when representing the same terrain. She also draws attention to what information various cartographers have marked and foregrounded, and what they have chosen to marginalize. Brand argues that this cartographic mutability "proves to me something of which I've had a nagging inkling – that places and those who inhabit them are indeed fictions. This news has cemented the idea that in order to draw a map only the skill of listening may be necessary. And the mystery of interpretation" (18). In this

observation, she recognizes that mapping can never be simply mimetic; all mapping is both a representative and a political act.

4 For a more sustained discussion of this issue see Leow, who examines the representation of Quy to challenge prematurely celebratory notions of global citizenship and cosmopolitanism. She argues that, via Quy, "the novel is a sustained examination of how multicultural Toronto is implicated in a distinctively unequal form of globalization" (193).

5 In its references to people who are not of English, French, or First Nations heritage or origin, the Canadian Multiculturalism Act makes use of the word "preserve" or "preservation" eight times, suggesting that this both is and should be the predominant cultural activity of those within the nation who are defined as "multicultural." By contrast, there is no language of "development," nor is there any suggestion that these cultural groups might also change the dominant construction of what it means to be "Canadian."

6 For a more detailed discussion of the historical feminization of the "natural" landscape and masculinization of developed or urban spaces, see also Peake and Kobayashi, "Unnatural Discourse." McDowell's *Gender, Identity and Place* and Massey's *Space, Place and Gender* also elaborate on the various genderings of public and private spaces.

2. "Belonging Is What You Give Yourself"

1 See for example Allan Gregg's 2006 article in *The Walrus*, "Identity Crisis," in which he attributes contemporary crises in large part to the "problem" that visible minority children of immigrants have little sense of connection to their "adopted state," rather than to a broader discourse that might alienate those children by framing them as perpetual outsiders in Canada.

2 McWatt has commented on the importance of Charlotte Brontë and also Jean Rhys to her writing. At a public reading and talk held on 30 March 2006 at York University, she referred to *Out of My Skin* as "my fictionalized Master's Thesis," which was a comparative study of Brontë's *Jane Eyre* and Rhys's *Wide Sargasso Sea*. McWatt stated that in writing her first novel she wanted to translate themes of madness and colonialism into a Canadian–Caribbean context.

3 I borrow this term from Maracle as she articulated it during the conference "TransCanada: Literature, Institutions, Citizenship" (Wosk Centre for Dialogue, Simon Fraser University, 23–6 June 2005).

4 This was not the first time police had used violent, confrontational means to regulate Native protesters. As York and Pindera observed in *People of*

the Pines, "the SQ [Sûreté du Québec, the Quebec provincial police], were heavily armed, obviously prepared to use force. They had a long history of using truncheons and tear gas to quell disturbances by native people" (27). But this was the first time the police opened fire on native protesters using semi-automatic rifles and other assault weapons.

5 This pamphlet focuses on the turbulent relationship Mohawks had with the Catholic Order of Saint Sulpice, which was granted the disputed territory by the French king in 1717, and later with the Department of Indian Affairs. Neither recognized Mohawk claims to the land. A more detailed history of these land claims is described in York and Pindera, and in Amelia Kalant's *National Identity and the Conflict at Oka*. Kalant notes that when the Sulpicians sought to transfer the largely Mohawk community occupying this land to another area north of Montreal, the Mohawk made the move under the assumption that the land was being held for them. But no ownership was transferred, and no treaty was ever signed (207). Following the British conquest of 1763, the Algonquin and Iroquois Confederacy lodged a series of complaints to have the land returned to them, but petitions in 1781, 1787, and 1795 were rejected. A 1788 claim to the Crown "for full title to the area was denied, despite proof that recorded it as theirs" (208). In the nineteenth century the Mohawk came into numerous conflicts with the Sulpicians, many of which are discussed in the pamphlet McWatt includes. An 1883 government report "denied that the Indians had valid title to the lands [and] conced[ed] full title to the seminary" (209). In the early twentieth century, the Mohawk redoubled their efforts to have the land recognized as theirs. But "the Privy council rejected another petition in 1912, and throughout the twentieth century Kanesatake complaints met with little or no response from Ottawa" (209–10). York and Pindera discuss at length the Mohawk efforts since 1973, when the Canadian government began to recognize the concept of Aboriginal land title. At this time the federal government "agreed to recognize two kinds of land claims: comprehensive land claims, which can be filed in regions where an Indian band has never signed a treaty to surrender its rights, and specific claims, when a government has violated a treaty by seizing Indian land or failing to provide the land it had promised" (275). They observe that both processes are "agonizingly slow" (275) and rarely result in favourable verdicts for Aboriginal groups. The Kanesatake Mohawk filed a comprehensive claim in 1975, which was rejected immediately because they could not prove occupation of the land for "time immemorial," one of the requisites for this type of claim. They then filed a specific land claim in 1977 that was considered for nine years

and eventually also rejected (276). At the time of the Oka Crisis in 1990, the land claim had not been resolved. Thomas King observes that seven years after the Oka Crisis, in 1997, "the Department of Indian Affairs and Northern development quietly purchased the disputed land for $5.2 million and 'gave' it to the Mohawk for their use. At the discretion of the federal government of course" (235).

6 I am grateful to David McNab for bringing this point to my attention.

7 Alanis Obomsawin's 1993 documentary *Kanehsatake: 270 Years of Resistance* does a superb job of foregrounding the voices of Mohawk women through numerous interviews with female protesters.

8 Caribbean-descended Canadian filmmakers have made similar visual interventions that place racialized characters squarely within the Canadian landscape. See for example the experimental videos by Richard Fung (*Out of the Blue*, 1991) and Shani Mootoo and Wendy Oberlinder (*A Paddle and A Compass*, 1992). I have written at length about Dionne Brand's engagement with the dominant discourses of the Canadian wilderness in "Roughing it In Bermuda."

3. "I Knew This Was England"

1 Levy's visual references and invocation of William Blake's "Jerusalem" might be read as an intertextual conversation with Caribbean-descended artist Ingrid Pollard's photograph series *Pastoral Interludes* (1984). Pollard's five photographs depict lone black figures in the English countryside. In two, men are fishing in streams; the other three feature Pollard herself looking through a gate, peering over a stone fence, or sitting in front of barbed wire while contemplating the hills and pastures beyond. The captions below the photographs similarly quote "Jerusalem" and Wordsworth's "I Wandered Lonely As a Cloud." Just as Pollard "wander[s] lonely as a black face in a sea of white," so too does Faith experience moments of crushing alienation when she visits Simon's country retreat. Pollard's captions also relate her feelings of unease in what she perceives to be a hostile rural landscape, drawing attention to dominant discourses that racialize the countryside as a white space, while "it's as if the Black experience is only lived within an urban environment." James Procter argues that "stylized and 'artificial,' these images are 'posed' in a way that denaturalizes both the English countryside, and the black subject's relationship to it" (181). Pollard's images work to point out that while this constitutive outside has historically been rendered both

geographically and conceptually distant, it has nonetheless played an important role in maintaining the English "green and pleasant land."

2 The National Front is a far-right white supremacist neo-Nazi organization founded in Britain in 1967. Their notorious anti-immigration stance and their violent actions fuelled racial tensions in Britain throughout the 1970s and 80s.

3 This term might have been borrowed from John Solomos and colleagues' article "The Organic Crisis of British Capitalism and Race." They observe that by the early 1980s, "the bastard children of Empire set up 'camps' in the heartlands of the mother country" (30).

4. "The Abuses of Settlement"

1 A.A. Knopf and Vintage are divisions of Random House of Canada. Most international editions of the novel are based on the second Vintage edition.

2 In the first edition there is only brief reference to a possible arsonist in Aster before the Tyne family's arrival. In the second edition, a potential earlier arsonist, Mr John Rodale, is named explicitly by Ray and Eudora Frank, who also state that after he moved away from Aster the fires ceased for several months, resuming only after the Tynes moved there.

3 Edugyan discussed with me how these changes emerged from the novel's publishing history. She told me: "Regarding the two differing editions of *Samuel Tyne*: the changes were initiated by feedback from my British publisher, who issued the novel a full year after its Canadian release. I altered the text based on her suggestions, but also on my own perceived flaws of the first Canadian edition. Subsequently, the American hardcover and paperback editions, as well as the Canadian paperback, were re-edited to incorporate these late changes (only the Dutch edition takes as its basis the first Canadian edition)" (personal email correspondence, 20 March 2007). Because she did not specify, I do not know if her erasure of indigenous presences was a personal decision or one that was suggested, encouraged, or compelled by her publishers, nor do I know which changes were made potentially in the interest of appealing to a non-Canadian audience.

4 See for example Edugyan's 2005 interview in *The Tyee* with Wayde Compton and Karina Vernon, "Black Writers in Search of Place." Compton observes that all three of their creative/scholarly pursuits deal with "the recovery of certain aspects of black history in Western Canada." They discuss black prairie settlements such as Amber Valley, Keystone (now called Breton,

near Edmonton), and Maidstone, Saskatchewan. Edugyan tells them: "Having grown up in 1970s–80s Alberta, in which there seemed to be very few black people, I was fascinated to discover the existence of these black settlements." Vernon had a similar experience, growing up only a short drive from Amber Valley, yet not even knowing about its existence: "When I found out about these historic black communities they seemed to me like buried, mythical places. The Black Atlantis."

5 For more extended historical discussions about black settlement on the prairies, see Winks, *The Blacks in Canada*; and especially Shepard's, *Deemed Unsuitable*. Edugyan consulted these and other sources in researching the novel.

6 Edugyan states that Stone Road is a fictional creation, which she included in the novel because she felt that this symbol spoke to the extent of racial antagonism that would have existed in the town at the time. She says: "As far as Stone Road is concerned, it's entirely a fabrication. But I liked the direness of that image, for it strikes me as something that might have happened during such racially charged times, though it is given an almost fabulist treatment in the book. But I also liked the psychological connotations, as Aster seems a town in which the wall still remains in the minds of its townfolk" (personal email correspondence, 16 July 2006).

7 To offer a few of the most relevant examples, in 1872 the first Order in Council amending the Immigration Act was passed, prohibiting the entry of poor and destitute immigrants. The government's restriction of black migrants from Oklahoma in the early twentieth century was also expressed in an Order in Council, passed on 12 August 1911, which stated: "For a period of one year from and after the date here of the landing in Canada shall be and the same is prohibited of any immigrants belonging to the Negro race, which race is deemed unsuitable to the climate and requirements of Canada" (qtd in Shepard, 1). In 1919 another amendment restricted the entry of prospective immigrants because of "their peculiar customs, habits, modes of living, and methods of holding property" (qtd in Knowles, 105).

5. "When Roots Won't Matter Any More"

1 Smith has remarked on this issue. When asked about the ways she represents multiracial London, she replied: "I was just trying to approach London. I don't think of it as a theme, or even a significant thing about the city. This is what modern life is like. If I were to write a book about London in which there were only white people, I think that would be kind

of bizarre. People do write books like that, which I find bizarre because it's patently not what London is, nor has it been for fifty years" (https://www.pbs.org).

2 Two notable exceptions are essays by Pirjo Akohas ("Transcending Binary Divisions") and Pascal Nicklas ("The Feminine Voice of Zadie Smith").

3 See in particular chapter 2 of Procter's *Dwelling Places*.

4 Enoch Powell's infamous "Rivers of Blood" speech was actually delivered at the West Midlands Conservative Political Centre in Birmingham on 20 April 1968.

5 I borrow these terms from Deleuze and Guattari's *A Thousand Plateaus*.

6 For an extended analysis of the relationship between familial descent and property relations, see for example Engels's *The Origin of the Family, Private Property and the State*.

7 John Clement Ball also explores Smith's challenge to "neutral spaces" in *Imagining London*. But while he focuses largely on the impossibility of these spaces ever being historically neutral, I also emphasize the impossibility of spatial/geographical neutrality by drawing on geographers like Lefebvre, Edward Soja, and McKittrick.

8 Only a few critics have even mentioned Irie's baby in their analyses. These include Akohas (see note 2 above), Walters, and Thompson). None of these articles make more than passing reference to the unborn child. Ironically, James Wood's negative review is the most extended discussion of Irie's baby.

9 Goulbourne, in *Race Relations*, also points out that conversely, "the children born outside the UK to registered citizens are also regarded as British citizens."

Works Cited

Ahmed, Sara, Claudia Castañeda, Anne-Marie Fortier, and Mimi Sheller. "Introduction." *Uprootings/Regroundings: Questions of Home and Migration*. Ed. Ahmed, Castañeda, Fortier, and Sheller. Oxford: Berg, 2003. 1–19.

Aidoo, Ama Ata. "The African Woman Today." *Sisterhood, Feminisms, and Power: From Africa to the Diaspora*. Ed. Obioma Nnaemeka. Trenton: Africa World Press. 39–50.

Akohas, Pirjo. "Transcending Binary Divisions: Constructing a Postmodern Female Urban Identity in Louise Erdrich's *The Antelope Wife* and Zadie Smith's *White Teeth*." *Sites of Ethnicity: Europe and the Americas*. Ed. William Boelhower, Rocio G. Davis, and Carmen Birkle. Heidelberg: Universitatsverlang Winter, 2004. 115–29.

Allen, Lillian. *Psychic Unrest*. Toronto: Insomniac, 1999.

Amin, Ash, and Nigel Thrift. "The 'Emancipatory' City?" *The Emancipatory City? Paradoxes and Possibilities*. Ed. Loretta Lees. London: Sage, 2004. 231–5.

Anderson, Benedict. *Imagined Communities: Reflections on the Origin and Spread of Nationalism*. Revised ed. London: Verso, 1991.

– Introduction. *Mapping the Nation*. Ed. Gopal Balakrishnan. London: Verso, 1996. 1–16.

Anthias, Floya, and Nira Yuval-Davis. *Woman, Nation, State*. London: Macmillan, 1989.

Appiah, Kwame Anthony. *The Ethics of Identity*. Princeton: Princeton UP, 2005.

Armah, Ayi Kwei. *The Beautyful Ones Are Not Yet Born*. London: Heinemann, 1969.

Atwood, Margaret. *Surfacing*. Toronto: Paper Jacks, 1972.

Augé, Mark. *Non-Places: Introduction to an Anthropology of Supermodernity*. Trans. John Howe. London: Verso, 1995.

Bakhtin, Mikhail. *The Dialogic Imagination: Four Essays*. Trans. Caryl Emerson and Michael Holquist. Austin: U of Texas P, 1981.

Balibar, Étienne. "The Nation Form: History and Ideology." *Race Critical Theories*. Ed. Philomena Essed and David Theo Goldberg. Oxford: Blackwell, 2002. 220–30.

Balibar, Étienne, and Emmanuel Wallerstein. *Race, Nation, Class: Ambiguous Identities*. London: Verso, 1991.

Ball, John Clement. *Imagining London: Postcolonial Fiction and the Transnational Metropolis*. Toronto: U of Toronto P, 2004.

Bannerji, Himani. *The Dark Side of the Nation: Essays on Multiculturalism, Nationalism, and Gender*. Toronto: Canadian Scholars' Press, 2000.

Baucom, Ian. *Out of Place: Englishness, Empire, and the Locations of Identity*. Princeton: Princeton UP, 1999.

Bauman, Zygmunt. "Soil, Blood, and Identity." *Sociological Review* 40.4 (1992): 675–701.

– *Life in Fragments: Essays in Postmodern Morality*. Oxford: Blackwell, 1995.

– *Globalization: The Human Consequences*. New York: Columbia UP, 1998.

Bhabha, Homi. *The Location of Culture*. London: Routledge, 1994.

Borden, Iain, Joe Kerr, Jane Rendall, and Alicia Pivaro. "Things, Flows, Filters, Tactics." *The Unknown City: Contesting Architecture and Social Space*. Ed. Borden, Kerr, Rendall, and Pivaro. Cambridge: MIT P, 2001. 3–28.

Boyce Davies, Carole. *Black Women, Writing, and Identity: Migrations of the Subject*. New York: Routledge, 1994.

Brah, Avtar. *Cartographies of Diaspora: Contesting Identities*. London: Routledge, 1996.

Brand, Dionne. "Bathurst." *Bread Out of Stone*. Toronto: Coach House, 1994. 25–38.

– "Brownman, Tiger." *Bread Out of Stone*. Toronto: Coach House, 1994. 57–75.

– *In Another Place, Not Here*. Toronto: A.A. Knopf, 1996.

– *Land to Light On*. Toronto: McClelland and Stewart, 1997.

– *At the Full and Change of the Moon*. Toronto: A.A. Knopf, 1999.

– *A Map to the Door of No Return*. Toronto: Vintage, 2002.

– *Thirsty*. Toronto: McClelland and Stewart, 2002.

– *What We All Long For*. Toronto: A.A. Knopf, 2005.

– "An Ars Poetica From the Blue Clerk." *Black Scholar* 47.1 (2017): 58–77. Web.

Brand, Dionne, Tessa McWatt, and Rabindranath Maharaj, eds. *Luminous Ink: Writers on Writing in Canada*. Toronto: Cormorant Books, 2018.

British Nationality Act. 1981. <https://www.legislation.gov.uk/ukpga/1981/61>.

Brontë, Charlotte. *Jane Eyre*. 1847. London: Penguin, 1996.

Brubaker, Rogers. "The 'Diaspora' Diaspora." *Ethnic and Racial Studies* 28.1 (2005): 1–19.

Brydon, Diana. "Post-Colonialism Now: Autonomy, Cosmopolitanism, and Diaspora." *University of Toronto Quarterly* 73.2 (2004): 691–706.

Brysk, Alison, and Gershon Shafir. "Globalization and the Citizenship Gap." *People Out of Place: Globalization, Human Rights, and the Citizenship Gap*. Ed. Brysk and Shafir. New York: Routledge, 2004. 3–10.

Canadian Multiculturalism Act. 1988. *Other Solitudes: Canadian Multicultural Fictions*. Ed. Linda Hutcheon and Marian Richmond. Toronto: Oxford UP, 1990. 369–74.

Chambers, Iain. "Narratives of Nationalism: Being 'British.'" *Space and Place: Theories of Identity and Location*. Ed. Erica Carter, James Donald, and Judith Squires. London: Lawrence and Wishart, 1993. 145–64.

– *Migrancy, Culture, Identity*. London: Routledge, 1994.

Cho, Lily. "The Turn to Diaspora." *Topia: Canadian Journal of Cultural Studies* 17 (2007): 11–30.

Christian, Barbara. "The Race for Theory." *Feminist Studies* 14.1 (1988): 67–79.

Clarke, Austin. *The Meeting Point*. Toronto: Macmillan, 1967.

– *Storm of Fortune*. Boston: Little Brown, 1973.

– *The Bigger Light*. Boston: Little Brown, 1975.

Clifford, James. "Travelling Cultures." *Cultural Studies*. Ed. L. Grossberg et al. London: Routledge, 1992. 96–116.

– "Diasporas." *Cultural Anthropology* 9.3 (1994): 302–38.

Coleman, Daniel. *White Civility: The Literary Project of English Canada*. Toronto: U of Toronto P, 2006.

Collins, Patricia Hill. "It's All in the Family: Intersections of Gender, Race, and Nation." *Decentering the Center: Philosophy for a Multicultural, Postcolonial and Feminist World*. Ed. Uma Narayan and Sandra Harding. Bloomington: Indiana UP, 2000. 156–76.

Compton, Wayde, and Karina Vernon. "Black Writers in Search of Place." *The Tyee*, 28 February 2005. https://thetyee.ca/Life/2005/02/28/BlackWriters

Davies, Robertson. *The Merry Heart: Selections 1980–1995*. Toronto: McClelland and Stewart, 1996.

Davis, Andrea. "Black Canadian Literature as Diaspora Transgression: *The Second Life of Samuel Tyne*." *TOPIA: Canadian Journal of Cultural Studies* 17 (2007): 31–49.

Davis, Nira Yuval. *Gender and Nation*. London: Sage, 1997.

Dawson, Ashley. *Mongrel Nation: Diasporic Culture and the Making of Postcolonial Britain*. Ann Arbor: U of Michigan P, 2007.

de Certeau, Michel. *The Practice of Everyday Life*. Trans. Steven Rendall. Berkeley: U of California P, 1984.

– *Culture in the Plural*. Trans. Tom Conley. Minneapolis: U of Minnesota P, 1997.

Delaney, David. "The Space That Race Makes." *Professional Geographer* 54.1 (2002): 6–14.

Deleuze, Gilles, and Felix Guattari. *A Thousand Plateaus: Capitalism and Schizophrenia*. Trans. Brian Massumi. Minneapolis: U of Minnesota P, 1987.

Derrida, Jacques. *On Cosmopolitanism and Forgiveness*. Trans. Mark Dooley and Michael Hughes. London: Routledge, 2001.

– "The Last of the Rogue States: The 'Democracy to Come,' Opening in Two Turns." *South Atlantic Quarterly* 103.2–3 (2004): 323–41.

DeVere Brody, Jennifer. "Hyphen-Nations." *Cruising the Performative: Interventions into the Representation of Ethnicity, Nationality, and Sexuality*. Ed. Sue-Ellen Case, Philip Brett, and Susan Leigh Foster. Bloomington: Indiana UP, 1995. 149–62.

Dobson, Kit. "'Struggle Work': Global and Urban Citizenship in Dionne Brand's *What We All Long For*." *Studies in Canadian Literature* 31.2 (2006): 88–104.

Donald, James. "'How English Is It?' Popular Literature and National Culture." *Space and Place: Theories of Identity and Location*. Ed. Erica Carter, James Donald, and Judith Squires. London: Lawrence and Wishart, 1993. 165–86.

Donnell, Alison. "Nation and Contestation: Black British Writing." *Wasafiri* 36 (2002): 11–17.

Duncan, Nancy. "Renegotiating Gender and Sexuality in Public and Private Spaces." *BodySpace: Destabilizing Geographies of Gender and Sexuality*. Ed. Duncan. London: Routledge, 1996. 127–45.

Edugyan, Esi. *The Second Life of Samuel Tyne*. Toronto: A.A. Knopf, 2004.

Engels, Frederich. *The Origin of the Family, Private Property, and the State*. 1884. New York: International Publishers, 1970.

Fanon, Frantz. *The Wretched of the Earth*. 1961. New York: Grove, 1963.

– *Black Skin, White Masks*. 1952. New York: Grove, 1967.

Findlay, Len. "Always Indigenize! The Radical Humanities in the Postcolonial Canadian University." *Unhomely States: Theorizing English-Canadian Postcolonialism*. Ed. Cynthia Sugars. Peterborough: Broadview, 2004. 367–82.

Foucault, Michel. "Truth and Power." *Power/Knowledge: Selected Interviews and Other Writings, 1972–1977*. Ed. Colin Gordon. New York: Pantheon, 1980.

Fung, Richard. *Out of the Blue*. Trinity Square Video, 1991.

Gates, Henry Louis. *The Signifying Monkey: A Theory of African American Literary Criticism*. New York: Oxford UP, 1988.
Gilroy, Paul. *There Ain't No Black in the Union Jack*. London: Hutchinson, 1987.
– *The Black Atlantic: Modernity and Double Consciousness*. Cambridge: Harvard UP, 1993.
– *Small Acts: Thought on the Politics of Black Cultures*. London: Serpent's Tail, 1993.
– "'A London sumting dis …'" *Critical Quarterly* 41.3 (1999): 57–69.
– *Against Race: Imagining Political Culture beyond the Color Line*. Cambridge: Harvard UP, 2000.
– *Postcolonial Melancholia*. New York: Columbia UP, 2005.
Glissant, Edouard. *Caribbean Discourse: Selected Essays*. Trans. J. Michael Dash. Charlottesville: UP of Virginia, 1989.
– *Poetics of Relation*. Trans. Betsey Wing. Ann Arbor: U of Michigan P, 1997.
Goldie, Terry. *Fear and Temptation: The Image of the Indigene in Canadian, Australian, and New Zealand Literatures*. Kingston and Montreal: McGill–Queen's UP, 1989.
Goldman, Marlene. "Mapping the Door of No Return: Deterritorialization and the Work of Dionne Brand." *Canadian Literature* 182 (2004): 13–28.
Goulbourne, Harry. *Race Relations in Britain Since 1945*. London: Macmillan, 1998.
Gregg, Allan. "Identity Crisis: Is Canadian Multiculturalism Dangerously Outdated?" *The Walrus*, March 2006, 38–47.
Gregory, Derek. *Geographical Imaginations*. Cambridge: Blackwell, 1994.
Grosz, Elizabeth. "Bodies-Cities." *The Blackwell City Reader*. Ed. Gary Bridge and Sophie Watson. Oxford: Blackwell, 2002. 297–303.
Grove, Frederick Philip. *Over Prairie Trails*. Toronto: McClelland and Stewart, 1922.
Hall, Stuart. "New Ethnicities." *Stuart Hall: Critical Dialogues in Cultural Studies*. Ed. David Morley and Kuan Hsing Chen. London: Routledge, 1996. 441–9.
– "Minimal Selves." *Black British Cultural Studies*. Ed. Houston A. Baker Jr., Manthia Diawara, and Ruth Lindeborg. Chicago: U of Chicago P, 1996. 114–19.
– "When Was the Post-Colonial? Thinking at the Limit." *The Post-Colonial Question: Common Skies, Divided Horizons*. Ed. Iain Chambers and Lidia Curti. London: Routledge, 1996. 242–60.
– "Old and New Identities, Old and New Ethnicities." *Culture, Globalization, and the World System*. Ed. Anthony King. Minneapolis: U of Minnesota P, 1997. 41–68.

– "The Local and the Global: Globalization and Ethnicity." *Culture, Globalization, and the World System*. Ed. Anthony King. Minneapolis: U of Minnesota P, 1997. 19–39.

– "Whose Heritage? Un-settling 'The Heritage,' Re-imagining the Post-nation." *Third Text* 49 (1999–2000): 3–13.

– "The Multicultural Question." *Un/Settled Multiculturalisms: Diasporas, Entanglements, Transruptions*. Ed. Barnor Hesse. London: ZED Books, 2000. 209–41.

Haraway, Donna. *Modest_Witness@Second_Millenium: Female Man©_Meets_OncoMouse™: Feminism and TechnoScience*. New York: Routledge, 1997.

Hardt, Michael, and Antonio Negri. *Empire*. Cambridge: Harvard UP, 2000.

Harvey, David. "The Right to the City." *The Emancipatory City? Paradoxes and Possibilities*. Ed. Loretta Lees. London: Sage, 2004. 236–9.

Hassan, Jamelie. *Because there was and there wasn't a city of Baghdad*. Billboard installation, Windsor, London, and Vancouver, Canada, 1991–2.

Hawkins, Freida. *Canada and Immigration: Public Policy and Public Concern*. Second Ed. Kingston and Montreal: McGill–Queen's UP, 1988.

Head, Bessie. *A Question of Power*. London: Heinemann, 1974.

Hedetoft, Ulf, and Mette Hjort. Introduction. *The Postnational Self*. Ed. Hedetoft and Hjort. Minneapolis: U of Minnesota P, 2002. vii–xxxii.

Helsinger, Elizabeth. "Turner and the Representation of England." *Landscape and Power*. Ed. W.J.T. Mitchell. Chicago: U of Chicago P, 1994. 103–25.

Hesse, Barnor. "Black to Front and Back Again: Racialization through Contested Times and Spaces." *Place and the Politics of Identity*. Ed. Michael Keith and Steve Pile. London: Routledge, 1993. 162–82.

– "Un/Settled Multiculturalisms." *Un/Settled Multiculturalisms: Diasporas, Entanglements, Transruptions*. Ed. Hesse. London: ZED Books, 2000. 1–30.

Hewison, Robert. *The Heritage Industry: Britain in a Climate of Decline*. London: Methuen, 1987.

Iton, Richard. *In Search of the Black Fantastic: Politics and Popular Culture in the Post-Civil Rights Era*. New York: Oxford UP, 2008.

Jacobs, Jane. "Staging Difference: Aestheticization and the Politics of Difference in Contemporary Cities." *Cities of Difference*. Ed. Jacobs and Ruth Fincher. New York: Guilford Press, 1998. 252–78.

Jaggi, Maya. "Redefining Englishness." *Waterstone's Magazine* 6 (1996): 62–9.

James, C.L.R. *Beyond a Boundary*. 1963. Durham, NC: Duke University Press, 1993.

Johanson, Emily. "'Streets Are the Dwelling Place of the Collective': Public Space and Cosmopolitan Citizenship in Dionne Brand's *What We All Long For*." *Canadian Literature* 196 (2008): 48–62.

Kalant, Amelia. *National Identity and the Conflict at Oka: Native Belonging and the Myths of Postcolonial Nationhood in Canada*. New York: Routledge, 2004.

Kalliney, Peter J. *Commonwealth of Letters: British Literary Culture and the Emergence of Postcolonial Aesthetics*. Oxford: Oxford UP, 2013.

Kastoryano, Riva. "Citizenship and Belonging: Beyond Blood and Soil." *The Postnational Self*. Ed. Ulf Hedetoft and Mette Hjort. Minneapolis: U of Minnesota P, 2002. 120–36.

Kerr, Joe. "The Uncompleted Monument: London, War, and the Architecture of Remembrance." *The Unknown City: Contesting Architecture and Social Space*. Ed. Iain Borden, Jane Rendell, Joe Kerr, and Alicia Pivaro. Cambridge: MIT P, 2001. 69–90.

Kim, Christine, Sophie McCall, and Melina Baum Singer, eds. *Cultural Grammars of Nation, Diaspora, and Indigeneity in Canada*. Waterloo: Wilfrid Laurier UP, 2012.

King, Thomas. *The Inconvenient Indian: A Curious Account of Native People in North America*. Toronto: Doubleday, 2012.

Knowles, Valerie. *Strangers at Our Gates: Immigration and Immigration Policy, 1540–1997*. Toronto: Dundurn, 1997.

Lamming, George. 1954. *The Emigrants*. London: M. Joseph, 1954.

Lefebvre, Henri. *The Production of Space*. 1974. Trans. Donald Nicholson-Smith. Oxford: Blackwell, 1991.

– *Writings on Cities*. Trans. and Ed. Elonore Kofman and Elizabeth Lebas. Oxford: Blackwell, 1996.

– "The Right to the City." *The Emancipatory City? Paradoxes and Possibilities*. Ed. Loretta Lees. London: Sage, 2004. 367–74.

Leow, Joanne. "Beyond the Multiculture: Transnational Toronto in Dionne Brand's *What We All Long For*." *Studies in Canadian Literature* 37.2 (2012): 192–212.

Levy, Andrea. *Every Light in the House Burnin'*. London: Review, 1994.

– *Never Far From Nowhere*. London: Review, 1996.

– *Fruit of the Lemon*. London: Review, 1999.

– "This Is My England." *The Guardian*, 19 February 2000. http://books.guardian.co.uk

– *Small Island*. London: Headline, 2004.

– *The Long Song*. London: Headline, 2010.

Mackey, Allison. "Postnational Coming of Age in Contemporary Anglo-Canadian Fiction." *English Studies in Canada* 38.3–4 (2012): 227–53.

Mackey, Eva. *The House of Difference: Cultural Politics and National Identity in Canada*. Toronto: U of Toronto P, 2002.

Maczynska, Magdalena. "The Aesthetics of Realism in Contemporary Black London Fiction." *The Cambridge Companion to Black and Asian Literature (1945–2010)*. Ed. Dierdre Osborne. Cambridge: Cambridge UP, 2016. 135–49.

Maracle, Lee. *Talking to the Diaspora*. Winnipeg: ARP, 2015.

Marlyn, John. *Under the Ribs of Death*. Toronto: McClelland and Stewart, 1957.

Marston, Sallie. "The Social Construction of Scale." *Progress in Human Geography* 24.2 (2000): 219–42.

Massey, Doreen. *Space, Place, and Gender*. Cambridge: Polity, 1994.

Matera, Marc. *Black London: The Imperial Metropolis and Decolonization in the Twentieth Century*. Oakland: U of California P, 2015.

McClintock, Anne. *Imperial Leather: Race, Gender, and Sexuality in the Colonial Contest*. New York: Routledge, 1995.

– *Double Crossings: Madness, Sexuality, and Imperialism*. Vancouver: Rosedale, 2001.

McDowell, Linda. *Gender, Identity, and Place; Understanding Feminist Geographies*. Minneapolis: U of Minnesota P, 1999.

McKittrick, Katherine. "'Their Blood Is There, and They Can't Throw It Out': Honouring Black Canadian Geographies." *Topia* 7 (2002): 27–37.

– *Demonic Grounds: Black Women and the Cartographies of Struggle*. Minneapolis: U of Minnesota P, 2006.

McKittrick, Katherine, and Clyde Woods, eds. *Black Geographies and the Politics of Place*. Toronto: Between the Lines, 2007.

McLeod, John. *Postcolonial London: Rewriting the Metropolis*. London: Routledge, 2004.

McNab, David. *Circles of Time: Aboriginal Land Rights and Resistance in Ontario*. Waterloo: Wilfrid Laurier UP, 1999.

McNab, David, Bruce W. Hodgins, and Dale Standen. "'Black With Canoes.' Aboriginal Resistance and the Canoe: Diplomacy, Trade, and Warfare in the Meeting Grounds of Northeastern North America." *Technology, Disease, and Colonial Conquests, Sixteenth to Eighteenth Centuries*. Ed. George Raudzens. Amsterdam: BRILL International, 2001. 237–92.

McWatt, Tessa. *Out of My Skin*. Toronto: Riverbank, 1998.

– *Dragons Cry*. Toronto: Riverbank, 2000.

– *This Body*. Toronto: HarperCollins, 2004.

– *Higher Ed*. Toronto: Penguin Random House, 2015.

Medovarski, Andrea. "Roughing It in Bermuda: Susanna Strickland Moodie, Mary Prince, Dionne Brand, and the Black Diaspora." *Canadian Literature* 220 (2014): 94–114.

Mercer, Kobena. *Welcome to the Jungle: New Positions in Black Cultural Studies*. London: Routledge, 1994.

Mistry, Rohinton. *Tales from Firozsha Baag*. Toronto: Penguin, 1987.

Mitchell, Don. *Cultural Geography*. Oxford: Blackwell, 2000.

Mitchell, W.J.T. Introduction. *Landscape and Power*. Ed. Mitchell. Chicago: U of Chicago P, 1994. 1–4.

Mootoo, Shani, and Wendy Oberlinder. *A Paddle and a Compass*. V-Tape, 1992.

Nash, Catherine. "'They're family!': Cultural Geographies of Relatedness in Popular Genealogy." *Uprootings/Regroundings: Questions of Home and Migration*. Ed. Sara Ahmed, Claudia Castaneda, Anne-Marie Fortier, and Mimi Sheller. Oxford: Berg, 2003. 179–203.

New, W.H. *Land Sliding: Imagining Space, Presence, and Power in Canadian Writing*. Toronto: U of Toronto P, 1997.

Nicklas, Pascal. "The Feminine Voice of Zadie Smith." *Anglistik* 24.1 (2013): 125–35.

Obomsawin, Alanis. *Kanehsatake: 270 Years of Resistance*. National Film Board of Canada, 1993.

Osborne, Dierdre. "Introduction." *The Cambridge Companion to Black and Asian Literature (1945–2010)*. Ed. Osborne. Cambridge: Cambridge UP, 2016. 1–20.

Peake, Linda, and Audrey Kobayashi. "Unnatural Discourse, 'Race,' and Gender in Geography." *Gender, Place, and Culture* 1.2 (1994): 225–43.

Peake, Linda, and Brian Ray. "Racializing the Canadian Landscape: Whiteness, Uneven Geographies, and Social Justice." *Canadian Geographer* 45.1 (2001): 180–6.

Pollard, Ingrid. *Pastoral Interludes*. Hand-tinted photographs. InIVA archive, 1986.

Powell, Enoch. "From 'Still to Decide.'" *Hurricane Hits England: An Anthology of Writing about Black Britain*. Ed. Onyekachi Wambu. New York: Continuum, 1998. 139–45.

Procter, James. *Dwelling Places: Postwar Black British Writing*. Manchester: Manchester UP, 2003.

Rastogi, Pallavi. 2016. "Women's Fiction and Literary (Self-)Determination." *The Cambridge Companion to Black and Asian Literature (1945–2010)*. Ed. Dierdre Osborne. Cambridge: Cambridge UP, 2016. 77–94.

Rushdie, Salman. *The Satanic Verses*. New York: Viking, 1988.

Rybczynski, Witold. *Home: A Short History of an Idea*. New York: Penguin, 1986.

Said, Edward. *Culture and Imperialism*. New York: A.A. Knopf, 1993.

Saloojee, Anver. "Social Cohesion and the Limits of Multiculturalism in Canada." *Racism, Eh? A Critical Interdisciplinary Anthology of Race in Canada*. Ed. Camille Nelson and Charmaine Nelson. Concord: Captus, 2004. 410–28.

Samarantrai, Ranu. *AlterNatives: Black Feminism in the Postimperial Nation*. Stanford: Stanford UP, 2002.

Sassen, Saskia. "The Repositioning of Citizenship." *People Out of Place: Globalization, Human Rights, and the Citizenship Gap*. Ed. Alison Brysk and Gershon Shafir. New York: Routledge, 2004. 191–208.

Scott, David. *Refashioning Futures: Criticism after Postcoloniality*. Princeton: Princeton UP, 1999.

– 2004. *Conscripts of Modernity: The Tragedy of Colonial Enlightenment*. Durham: Duke UP, 2004.

Selvon, Samuel. *The Lonely Londoners*. London: A. Wingate, 1956.

– *Moses Ascending*. London: Davis-Poynter, 1975.

– *Moses Migrating*. Harlow: Longman, 1983.

Shepard, R. Bruce. *Deemed Unsuitable: Blacks from Oklahoma Move to the Canadian Prairies in Search of Equality in the Early Twentieth Century Only to Find Racism in Their New Home*. Toronto: Umbrella, 1997.

Smith, Neil. "Contours of a Spatialized Politics: Homeless Vehicles and the Production of Geographical Scale." *Social Text* 33 (1992): 54–81.

Smith, Sidone, and Gisela Brinkler-Gabler. "Gender, Nation, and Immigration in the New Europe." *Writing New Identities: Gender, Nation, and Immigration in Contemporary Europe*. Ed. Brinkler-Gabler and Smith. Minneapolis: U of Minnesota P, 1997. 1–27.

Smith, Zadie. *White Teeth*. London: Penguin, 2000.

– *On Beauty*. Toronto: Penguin Canada, 2005.

Smyth, Heather. "'The Being Together of Strangers': Dionne Brand's Politics of Difference and the Limits of Multicultural Discourse." *Studies in Canadian Literature* 33.1 (2008): 272–90.

Soja, Edward. *Postmodern Geographies: The Reassertion of Space in Critical Social Theory*. London: Verso, 1989.

Solomos, John, Bob Findlay, Simon Jones, and Paul Gilroy. "The Organic Crisis of British Capitalism and Race: The Experience of the Seventies." *The Empire Strikes Back: Race and Racism in 70s Britain*. Centre for Contemporary Cultural Studies, Birmingham. London: Hutchinson, 1982. 9–46.

Stein, Marc. *Black British Literature: Novels of Transformation*. Columbus: Ohio State UP, 2004.

Szeman, Imre. *Zones of Instability: Literature, Postcolonialism, and the Nation*. Baltimore: Johns Hopkins UP, 2003.

Taylor, Charles. *Multiculturalism and "The Politics of Recognition."* Princeton: Princeton UP, 1992.

Thobani, Sunera. *Exalted Subjects: Studies in the Making of Race and Nation in Canada*. Toronto: U of Toronto P, 2007.

Thompson, Molly. "'Happy Multicultural Land'? the Implications of an 'Excess of Belonging' in Zadie Smith's *White Teeth*." *Write Black, Write*

British: From Post Colonial to Black British Literature. Ed. Kadija Sesay. Hertford: Hansib, 2005. 122–44.

Walcott, Rinaldo. *Black Like Who? Writing Black Canada.* Toronto: Insomniac, 1997.

– "Rhetorics of Blackness, Rhetorics of Belonging: The Politics of Representation in Black Canadian Expressive Culture." *Canadian Review of American Studies* 29.2 (1999): 1–24.

– "'Who is she and what is she to you?': Mary Ann Shadd Cary and the (Im)Possibility of Black/Canadian Studies." *Rude: Contemporary Black Canadian Cultural Criticism.* Ed. Walcott. Toronto: Insomniac, 2000. 27–47.

– Rev. of *What We All Long For* by Dionne Brand. *Globe and Mail,* 22 January 2005, D6.

– "Land to Light On? Making Reparation in a Time of Transnationality." *Metaphoricity and the Politics of Mobility.* Ed. Maria Margaroni and Effie Yiannopolou. New York: Rodopi, 2006. 87–99.

– "Genres of Human: Multiculturalism, Cosmo-politics, and the Caribbean Basin." *Sylvia Wynter: On Being Human as Praxis.* Ed. Katherine McKittrick. Durham: Duke UP, 2015. 183–202.

Walters, Tracey. "'We're All English Now Mate Like It or Lump It': The Blackness/Britishness of Zadie Smith's *White Teeth.*" *Write Black, Write British: From Post Colonial to Black British Literature.* Ed. Kadija Sesay. Hertford: Hansib, 2005. 314–22.

Winks, Robin. *The Blacks in Canada: A History.* Montreal: McGill–Queen's UP, 1971.

Wood, James. "Human, All Too Inhuman: *White Teeth* by Zadie Smith." *The New Republic* (2000): 41–5.

Wynter, Sylvia. "On Disenchanting Discourse: 'Minority' Literary Criticism and Beyond." *Cultural Critique* 7 (1987): 207–44.

Yaeger, Patricia. "Narrating Space." *The Geography of Identity.* Ed. Yaeger. Ann Arbor: U of Michigan P, 1996. 1–38.

York, Geoffrey, and Laureen Pindera. *People of the Pines: The Warriors and the Legacy of Oka.* Toronto: McArthur and Company, 1999.

Yuval-Davis, Nira. *Gender and Nation.* London: Sage Publications, 1997.

Index

www.ingramcontent.com/pod-product-compliance
Lightning Source LLC
LaVergne TN
LVHW090159080826
844660LV00013B/876/J

* 9 7 8 1 4 4 2 6 4 0 3 7 5 *